Nature
Quest

Nature Quest

---

*An Anthology of
Wild Life
Stories*

Chosen by
ALAN C. JENKINS

BLACKIE: LONDON AND GLASGOW

Other anthologies chosen by Alan C. Jenkins:

ANIMAL STORIES

THIN AIR
An Anthology of Ghost Stories

ESCAPE!
An Anthology of Action Stories

SPY!
An Anthology of Espionage Stories

MYSTERY!
An Anthology of Baffling Stories

GHOSTS!
An Anthology of Spectral Stories

A/591

ISBN 0 216 89312 7

Blackie & Son Limited,
5 Fitzhardinge Street, London, W.1
Bishopbriggs, Glasgow

Printed in Great Britain by
Robert Cunningham and Sons Limited
Alva, Scotland

Contents

Acknowledgements

For permision to reprint copyright material in this anthology I have to thank the following:

The Author and Messrs Methuen for the use of 'How Man Met Dog' from '*Man Meets Dog*' by Konrad Z. Lorenz

The Author and Messrs Little, Brown & Company for the use of 'Wolf Watch' from '*Never Cry Wolf*' by Farley Mowat

The Author and Messrs Thames & Hudson for 'The Flying Ark' from '*No Room for Wild Animals*' by Dr Bernhard Grzimek

Messrs Macmillan for the use of 'Reign of Terror' from '*The Maneaters of Tsavo*' by Lieutenant-Colonel J. H. Patterson

Messrs Hutchinson Publishing Group for the use of '*Quest for the Horned Horse*' from '*The Uganda Protectorate*' by Sir Harry Johnston

The Author and Messrs Hamish Hamilton for the use of 'Snake Man' from the book of that name by Alan Wykes

The Author and 'Animals Magazine' for the use of '*Operation Oryx*' by M. H. Woodford

Crispin Fisher Esq. and the Estate of the late James Fisher for the use of 'First Catch Your Goose' from '*One Thousand Geese*' by Peter Scott & James Fisher

The Author and Granada Publishing Ltd for the use of 'Mammoth Mystery' from '*On the Track of Unknown Animals*' by Bernard Heuvelmans

Messrs George Allen & Unwin for the use of 'A Journey to the Kuldur' from '*Beyond the Ural Mountains*' by Ivan Aramilev, translated and adapted by Michael Heron

Messrs W. & R. Chambers for the use of 'On the Trail of the Brontosaurus' by Fulahn

The Author and Messrs Sidwick & Jackson for the use of 'The Story of the Milu' from '*Dragons in Amber*' by Willy Ley

The Author and the Hutchinson Publishing Group for the use of 'Island of Dragons' from '*No tears for the Crocodile*' by Paul Potous

Messrs Cassell for the use of 'Pioneer Methods' from '*With Nature and Camera*' by Richard Kearton

The Author and the Hutchinson Publishing Group for the use of 'The Way of an Eagle' from '*Portrait of a Wilderness*' by Guy Mountfort

The Author and Messrs J. M. Dent for the use of 'Taping the Swan' from '*Memoirs of a Birdman*' by Ludwig Koch MBE

The Author and the Lutterworth Press for the use of 'Catching a Mermaid' from '*Zoo Quest to Guiana*' by David Attenborough

The Author and Messrs Collins for the use of 'I Mean No Harm' from '*The Year of the Gorilla*' by George B. Schaller

The Author and Messrs Heinemann for the use of 'A Falcon, Towering in her Pride' from ' "*As the Falcon Her Bells*" ' by Philip Glasier

The Author and Messrs Collins for the use of 'Rescue Operation' from '*Gara-Yaka*' by Desmond Varaday

The Author and Messrs Faber & Faber for the use of 'The Forest by Night' from '*The Overloaded Ark*' by Gerald Durrell

The Author and Messrs Thomas Nelson for the use of 'To Cure Sometimes' from '*Bird Doctor*' by Katharine Tottenham

Every effort has been made to trace the owners of copyright and if any omissions have occurred it is hoped that my apologies will be accepted.

Introduction

Man not only belongs to the animal kingdom but, from the beginning of his existence, his life has been intimately bound up with nature and the lives of his fellow-creatures. In one way or another he has unceasingly pursued a 'Nature Quest' of great complexity. At first he hunted simply for food – and in some parts of the world still does. At the same time he had to defend himself against predatory beasts – and occasionally, as one of the incidents in this book shows, he still does.

He took to domesticating animals, both for food and for work-purposes, and as he developed husbandry he was, generally speaking, no longer obliged to hunt for the pot. Instead, particularly with the invention of fire-arms, he took to hunting for sport and gain. This, together with the destruction of natural habitat, had a disastrous effect on animals, and only in recent generations have we realized belatedly the wanton damage we have committed and have started flimsily to make amends.

This collection of incidents and adventures attempts to illustrate part of this nature quest, and also, here and there, to show the change in man's attitude to nature. In the past – the not so distant past – man killed ruthlessly and greedily, whereas nowadays he finds that camera and tape-recorder require more skill and give more satisfaction than the gun. Instead of sallying forth to bag a head or a skin to fulfil his pride or bloodlust, he endures equal hardship in studying wildlife at close quarters in the interest of research – and because of that 'divine curiosity' which has always impelled him. He attempts to rescue endangered animals by captive breeding. He has taken to ranching wild animals for meat, instead of slaughtering them thoughtlessly. He has in living memory 'discovered' animals never thought to exist – witness Sir Harry Johnston's successful quest for the strange okapi, cousin of the giraffe, in the depths of the Congo seventy years ago. In other cases, man has 'rediscovered' a creature such as the coelacanth, thought to have been extinct for millions of years. He still hankers at the idea that other 'unknown' animals may still exist – and great was the disappointment at the realization that the so-called Abominable Snowman was not really as sensational as many had hoped!

The 'nature quest' that has so keenly exercised man is indeed far-flung and varied; in this book it has been possible to show only a few aspects of it. Nevertheless, anyone who is interested in nature and animals will find a wide-ranging cross-section of it and through it will perhaps appreciate both man's contrasting attitudes to nature and a little of nature's own 'infinite variety'.

A. C. J.

How Man Met Dog

Konrad Z. Lorenz

Although this anthology does not set out to follow a chronological pattern, this first story is a feasible theory by a world-famous scientist of how man first started to exploit the 'dog' and eventually to domesticate it.

Through the tall grass of the plain a little group of people makes its way, an unclothed, uncivilized band. They are certainly human beings like ourselves, their build no different from that of present-day man. In their hands they carry bone-tipped spears, some even have bows and arrows, but in their behaviour there is something which would be foreign even to present-day savages of the lowest cultural type, and which would strike a modern observer as being an animal trait. These men are no lords of creation that look fearlessly out into the world; instead, their dark eyes move to and fro restlessly as they turn their heads, glancing from time to time fearfully over their shoulders. They remind one of deer, hunted animals that must always be watchful. They give wide berth to bushes and the taller vegetation of the steppes which may easily shelter a large beast of prey, and, on one occasion, a big antelope breaks cover with a loud rustling: they start nervously, hastily adjusting their spears for action. The next moment, recognizing the harmlessness of the animal, their fear gives place to relieved but excited chatter and finally to hilarious laughter. But this cheerful mood soon subsides: the band is downcast and with good reason. In the course of the last month, they have been forced by stronger, more populous tribes to relinquish their original hunting grounds for the plains of the West, a country which they do not know and where large beasts of prey are much more prevalent than in the abandoned territory. The knowing old hunter who was their leader lost his life a few weeks ago; he was wounded by a sabre-toothed tiger which tried one night to steal a young girl from the band. In a fever of excitement, all the men set their spears at the tiger, the leader at their head, but unluckily it was he that received the brunt of its attack. The girl was already dead and the leader died of his wounds the next day. The fact that the tiger also died a week later of peritonitis caused by a spear wound in his abdomen was of small direct advantage to the little band of people. This now consisted of but five grown men, the rest being women and children, and five men are not enough to beat off the attacks of a large beast of prey. Nor is the man who has assumed the leadership so endowed with experience and muscle-power as was the former leader. But his eyes are brighter and his forehead higher and more arched than that of the other. The depleted group suffers most from lack of sleep. In their own territory they used to sleep round the fire, and, moreover, they possessed a guard of which, till now, they were unaware. The jackals that followed in the tracks of the human hordes, scavenging the refuse from slaughtered animals, surrounded their camp at night in a close circle. No feelings of friendship united the humans with their troublesome followers. Missiles greeted every jackal that dared approach too near the fire, and occasionally an arrow was aimed at them, though it was seldom that one was wasted on such unappetizing creatures.

Even today, in the eyes of many peoples, the dog is still marked out as an unclean animal in consequence of his disreputable ancestors. Nevertheless, the jackals were a definite help to the human beings whose footsteps they followed: to some extent, they saved them the trouble of setting a watch, since the clamour they set up on the approach of a beast of prey announced from afar the appearance of the marauder.

These primitive human beings, careless and unthinking, were unaware of this usefulness of their four-legged retinue; but now that it was missing, the uncanny stillness around the camp was so sinister that even those who were not entrusted with the watch hardly dared to close an eye; and this proved most exhausting, since their vigilance was already overtaxed owing to the small number of able-bodied men that their band included. And so the little company, tired and nervous and thoroughly disconsolate, pursued its way, jumping at every sound and seizing its weapons, and now very seldom bursting into guffaws when the alarm proved to be a false one. At the approach of evening, the dread of the coming night began to weigh heavy on every mind; they were obsessed by that fear of the unknown which, engraved in bygone eras into the convolution of our brain, renders even today the darkness of night a source of terror to the child and, to the adult, the symbol of all things evil. This is an age-old memory of the time when the powers of darkness, in the form of flesh-eating beasts of prey, sprang out of the night upon human beings. For our forefathers the night must indeed have held unlimited terrors.

The silent group of people presses closer together and begins searching for a place far from any bushy cover, where they will be safe from the attack of predatory beasts. Here, by a slow and tiresome procedure, they will light their camp fire and roast and divide the meagre spoils of the day. The repast consists today of the already 'high' remains of a wild boar, the leavings from the meal of the sabre-toothed tiger, from which the men had driven off, after a struggle, a pack of hyena dogs. Such a mutilated carcase would hardly seem appetizing to us, but the members of the band cast hungry looks at their leader who is carrying the half-eaten skeleton himself in order to save any less responsible person from temptation. Suddenly the footsteps of the band halt as if at an order. All heads are turned in the direction whence they have come and, like a herd of startled deer, they all focus their senses in that one direction. They have heard a sound, the call of an animal which, strangely enough, brings no threat with it as most animal calls do: for only the hunting animal gives tongue – the hunted have long ago learned to be silent. But this sound seems to the wanderers like a message from home, a reminder of happier and less dangerous times, for it is the howl of a jackal. It almost seems as though the band, in its childlike, almost ape-like impulsiveness, will hurry back in the direction whence the howling proceeds. Strangely moved, they stand in anticipation. Then suddenly the young leader with the high forehead does something remarkable and, to the others, inexplicable: he throws the carcase to the ground and begins to rip off a large piece of skin to which some flesh still adheres. Some young members of the band, thinking that a meal is about to be distributed, come close, but with furrowed brow, the leader repulses them with a deep grunt of anger. Leaving the detached pieces of meat on the ground, he picks up the rest of the carcase and gives a signal for marching. They have hardly advanced a few steps when the man who stands nearest the leader in rank, and who is physically stronger though mentally less active, challenges him, indicating with his eyes and with head movements – not as we would do it, with the hands – the abandoned piece of meat. The leader reproaches him and presses onward. After another ten yeards, the second man falls back and moves towards the meat. The leader, throwing his booty on to the grass, pursues him and, as the other raises the reeking flesh to his mouth, he rams his shoulder against him causing him to totter sideways. For a few seconds the two face each other threateningly, their foreheads puckered, their faces distorted with rage; then the second man drops his eyes and, muttering, follows the group, which is now once more in motion.

Not a man is conscious that he has just witnessed an epoch-making episode, a stroke of genius whose meaning in world history is greater than that of the fall of Troy or the discovery of gunpowder. Even the high-browed leader himself does not know it. He acted on impulse, hardly realizing that the motive for his action was the wish to have the jackals near him. He had instinctively and rightly calculated that since the wind was blowing against them it was bound to waft the scent of the meat into the nostrils of the howling jackals. The band moves on, but still no open space is to be found which could offer them a safe camping place. After a few hundred yards, the leader repeats his strange action, whereupon a loud protest is raised by the other men. The third time he repeats it something like a revolt breaks out, and it is only by recourse to an outburst of primitive fury that the leader is able to enforce his will. But shortly afterwards the bushes clear and a large expanse of open plain affords them some measure of safety. The men gather round the remains of the wild boar and begin, amidst continual grumbling and mutual threats, to carve the aromatic delicacy in pieces, while the women and children gather a pile of fuel sufficient for the whole night.

The wind has dropped and in the stillness the sensitive ear of the wild man can detect sounds a long distance away. Then suddenly the leader utters that quiet sound, fraught with meaning, that commands the absolute silence and attention of the others. All turn to statues, for in the distance the cry of an animal is again audible and this time louder than before: the jackals have found the first piece of meat and, with unmistakable sounds, two of them are fighting for the plunder. The leader smiles and gives the signal for his companions to continue. A little later, the same growling and snapping of the jaws can be heard, this time still nearer. Again the humans listen attentively. Suddenly the second man jerks round his head and, with a peculiar, tense expression, stares into the face of the leader who, with a satisfied grin, is listening to the fight of the jackals. Now at last, the second man has begun to grasp the leader's intentions. Seizing a few detached ribs, nearly bare of meat, he approaches him, grinning. Then he nudges him and, imitating the barking sound of the jackals, he carries off the bones in the direction from which the band has come. In its tracks, not far from the camp, he stoops to lay them down, then, rising, he looks questioningly at the leader, who has been following his actions with interest. They grin at each other and suddenly burst into loud laughter, that same unrestrained mirth that little boys might indulge in today when they have succeeded in some particular piece of mischief.

It is already dark and the camp fire is burning as the leader of the band again gives the signal for silence. A gnawing of bones can be heard and, in the light of the fire, the party suddenly see a jackal revelling in the pieces of meat. Once he raises his head, glancing apprehensively towards them, but as nobody attempts to move, he returns again to the feast, and they continue to watch him quietly. In the truest sense, an epoch-making happening: the first time a useful animal has been fed by man! And as at last they lie down to sleep they do so with a feeling of safety which they have not had for a long time.

Many years have passed, many generations. The jackals have become tamer and bolder, and now surround the camps of man in larger packs. Men have now added wild horses and stags to their prey and the jackals too have altered their habits: whereas formerly they remained concealed by day and only ventured abroad by night, now the strongest and cleverest amongst them have become diurnal and follow men on their hunting expeditions. And so some such episode as the following may well have taken place when hunters were following the trail of a pregnant wild mare that has been lamed by a spear wound: they are highly elated, their rations have been meagre for some time now, and the jackals are following them more eagerly than usual since they too have received little or no share of the spoils for an equal period. The mare, weakened by her condition and by loss of blood, resorts to an age-old strategy of her species and lays a false trail, that is, she doubles back in her tracks, runs on for some distance and finally turns off into a clump of bushes at right angles to her path. This strategy has often saved a hunted animal, and on this occasion too the hunters stand baffled at the point where the tracks apparently ended.

The jackals follow at a safe distance, still fearing to approach too close to the clamorous hunters. They follow the trail of the humans and not of the wild mare, since, as can be readily understood, they have no desire to overtake on their own an animal which is far too large a prey for them. But these jackals have often been given scraps of large animals whose scents have thus acquired for them a special meaning, and at the same time they have conceived an association of thought between a trail of blood and the near prospect of a feed. Today the jackals, being particularly hungry, are strongly stimulated by the fresh blood, and now something happens which inaugurates a new form of relationship between man and his band of retainers: the old, grey-muzzled bitch, the potential leader of the pack, notices something which the human hunters have overlooked, namely, the deflection of the trail of blood. The jackals turn off at this point and follow the trail independently, and the hunters, realizing that a false trail has been laid, turn back too. On their arrival at the junction of the paths they hear the jackals howling from one side, and, following the sound, they see the tracks where the many jackals have trodden down the grass of the plain. And here, for the first time, the order is laid down in which man and dog shall pursue their quarry from this day forth: first the dog and then the man. The jackals are swifter than the hunters in overtaking the mare and bringing it to bay.

When a large wild animal is brought to bay by dogs, a particular psychological mechanism plays an essential role: the hunted stag, bear or wild boar which flees from man but does not hesitate to defend itself against dogs, forgets its more dangerous enemy in its anger at its impertinent smaller aggressors. The weary mare, which sees in the jackals only a set of cowardly yappers, takes up a defensive attitude and lashes out wildly with one forefoot at a jackal which has ventured too close. Now, breathing heavily, the mare circles but does not resume its flight. In the meanwhile, the hunters, hearing the sound of the jackals now concentrated on one spot, soon reach the scene of action and, at a given signal, distribute themselves silently around their prey. At this, the jackals move as though to disperse but, seeing that nobody interferes with them, decide to remain. The leader of the pack, now devoid of all fear, barks furiously at the mare, and when it sinks down, impaled by a spear, buries her teeth ravenously in its throat and only retreats when the leader of the hunters approaches the carcase. This man, perhaps the great, great, great grandson of the one who first threw a piece of meat to the jackals, slits open the belly of the still twitching mare and tears out a portion of gut. Without looking directly at the jackals – an act of intuitive tact – he throws it, not at, but to the side of the animals – another instance of the same tact. The grey pack leader shrinks back a little, then, seeing that the man makes no threatening gesture, but only utters a friendly sound, such as the jackals have often heard from the side of the camp fire, she falls upon the piece of entrail. As she withdraws, holding the booty between her fangs and hurriedly chewing it, she glances back furtively at the man and at the same time her tail begins to move in little short strokes from side to side. For the first time a jackal has wagged its tail to a man and thus we get a step nearer to friendship between mankind and the dog. Even such intelligent animals as canine beasts of prey do not acquire an entirely new type of behaviour reaction through a sudden experience, but rather by an association of ideas which is only built up after many recurrences of the same situation.

Months elapsed probably before this jackal bitch again ran before the hunter after a big-game animal which had laid a false trail, and perhaps it was an even later descendant which regularly and consciously led human beings and brought the game to bay.

But man had taken the first step towards domesticating the dog, as it was to become.

Wolf Watch

Farley Mowat

Nowadays many of man's concepts about wild animals have been changed by scientific and sympathetic observation of them. Working for the Canadian Wildlife Service, this author made an extraordinarily detailed and intimate study of a family of wolves – and his findings (so well related in 'Never Cry Wolf!') show that the wolf is far from being the maligned villain of innumerable legends.

Very early in my observations I discovered that the wolves led a well-regulated life, although they were not slavish adherents to fixed schedules. Early in the evenings the males went off to work. They might depart at four o'clock or they might delay until six or seven, but sooner or later off they went on the nightly hunt. During this hunt they ranged far afield, although always – as far as I could tell – staying within the limits of the family territory. I estimated that during a normal hunt they covered thirty or forty miles before dawn. When times were hard they probably covered even greater distances, since on some occasions they did not get home until the afternoon. During the balance of the daylight hours they slept – but in their own peculiarly wolfish way, which consisted of curling up for short wolf-naps of from five to ten minutes' duration; after each of which they would take a quick look about, and then turn round once or twice before dozing off again.

The female and the pups led a more diurnal life. Once the males had departed in the evening, the female usually went into the den and stayed there, emerging only occasionally for a breath of air, a drink, or sometimes for a visit to the meat cache for a snack.

This cache deserves special mention. No food was ever stored or left close to the den; and only enough was brought in at one time for immediate consumption. Any surplus from a hunt was carried to the cache, which was located in a jumble of boulders half a mile from the den, and stuffed into crevices, primarily for the use of the nursing female who, of course, could not join the male wolves on extended hunting trips.

The cache was also used surreptitiously by a pair of foxes who had their own den close by. The wolves must have known of the location of the foxes' home, and probably knew perfectly well that there was a certain amount of pilfering from their cache; but they did nothing about it even though it would have been a simple matter for them to dig out and destroy the litter of fox pups. The foxes, on their side, seemed to have no fear of the wolves, and several times I saw one flit like a shadow across the esker (a post-glacial ridge) within a few yards of a wolf without eliciting any response.

Later I concluded that almost all the dens used by the Barren Land wolves were abandoned fox burrows which had been taken over and enlarged by the wolves. It is possible that the usefulness of the foxes as preliminary excavators may have guaranteed them immunity; but it seems more likely that the wolves' tolerance simply reflected their general amiability.

During the day, while the males wolves took it easy, the female would be reasonably active about her household chores. Emerging boisterously from the close confines of the den, the pups also became active – to the point of total exhaustion. Thus throughout the entire twenty-four-hour period there was usually something going on, or at least the expectation of something, to keep me glued to the telescope.

After the first two days and nights of nearly continuous observing I had about reached the limits of my endurance. It was a most frustrating situation. I did not dare go to sleep for fear of missing something vital. On the other hand, I became so sleepy that I was seeing double and saw that something drastic would have to be done or my whole programme would founder. I could think of nothing adequate until, watching one of the males dozing comfortably on a hillock near the den, I recognized the solution to my problem. It was simple. I had only to learn to nap like a wolf.

It took some time to get the knack of it. I experimented by closing my eyes and trying to wake up again five minutes later, but it didn't work. After the first two or three naps I failed to wake up at all until several hours had passed.

The fault was mine, for I had failed to imitate *all* the actions of a dozing wolf, and, as I eventually discovered, the business of curling up to start with, and spinning about after each nap, was vital to success. I don't know why this is so. Perhaps changing the position of the body helps to keep the circulation stimulated. I *do* know, however, that a series of properly conducted wolf-naps is infinitely more refreshing than the unconscious coma of seven or eight hours' duration which represents the human answer to the need for rest.

As I grew more completely attuned to their daily round of family life I found it increasingly difficult to maintain an impersonal attitude towards the wolves. No matter how hard I tried to regard them with scientific objectivity, I could not resist the impact of their individual personalities. Because he reminded me irresistibly of a Royal Gentleman for whom I worked as a simple soldier during the war, I found myself calling the father of the family George, even though in my notebooks he was austerely identified as Wolf 'A'.

George was a massive and eminently regal beast whose coat was silver-white. He was about a third larger than his mate, but he hardly needed this extra bulk to emphasize his air of masterful certainty. George had presence. His dignity was unassailable, yet he was by no means aloof. Conscientious to a fault, thoughtful of others, and affectionate within reasonable bounds, he was the kind of father whose idealized image appears in many wistful books of human family reminiscences, but whose real prototype has seldom paced the earth upon two legs. George was, in brief, the kind of father every son longs to acknowledge as his own.

His wife was equally memorable. A slim, almost pure-white wolf with a thick ruff around her face, and wide-spaced, slightly slanted eyes, she seemed the picture of a minx. Beautiful, ebullient, passionate to a degree, and devilish when the mood was on her, she hardly looked like the epitome of motherhood; yet there could have been no better mother anywhere. I found myself calling her Angeline, although I have never been able to trace the origin of that name in the murky depths of my own subconscious. I respected and liked George very much, but I became deeply fond of Angeline, and still live in hopes that I can somewhere find a human female who embodies all her virtues!

Angeline and George seemed as devoted a mated pair as one could hope to find. As far as I could tell they never quarrelled, and the delight with which they greeted each other after even a short absence was obviously unfeigned. They were extremely affection-ate with one another and whereas the phrase 'till death us do part' is one of the more amusing mockeries in the nuptial arrangements of a large proportion of the human race, with wolves it is a simple fact. Wolves are also strictly monogamous; and although I do not necessarily consider this an admirable trait, it does make the reputation for unbridled promiscuity which we have bestowed on the wolf somewhat hypocritical.

While it was not possible for me to know with exact certainty how long George and Angeline had been mated, I was able to discover from my Eskimo friends that they had been together for at least five years – or the equivalent of thirty years in terms of the relative longevity of wolves and men. The Eskimos recognized the wolves in their area as familiar individuals and held them in such high regard that they would not have thought of killing them or doing them an injury. Thus not only were George, Angeline and other members of the family well known to the Eskimos, but the site of their den had been known for some forty or fifty years, during which time generations of wolves had raised families there.

One factor concerning the organization of the family mystified me very much at first. During my early visit to the den I had seen *three* adult wolves; and during the first few days of observing the den I had again glimpsed the odd-wolf-out several times. He posed a major conundrum, for while I could accept the idea of a contented domestic group consisting of mated male and female and a bevy of pups, I had not yet progressed far enough into the wolf world to be able to explain, or to accept, the apparent existence of an eternal triangle.

Whoever the third wolf was, he was definitely a character. He was smaller than George, not so lithe and vigorous, and with a grey overcast to his otherwise white coat. He became 'Uncle Albert' to me after the first time I saw him with the pups.

The sixth morning of my vigil had dawned bright and sunny, and Angeline and the pups took advantage of the good weather. Hardly was the sun risen (at 3 a.m.) when they all left the den and adjourned to a near-by sandy knoll. Here the pups worked over their mother with an enthusiasm which would certainly have driven any human female into hysterics. They were hungry; but they were also full to the ears of hellery. Two of them did their best to chew off Angeline's tail, worrying it and fighting over it until I thought I could actually see her fur flying like spindrift; while the other two did what they could to remove her ears.

Angeline stood it with noble stoicism for about an hour and then, sadly dishevelled, she attempted to protect herself by sitting on her tail and tucking her mauled head down between her legs. This was a fruitless effort. The pups went for her feet, one to each paw, and I was treated to the spectacle of the demon killer of the wilds trying desperately to cover her paws, her tail, and her head at one and the same instant.

Eventually she gave it up. Harrassed beyond endurance she leapt away from her brood and raced to the top of a high sand ridge behind the den. The four pups rolled cheerfully off in pursuit, but before they could reach her she gave vent to a most peculiar cry.

The whole question of wolf communications was to intrigue me more and more as time went on, but on this occasion I was still labouring under the delusion that complex communications among animals other than man did not exist. I could make nothing definite of Angeline's high-pitched and yearning whine-cum-howl. I did, however, detect a plaintive quality in it which made my sympathies go out to her.

I was not alone. Within seconds of her *cri-de-coeur*, and before the mob of pups could reach her, a saviour appeared. It was the third wolf. He had been sleeping in a bed hollowed in the sand at the southern end of the esker where it dipped down to disappear beneath the waters of the bay. I had not known he was there until I saw his head come up. He jumped to his feet, shook himself, and trotted straight towards the den – intercepting the pups as they prepared to scale the last slope to reach their mother.

I watched fascinated as he used his shoulder to bowl the leading pup over on its back and send it skidding down the lower slope towards the den. Having broken the charge, he then nipped another pup lightly on its fat behind; then he shepherded the lot of them back to what I later came to recognize as the playground area.

I hesitate to put human words into a wolf's mouth, but the effect of what followed was crystal clear. 'If it's a work-out you kids want,' he might have said, 'then I'm your wolf!'

And so he was. For the next hour he played with the pups with as much energy as if he were still one himself. The games were varied, but many of them were quite recognizable. Tag was the stand-by, and Albert was always 'it'. Leaping, rolling and weaving amongst the pups, he never left the area of the nursery knoll, while at the same time leading the youngsters such a chase that they eventually gave up.

Albert looked them over for a moment and then, after a quick glance towards the crest where Angeline was now lying in a state of peaceful relaxation, he flung himself in among the tired pups, sprawled on his back, and invited mayhem. They were game. One by one they roused and went into battle. They were really roused this time, and no holds were barred – by them, at any rate.

Some of them tried to choke the life out of Albert, although their small teeth, sharp as they were, could never have penetrated his heavy ruff. One of them, in an excess of infantile sadism, turned its back on him and pawed a shower of sand into his face. The others took to leaping as high into the air as their bowed little legs would propel them; coming down with a satisfying thump on Albert's vulnerable belly. In between jumps they tried to chew the life out of whatever vulnerable parts came to tooth.

I began to wonder how much he could stand. Evidently he could stand a lot, for not until the pups were totally exhausted and had collapsed into complete somnolence did he get to his feet, careful not to step on the small, sprawled forms and disengage himself. Even then he did not return to the comfort of his own bed (which he had undoubtedly earned after a night of hard hunting) but settled himself on the edge of the nursery knoll, where he began wolf-napping, taking a quick look at the pups every few minutes to make sure they were still safely near at hand.

His true relationship to the rest of the family was still uncertain; but as far as I was concerned he had become, and would remain, 'good old Uncle Albert'.

After some weeks of study I still seemed to be as far as ever from solving the salient problem of how the wolves made a living. This was a vital problem, since solving it in a way satisfactory to my employers was the reason for my expedition.

Caribou are the only large herbivores to be found in any numbers in the arctic Barren Lands. Although once as numerous as the plains buffalo, they had shown a catastrophic decrease during the three or four decades preceding my trip to the Barrens. Evidence obtained by various Government agencies from hunters, trappers and traders seemed to prove that the plunge of the caribou towards extinction was primarily due to the depredations of the wolf. It therefore must have seemed a safe bet, to the politicians-cum-scientists who had employed me, that a research study of wolf-caribou relationships in the Barrens would uncover incontrovertible proof with which to damn the wolf wherever he might be found, and provide a more than sufficient excuse for the adoption of a general campaign for his extirpation.

I did my duty, but although I had searched diligently for evidence which would please my superiors, I had so far found none. Nor did it appear I was likely to.

Towards the end of June, the last of the migrating caribou herds had passed the area heading for the high Barrens some two or three hundred miles to the north, where they would spend the summer.

Whatever my wolves were going to eat during those long months, and whatever they were going to feed their hungry pups, it would not be caribou, for the caribou were gone. But if not caribou what *was* it to be?

I canvassed all the other possibilities I could think of, but there seemed to be no source of food available which would be adequate to satisfy the appetites of three adult and four young wolves.

Apart from myself (and the thought recurred several times) there was hardly an animal left in the country which would be considered suitable prey for a wolf. Arctic hares were present; but they were very scarce and so fleet of foot that a wolf could not hope to catch one unless he was extremely lucky. Ptarmigan and other birds were numerous; but they could fly, and the wolves could not. Lake trout, arctic grayling and whitefish filled the lakes and rivers; but wolves are not otters.

The days passed and the mystery deepened. To make the problem even more inscrutable, the wolves seemed reasonably well fed; and to baffle me to the point of near insanity, the two male wolves went off hunting every night and returned every morning, but never appeared to bring anything home.

As far as I could tell, the whole lot of them seemed to be existing on a diet of air and water. Once, moved by a growing concern for their well-being, I went back to the cabin and baked five loaves of bread, which I then took to the neighbourhood of the wolf-den and left beside one of the hunting paths. My gift was rejected. It was even scorned. Or perhaps Uncle Albert, who discovered them, simply thought the loaves were some new sort of boundary posts which I had erected, and that they were to be treated accordingly.

About this time I began having trouble with mice. The vast expanses of spongy sphagnum bog provided an ideal milieu for several species of small rodents who could burrow and nest-build to their hearts' content in the ready-made mattress of moss. As June waned into July the country seemed to become alive with little rodents. The most numerous species were the lemmings, which are famed in literature for their reputedly suicidal instincts, but which, instead, ought to be hymned for their unbelievable reproductive capabilities. Red-backed mice and meadow mice began invading the cabin in such numbers that it looked as if *I* would soon be starving unless I could thwart their appetites for my supplies. *They* did not scorn my bread. They did not scorn my bed, either; and when I awoke one morning to find that a meadow mouse had given birth to eleven naked offspring inside the pillow of my sleeping-bag, I began to know how Pharaoh must have felt when he antagonized the God of the Israelites.

I suppose it was only because my own wolf indoctrination had been so complete, and of such a staggeringly inaccurate nature, that it took me so long to account for the healthy state of the wolves in the apparent absence of any game worthy of their reputation and physical abilities. The idea of wolves not only eating, but actually thriving and raising their families on a diet of mice was so at odds with the character of the mythical wolf that it was really too ludicrous to consider. And yet, it was the answer to the problem of how my wolves were keeping the larder full.

Angeline tipped me off.

Late one afternoon, while the male wolves were still resting in preparation for the night's labours, she emerged from the den and nuzzled Uncle Albert until he yawned, stretched and got laboriously to his feet. Then she left the den site at a trot, heading directly for me across a broad expanse of grassy muskeg, and leaving Albert to entertain the pups as best he could.

There was nothing particularly new in this. I had several times seen her conscript Albert (and on rare occasions even George) to do duty as a babysitter while she went down to the bay to drink or, as I mistakenly though, simply went for a walk to stretch her legs.

Usually her peregrinations took her to the point of the bay farthest from my tent where she was hidden from sight by a low gravel ridge; but this time she came my way in full view and so I swung my telescope to keep an eye on her.

She went directly to the rocky foreshore, waded out until the icy water was up to her shoulders, and had a long drink. As she was doing so, a small flock of Old Squaw ducks flew around the point of the bay and pitched only a hundred yards away from her She raised her head and eyed them speculatively for a moment, then waded back to shore, where she proceeded to act as if she had suddenly become demented

Yipping like a puppy, she began to chase her tail; to roll over and over among the rocks; to lie on her back; to wave all four feet furiously in the air; and in general to behave as if she were clean out of her mind.

I swung my glasses back to where Albert was sitting amidst a gaggle of pups to see if he, too, had observed this mad display, and, if so, what his reaction to it was. He had seen it all right, in fact he was watching Angeline with keen interest but without the slightest indication of alarm.

By this time, Angeline appeared to be in the throes of a manic paroxysm, leaping wildly into the air and snapping at nothing, the while uttering shrill squeals. It was an awe-inspiring sight, and I realized that Albert and I were not the only ones who were watching it with fascination. The ducks seemed hypnotized by curiosity. So interested were they that they swam in for a closer view of this apparition on the shore. Closer and closer they came, necks outstretched, and gabbling incredulously among themselves. And the closer they came, the crazier grew Angeline's behaviour.

When the leading duck was not more than fifteen feet from shore, Angeline gave one gigantic leap towards it. There was a vast splash, a panic-stricken whacking of wings, and then all the ducks were up and away. Angeline had missed a dinner by no more than inches.

This incident was an eye-opener since it suggested a versatility at food-getting which I would hardly have credited to a human being, let alone to a mere wolf. However, Angeline soon demonstrated that the charming of ducks was a mere side line.

Having dried herself with a series of energetic shakes which momentarily hid her in a blue mist of water droplets, she padded back across the grassy swale. But now her movements were quite different from what they had been when she passed through the swale on the way to the bay.

Angeline was of a rangy build anyway, but stretching herself so that she literally seemed to be walking on tiptoe, and by elevating her neck like a camel, she seemed to gain several inches in height. She began to move infinitely slowly upwind across the swale, and I had the impression that both ears were cocked for the faintest sound, while I could see her nose wrinkling as she sifted the breeze for the most ephemeral scents.

Suddenly she pounced. Flinging herself up on her hind legs like a horse trying to throw its rider, she came down again with driving force, both forelegs held stiffly out in front of her. Instantly her head dropped; she snapped once, swallowed, and returned to her peculiar mincing ballet across the swale. Six times in ten minutes she repeated the straight-armed pounce, and six times she swallowed – without my having caught a glimpse of what it was she had eaten. The seventh time she missed her aim, spun around and began snapping frenziedly in a tangle of cotton grasses. This time when she raised her head I saw, quite unmistakably, the tail and hindquarters of a mouse quivering in her jaws. One gulp and it too was gone.

Although I was much entertained by the spectacle of one of the American continent's most powerful carnivores hunting mice, I did not really take it seriously. I thought Angeline was only having fun; snacking, as it were. But when she had eaten some twenty-three mice I began to wonder. Mice are small, but twenty-three of them adds up to a fair-sized meal, even for a wolf.

It was only later, by putting two and two together, that I was able to bring myself to an acceptance of the obvious. My wolves, and, by inference at least, all the Barren Land wolves who were raising families outside the summer caribou range, were living largely, if not entirely, on mice.

And how did they transport the catch of mice (which in the course of an entire night must have amounted to a formidable number of individuals) back to the dens to feed the pups? They took them home in their bellies and the wolf-pups were fed by regurgitation.

The Flying Ark

Dr Bernhard Grzimek

For many people pent up in cities, the only way of coming in contact with wild animals is by visiting them in zoos. Here a famous zoo-man describes how he brought back from Africa an aircraft full of wild animals for his zoo in Frankfurt.

While we were still in the middle of the Congo bush, making plans for taking home to Frankfurt Zoo our newly captured animals, I had my first qualms about air transport. I had been informed that the entrance door of the aircraft was 6 feet 6 inches high, and I had passed the information on to the okapi station which was to construct the travelling cage for me. Then all of a sudden I remembered how I myself always had to duck my head when boarding a plane – and my height is slightly less than 6 feet 3 inches. The confounded door can't be 6 feet 6 inches, I thought to myself, and I conjured up a vivid picture of what would happen if I arrived shortly before the take-off with a valuable okapi in a cage which could not be got aboard the aircraft. The thought just would not give me any peace, and in the end I hastily jumped into a plane at Irumu and flew the 350 miles over the Ituri forest to Stanleyville to check the measurements myself.

When finally a D.C.4 landed and had spewed out its passengers, I got busy with my tape-measure. I discovered the door was exactly 5 feet 3 inches high. My hop over the forest had indeed been worth while! When I got back to the okapi station, the first thing we had to do was to take to pieces the cage already made and start our calculations afresh. This was by no means easy and it gave me many a headache. The cage, obviously, could not be more than 5 feet 3 inches high; but my okapi, unless it happened at the moment to be hanging its head, stood just a shade under 5 feet 11 inches, and to make it keep its head bent for days on end was a bit too much to expect. In the end I designed an adjustable cage consisting of two sections. The upper half was the broader of the two and fitted closely over the lower half in such a manner that it could be raised or lowered and could be fixed at the desired height by means of four bolts and screws on the sides. To enable it to pass through the door of the aircraft the cage could thus be temporarily reduced in height, while giving the okapi full freedom of movement once it was inside. (This station, incidentally, at once adopted my design, and in future they will despatch all okapis in cages of this type.)

I had read all I could find and had kept my ears open for all I could hear about what had happened when okapis had been transported previously. On one occasion one of them had slipped on the slimy floor of the cage and had been unable to regain its feet. It had then become so agitated that it died of heart-failure. It was then found that someone had forgotten to put cross-slats on the floor of the cage. On another occasion the flap at the front of the cage for the insertion of fodder had been made far too big, and the animal had leapt out on the deck of the ship; in this case, however, it was swiftly recaptured and no harm was done. Again, when an okapi was being transported by air from Leopoldville, it was found that the cage was too big to go through the door of the aircraft – as would have been my original cage. In the end, rather in desperation, the people in charge canted the cage and tried to push it edgeways through the entrance. The okapi had then kicked its cage to pieces and freed itself, but was badly injured in the process. The width of the cage, I realized, was also an important factor. If it is too narrow the okapi is unduly cramped; and if it is too wide, the animal will try to turn round, and in doing so it can easily get stuck and break its neck.

The excessively hard African woods, which, unfortunately, are as heavy as they are hard, were another considerable source of worry. On a long journey such as this, every pound of freight by air costs a lot of money, and in Africa animal-boxes for transportation by sea were always made much heavier than the animal itself. In my case I was faced with the problem of constructing as light and airy a cage as possible, but one which, at the same time, could not be broken to pieces by the animal inside it.

One afternoon the Bambuti presented me with an animal of which I had never before seen a live specimen and which I had not even dreamed of obtaining and taking home with me – a *Hylochoerus meinertzhageni* or giant forest hog. As a matter of fact the name, in this case, sounded rather ridiculous, for this creature was in reality just a small black piglet; but it certainly possessed the broad nose which is a characteristic of its species and it was quite a truculent little beast. This species of hog also belongs to the Congo forest's museum of primeval animals. Stanley had heard of it; and, according to the Russo-German explorer, Wilhelm Junker, the natives asserted that, in addition to the red river-hog and the water-hog, there existed also a third species of pig. Junker himself, however, had never seen one. As the natives always insisted that this animal was very big, much bigger, indeed, than the normal type of wild boar, it had been assumed that they were in reality referring to the dwarf hippopotamus, which had been discovered as long ago as 1849, and no great credence was given to their tales. In 1904, however, Captain Meinertzhagen of the British East African Rifles sent to England the skull and the greater portion of the hide of one of this new species of pig, which had become very rare since the rinderpest epidemic of 1891. These forest-hogs grow to a height of four feet at the shoulder and weigh anything from 330 to 450 lb. The only time that these creatures have reached Europe alive – they were sent to Hamburg – they survived for no more than a few months.

These giant hogs are not always harmless. One night a farmer in Rutshuru, a place between Lake Edward and Lake Kiwu, went out with a torch to drive a herd of hogs off his plantation. Almost before he realized it, however, the hogs turned on him and he was compelled to scramble as quickly as he could up the nearest tree, leaving his gun lying on the ground below him. The same planter once unexpectedly encountered a boar in the bush, and he suddenly found himself sitting astride the animal, but facing its tail. It collapsed, however, immediately afterwards and died.

Helene, as we had named our red river-hog, was by no means such a rarity, but I found her a much more attractive animal, with the red down which covered her body, tufts of hair in her ears and her white beard. Above all, she was a most sociable creature; she always answered when spoken to, she allowed herself to be stroked and she would eat out of one's hand. The red river-hog is certainly the handsomest of the wild boar species, and I decided to take Helene home with me, too. Meanwhile the number of monkeys, duiker, situtunga and monitors ear-marked for my aerial Noah's ark continued to increase.

Our okapi, Epulu, walked quite happily into its cage. We had had a rehearsal a couple of days before, when we had driven it along a corridor, the farther end of which led back into its enclosure, and Epulu came to regard the whole business as a promenade. On the evening before, however, at the end of this corridor a ramp had been constructed, leading straight into the cage in which Epulu would travel to Frankfurt.

Dima, our little elephant, gave us much more trouble. On the journey from Gangala na Bodio to the okapi station, when she found out that she could not just walk out of her cage at will, she had expended much labour and effort in smashing up her first container. When, therefore, we tried to entice her into another cage, all our efforts proved in vain; she simply turned aside and charged her way through the whole bunch of us. And when we decided that we should have to use force, the diminutive little elephant brushed four of the natives aside, bowling them over like ninepins. There remained no alternative but to tie her up, for the second time in her life, expertly and efficiently with ropes and nooses, to lay her on her side and then, with the help of all available hands, to push her forcibly into the cage.

At three o'clock in the morning – four hours before sunrise – the convoy set forth. The first to leave was the slowest of the vehicles, namely the heavy truck with its load of many animal cages. An hour later Michael* left in our blue International, and an hour later still I myself took the road in Marinos's car, a big Chevrolet. We wanted, if possible, to cover the 350 miles through the forest in one and a half days and had therefore issued instruc-

* Dr Grzimek's son who was later killed when his aircraft crashed during an expedition in the Serengeti National Park.

tions that the heavy truck should keep moving and stop only when it became necessary to feed and water the animals. But within two hours we had overtaken it, and it was obvious that the native driver and attendants had been dawdling and must have halted at some village *en route*. After this we decided not to overtake it again, but to keep hard on its heels and see that our instructions were being obeyed. To sit once more, after an interval of six months, in a proper car with cushions and plaited seats – for cool travel – and with a radio, was a great treat.

In Bafwasende we found Michael waiting for us, and he drove with us as far as the big ferry over the Lindi. The road slopes somewhat steeply down to the water's edge, and vehicles have to wait their turn. Cars and white men have priority, and a certain number of native chauffeurs driving express trucks also carry a pass, which entitles them to be ferried across as quickly as possible; but this was a privilege which their less fortunate brethren fiercely contested.

Michael pointed silently to our International, and I hardly recognized it. Its radiator was pushed back on to the engine, the side windows were smashed, the fenders crumpled and the doors would no longer shut. While Michael was standing with the engine switched off and the brakes on behind a big truck at the end of the queue, another heavy truck laden with gravel had run into him from behind and pushed him violently into the back of the truck in front of him. Had this solid truck not been standing there, our International would certainly have plunged into the waters of the Lindi and disappeared, without giving Michael a chance to wake from the afternoon nap he had been enjoying; and if he had been in an ordinary car instead of the International, it would have been so firmly squashed between the two great trucks that we should probably have had to saw Michael out of it. This, of course, is just the sort of thing that would happen on the day before the end of the journey. By a bit of luck, however, the whole thing had happened within a hundred yards of the District Administrator's office, and a European police officer appeared at once and took charge of the whole affair – a veritable miracle where motor accidents in Africa are concerned. The truck which had run into ours had no brakes worth mentioning and belonged to the Colony. '*La Colonie payera tout*,' the bystanders assured us comfortingly. Yes – but when and where? We were flying with our animals the next day, and our special aircraft was already waiting for us at the airport. Michael remained behind to bring on our baggage and, if possible, the damaged International, and I drove on behind the 'German' okapi.

In the afternoon we came upon a truck with two natives sitting beside it and bemoaning their fate. The large wooden super-structure, which most trucks in Africa carry, had been smashed and half of it cut clean away. The two men, it transpired, were not merely chauffeurs, but they were the owners of the vehicle as well. A government truck had swept past them and done the damage, and they had noted its number on a piece of paper. Marinos, as a white man, felt it incumbent on him to give what help we could. He looked first at the number and then at me. The number was that of the truck carrying our animals!

For a moment we hesitated, and then Marinos said that, after all, they were only a couple of poor black devils, and that for decency's sake we must help them. '*La Colonie payera deux fois!*' – 'The Government will have to pay twice over,' he added, and he gave them a chit containing a confirmation of what had occurred and the address to which they should report the matter. I, however, was wondering what had happened to Dima, Epulu, Helene, the baby forest-hog and the forty other animals at the time of the crash. We put on speed and within an hour had overtaken our truck. The chauffeur and the native attendants, of course, said not a word about the accident, and there was not a scratch to be seen anywhere on the vehicle. All the damage seemed to have been suffered by the other one.

Driving through the night, we succeeded in reaching Stanleyville in the early hours of the morning and went straight to the enclosure which the Antwerp Zoo had constructed as an intermediate station for animals in transit. Having seen to the wants of man and beast, we made our way to the Sabena Hotel, to sleep in its regal rooms under huge ceiling fans which were kept going all night.

Very soon we were busy again, cooking milk and rice for the little elephant, obtaining green fodder for the okapi and the other animals; and then we went off to have a quick look at the hogs, which we had left overnight to run free in a small meadow.

Oh! Helene, spotless, burnished and most civilized of your species, the spoilt darling of us all – what did you look like! The whole grass plot had completely disappeared, most conscientiously ploughed up to reveal the fresh red earth. Helene must have worked furiously throughout the night. Her head was encrusted with mud to the tips of her ears, the lovely white beard was all smeared, and when we called her she took no notice but continued to dig zealously – for the last time in her life in the soil of Africa.

Export licences, permits, the Bank, the Customs, the Police veterinary certificates and finally a leave-taking from our boy. On my last expedition my erstwhile boy had pinched half my shirts. This time my wife had given me a complete list of all our linen to take with me, and this I translated into French with the aid of a dictionary and wrote neatly on a card. Our boy could, it is true, not read it, but I once noticed later on how, holding this list in his hand, he parleyed earnestly with other natives. The result certainly was that this time nothing of mine was missing. Whether a few odds and ends are stolen or whether one makes a present of them to one's boy on parting comes to much the same thing in the end; except, of course, that to be fleeced always makes one feel a fool. It was only at the very last moment that I found out that our boy, with his four wives, was a personage highly respected in the native quarter.

Between the enclosures in the small zoological station in Stanleyville lay a new elephant skull, evidence of a calamity which had recently occurred. The elephant station had quartered three elephants here – one bull and two cows – with their kornaks (mahouts); as usual the animals spent half the day grazing in the forest. The bull, which was the tamest of all the animals the elephant station possessed, had just sat down on the order of his kornak, when one of the cows bumped into him from behind. Under the impact the girth broke and the kornak was thrown to the ground. The native in charge of this small section came to his assistance somewhat hurriedly and must have startled the bull elephant, which at once transfixed him with his tusks, trampled him to death and then fled. The other two kornaks had then returned with their cows to the elephant enclosures. Two days later the bull elephant walked back through the streets of the city quite alone, and of his own accord took up his customary place in the enclosure. He was at once shackled to the stakes with three chains, but very soon he began to attack anyone who approached him. On the first day one of the chains broke, and when on the next day a second chain also gave way, the situation became menacing, and it was decided to give the animal twenty-seven grammes of gardenal to pacify it. The drug, however, had no effect, and the creature became fiercer than ever. The superintendent of the station thereupon ordered it to be shot . . .

The whole of the big aircraft had been stripped for our convenience. Its armchairs were piled in a corner of the waiting-room, and in the place itself only four seats remained bolted to the floor at one end for our own personal use. When conveying animals in this manner all sorts of unforeseen difficulties crop up; at the airport, for example, there were no scales on which an elephant and an okapi, complete with their cages, could be weighed. My suggestion that we might make an estimate did not appeal to the Sabena officials, and so we had to drive the laden lorry down to a factory on the banks of the Congo, where a weigh-bridge was available.

An elephant, an okapi, several antelopes and hogs drink quite a lot, and consequently make water in proportionately large quantities. The floor of the passenger compartment is not water-proof, and under it run the aircraft's electric leads. Were these to become wet, a short circuit might occur and cause a serious accident. First of all, therefore, we spread a large piece of water-proof tent-cloth on the floor, covered it with a liberal amount of sawdust and placed the cages on it; we then gathered up the ends of the canvas and tied them round the sides and ends of the cages in such a way that the latter remained standing, as it were, in a large canvas bath-tub.

The cages themselves had to be securely fastened to the floor of the aircraft to prevent them from shifting about, for the walls of a plane are, after all, made of very thin metal and could very easily be fractured. I took great care, therefore, to see that the elephant's cage was more securely fastened this time than it had been on the first occasion. In Wuppertal a small elephant, which was being conveyed on the overhead railway, battered its way through the sides of the waggon and fell into the River Wupper twenty-five feet below. The sides of an aircraft are much thinner than those of a goods waggon, and the elephant would not only fall ten thousand feet instead of twenty-five, but would also take the holed aircraft down with it. The loading all went very smoothly; the cases were lifted mechanically and passed through the bows of the aircraft. At one o'clock to the minute we took off and flew over the clean, orderly streets of Stan, over the broad expanse of the Congo river and on over the endless stretches of the virgin forest.

How amusingly rivers flow in those places where the irrigation engineer has not yet turned them into graduated gutters! A river will be running through the forest, with small islands and sand-banks dotted in its midst; and then suddenly it will turn and flow for hundreds of miles in the opposite direction, parallel to itself. At no point are its twin beds more than a couple of hundred yards apart, with the result that no engineer in the world could resist the temptation of making a cutting at the shortest point and leaving the endless bends and curves to dry up. (Then, of course, the ground water diminishes, and the farmer finds the crops in his fields dwindling.) The roads through the forest slipped away beneath us; then we saw two streams, one almost black and the other bright cocoa-reddish in colour, converging together, and from the point of their confluence one single river flowed on, one half of it black and the other half red, for mile after mile, until we ourselves sped over it and away in a matter of moments.

To have a whole aircraft to oneself gives one rather a bracing feeling. In the cock-pit six men were busy, flying the two of us punctually and safely to our destination. The steward came along to announce a meal for us, but at the moment we were engaged in serving meals to our animals. We spoke heartening words to them. From a can with a long spout we skilfully directed a stream of water into the drinking bowls down on the floor of the cages, opened up the doors with hammer and pliers to remove the droppings, and handed out bananas to some, to others cakes which we had bought at the weekly native market. In the end the steward gave the whole thing up as a bad job; he showed us the kitchen, from which he was wont to satisfy the needs of fifty passengers, and invited us to help ourselves. The kitchen had a refrigerator with beer, wine, champagne, soda-water, lemonade and milk, all at our disposal as the fancy took us. While one of us was busy with the animals, the other explored the aircraft. Up forward we found the buttons with which one can regulate the temperature of the entire cabin; we found drawers full of chocolates, boxes full of luscious pears, apples, bananas and oranges, many of which, of course, found their way to the animals; we found more boxes containing five different sorts of bread, hygienically packed cutlery, an assortment of pepper, salt and mustard, tiny tubes of sardine-paste, a basin full of potato salad, roast meats, ham and boned chicken by the pound, cakes, biscuits, life-belts, first-aid kit, maps and boxes everywhere – it is amazing how much an aircraft can stow away in its broad belly.

At Libenge, just on the Belgian side of the frontier with French Equatorial Africa, we landed at a tiny airport. This saves the Belgians the expense of paying landing dues in foreign exchange; for the same reason another airport is to be built in the near future close to the Sudan frontier, to enable the planes in transit over Egypt to fuel as far as possible in their own country. In Libenge, one by one great barrels were rolled up to the aircraft and 3,000 gallons of petrol were pumped into our tanks. Altogether it took well over 5,000 gallons of fuel to bring the first okapi from Stanleyville to Germany, and this alone, I felt, put an obligation on our Epulu to survive the journey! In the middle of it all, four natives came along, opened a flap in the under-belly of the aircraft and pitched in a number of small bars, each wrapped in cloth and sealed – a few hundredweight of gold from the Congo mines. In the films a consignment of gold is always accompanied by armoured cars and policemen flourishing automatics; here it was all done as casually as a bakery delivering a few loaves of bread. But to me the golden floor beneath our feet seemed a worthy concomitant for the rarest African guest that had ever journeyed to a German zoo.

It is quite incredible how busy our charges kept us. The okapi and the baby elephant, Dima, were completely unaffected by flying. Epulu calmly ate the fodder we gave him, and Dima thrust out her trunk every time we passed. The hogs slept peacefully. But the chimpanzees! When we first went aboard, and when the aircraft took off, they were very excited; but as we continued to climb, they became more and more torpid. We took Popeye out of her cage, but she merely yawned, and registered pained protest; the air-pressure was affecting her, and she was air-sick. Only Koki, the smallest of them all, ran round in a lively fashion, seizing bananas wherever she could find them and clinging to our legs.

In the grey dawn we are over the Mediterranean. Corsica rises above the horizon and sinks away behind us. I had succeeded in making it a condition that we should not fly over the Alps, as we had done on the way out; for, unlike the bigger D.C.6, our D.C.4 had no pressurized cabin. I had no idea how air-pressure at a height of 12,000 feet and more would affect an okapi, and I did not wish to run any unnecessary risks. So, while the day is still young, we slip up the Rhone valley, with the Alps on our right, an ocean of rolling cloud beneath us. At the first glimpse of the ground through a gap, I shiver; even though it is mid-May, everything looks so cold. The Rhine, the Main and then the red cathedral of Frankfurt . . . We land and the doors are thrown wide. The sun is shining, but a cold wind is blowing. Our zoo travelling companions, friendly familiar faces, look up at us.

We have brought them all home safely – and alive. One worry, at least, is off our minds; but another quickly takes its place. How long, I wonder, will we succeed in keeping them alive?

I have now had a thorough test and have put on weight again. As I sit on the fifth floor above the Frankfurt Zoo, looking back on those months passed among the 'wild beasts', I sometimes ask myself: Must one really and repeatedly make one's life so uncomfortable and wearisome?

According to the Bible, one of our ancestors once built a big vessel and, as the waters rose, he saved from drowning lions and tigers, horses and cattle, giraffes and camels, and all the animals two by two; by so doing Noah bestowed upon future generations a gift richer than all the works of art, the discoveries and the knowledge, the religions and inventions of great men throughout the history of the human race.

The swirling, ever-rising tide of humanity is today drowning the wild animals just as surely as did the Flood in the Bible. But this flood kills more surely and lasts much longer. Creation is in dire need of a second Noah. Someone, then, must enter the lists on behalf of the animals; and not for the animals' sake alone, but for the sake of all mankind.

'After He Was Thus Chained'

Paul B. du Chaillu

The exploits of this Franco-American explorer, a century or more ago, brought a virtually unknown animal to the attention of the world. Today we find his attitude to animals archaically callous; moreover, modern observation has shown the gorilla to be anything but the vicious creature du Chaillu suggests.

The next day we went out all together for a gorilla-hunt. The country hereabouts* is very rough, hilly, and densely crowded; consequently, hunting is scarcely to be counted sport. But a couple of days of rest had refreshed me, and I was anxious to be in at the death of a gorilla.

We saw several gorilla-tracks, and about noon divided our party, in the hope of surrounding the resting-place of one whose tracks were very plain. I had scarce got away from my party three hundred yards when I heard a report of a gun, then of three more, going off one after the other. Of course I ran back as fast as I could, and hoped to see a dead animal before me, but was once more disappointed. My Mbondemo fellows had fired at a female, had wounded her, as I saw by the clots of blood which marked her track, but she had made good her escape. We set out at once in pursuit; but these woods are so thick, so almost impenetrable, that pursuit of a wounded animal is not often successful. A man can only creep where the beast would run.

Night came upon us while we were still beating the bush, and it

* Central Africa.

was determined to camp out and try our luck again on the morrow. Of course, I was only too glad. We shot some monkeys and birds, built our camp, and, while the men roasted their monkey-meat over the coals, I held my birds before the blaze on a stick. Fortunately we had food enough, and of a good kind, for next day.

We started early, and pushed for the most dense and impenetrable part of the forest, in hopes to find the very home of the beast I so much wished to shoot. Hour after hour we travelled, and yet no signs of gorilla. Only the everlasting little chattering monkeys – and not many of these – and occasionally birds. In fact, the forests of this part of Africa are not so full of life as in some other parts to the south.

Suddenly Miengai uttered a little *cluck* with his tongue, which is the native's way of showing that something is stirring, and that a sharp look-out is necessary. And presently I noticed, ahead of us seemingly, a noise as of someone breaking down branches or twigs of trees.

This was the gorilla, I knew at once, by the eager and satisfied looks of the men. They looked once more carefully at their guns, to see if by any chance the powder had fallen out of the pans; I also examined mine, to make sure that all was right; and then we marched on cautiously.

The singular noise of the breaking of tree-branches continued. We walked with the greatest of care, making no noise at all. The countenances of the men showed that they thought themselves engaged in a very serious undertaking; but we pushed on, until finally we thought we saw through the thick woods the moving of branches and small trees which the great beast was tearing down, probably to get from them the berries and fruits he lives on.

Suddenly, as we were yet creeping along, in a silence which made a heavy breath seem loud and distinct, the woods were at once filled with the tremendous barking roar of the gorilla.

Then the underbush swayed rapidly just ahead, and presently before us stood an immense male gorilla. He had gone through the jungle on his all-fours; but when he saw our party he erected himself and looked us boldly in the face. He stood about a dozen yards from us, and was a sight I think I shall never forget. Nearly six feet high (he proved four inches shorter), with immense body, huge chest, and great muscular arms, with fiercely-glaring, large, deep-grey eyes, and a hellish expression of face, which seemed to me like some nightmare vision: thus stood before us this king of the African forest.

He was not afraid of us. He stood there, and beat his breast with his huge fists till it resounded like an immense bass-drum, which is their mode of offering defiance; meantime giving vent to roar after roar.

The roar of the gorilla is the most singular and awful noise heard in these African woods. It begins with a sharp *bark*, like an angry dog, then glides into a deep bass *roll*, which literally and closely resembles the roll of distant thunder along the sky, for which I have sometimes been tempted to take it where I did not see the animal. So deep is it that it seems to proceed less from the mouth and throat than from the deep chest and vast paunch.

His eyes began to flash fiercer fire as we stood motionless on the defensive, and the crest of short hair which stands on his forehead began to twitch rapidly up and down, while his powerful fangs were shown as he again sent forth a thunderous roar. And now truly he reminded me of nothing but some hellish dream creature

– a being of that hideous order, half-man, half-beast, which we find pictured by old artists in some representations of the infernal regions. He advanced a few steps – then stopped to utter that hideous roar again – advanced again, and finally stopped when at a distance of about six yards from us. And here, just as he began another of his roars, beating his breast in rage, we fired, and killed him.

With a groan which had something terribly human in it, and yet was full of brutishness, he fell forward on his face. The body shook convulsively for a few minutes, the limbs moved about in a struggling way, and then all was quiet – death had done its work, and I had leisure to examine the huge body. It proved to be five feet eight inches high, and the muscular development of the arms and breast showed what immense strength it had possessed.

My men, though rejoicing at our luck, immediately began to quarrel about the apportionment of the meat – for they really eat this creature. I saw that they would come to blows presently if I did not interfere, and therefore said I would myself give each man his share, which satisfied all. As we were too tired to return to our camp of last night, we determined to camp here on the spot, and accordingly soon had some shelters erected and dinner going on. Luckily, one of the fellows shot a deer just as we began to camp, and on its meat I feasted while my men ate gorilla.

I noticed that they very carefully saved the brain, and was told that charms were made of this – charms of two kinds. Prepared in one way, the charm gave the wearer a strong hand for the hunt and in another it gave him success with women. This evening we had again gorilla stories – but all to the same point, that there are gorillas inhabited by human spirits.

On the 4th of May I had one of the greatest pleasures of my whole life. Some hunters who had been out on my account brought in a young gorilla alive! I cannot describe the emotions with which I saw the struggling little brute dragged into the village. All the hardships I had endured in Africa were rewarded in that moment.

It was a little fellow of between two and three years old, two feet six inches in length, and as fierce and stubborn as a grown animal could have been.

My hunters, whom I could have hugged to my heart, took him in the country between the Rembo and Cape St Catherine. By their account, they were going, five in number, to a village near the coast, and walking very silently through the forest, when they heard what they immediately recognized as the cry of a young gorilla for its mother. The forest was silent. It was about noon; and they immediately determined to follow the cry. Presently they heard it again. Guns in hand, the brave fellows crept noiselessly towards a clump of wood, where the baby gorilla evidently was. They knew the mother would be near; and there was a likelihood that the male, the most dreaded of all, might be there too. But they determined to risk all, and, if at all possible, to take the young one alive, knowing what a joy it would be for me.

Presently they perceived the bush moving; and crawling a little further on in dead silence, scarce breathing with excitement they beheld, what has seldom been seen even by the Negroes, a young gorilla, seated on the ground, eating some berries which grew close to the earth. A few feet further on sat the mother also eating of the same fruit.

Instantly they made ready to fire; and none too soon, for the old female saw them as they raised their guns, and they had only to pull triggers without delay. Happily they wounded her mortally.

She fell. The young one, hearing the noise of the guns, ran to his mother and clung to her, hiding his face, and embracing her body. The hunters immediately rushed towards the two, hallooing with joy as they ran on. But this roused the little one, who instantly let go his mother and ran to a small tree, which he climbed with great agility, where he sat and roared at them savagely.

They were now perplexed how to get at him. No one cared to run the chance of being bitten by this savage little beast, and shoot it they would not. At last they cut down the tree, and as it fell, dexterously threw a cloth over the head of the young monster, and thus gained time to secure it while it was blinded. With all these precautions, one of the men received a severe bite on the hand, and another had a piece taken out of his leg.

As the little brute, though so diminutive, and the merest baby for age, was astonishingly strong and by no means good-tempered, they could not lead him. He constantly rushed at them. So they were obliged to get a forked stick in which his neck was inserted in such a way that he could not escape, and yet could be kept at a safe distance. In this uncomfortable way he was brought into the village.

There the excitement was intense. As the animal was lifted out of the canoe in which he had come a little way down the river, he roared and bellowed, and looked around wildly with his wicked little eyes, giving fair warning that if he could only get at some of us he would take his revenge. I saw that the stick hurt his neck, and immediately set about to have a cage made for him. In two hours we had built a strong bamboo house, with the slats securely tied at such distances apart that we could see the gorilla and it could see out. Here the thing was immediately deposited; and now for the first time, I had a fair chance to look at my prize.

It was a young male gorilla, evidently not yet three years old, fully able to walk alone, and possessed, for its age, of most extraordinary strength and muscular development. Its greatest length proved to be, afterwards, two feet six inches. Its face and hands were very black, eyes not so much sunken as in the adult. The hair began just at the eyebrows and rose to the crown, where it was of a reddish-brown. It came down the sides of the face in lines to the lower jaw much as our beards grow. The upper lip was covered with short coarse hair; the lower lip had longer hair. The eyelids very slight and thin. Eyebrows straight, and three-quarters of an inch long.

The whole back was covered with hair of an iron-grey, becoming dark nearer the arms, and quite white about the *anus*. Chest and abdomen covered with hair, which was somewhat thin and short on the breast. On the arms the hair was longer than anywhere on the body, and of a greyish-black colour, caused by the roots of the hair being dark and the ends whitish. On the hands and wrists the hair was black, and came down to the second joints of the fingers, though one could see in the short down the beginning of the long black hair which lines the upper parts of the fingers in the adult. The hair of the legs was greyish-black, becoming blacker as it reached the ankles, the feet being covered with black hair.

When I had the little fellow safely locked in his cage, I ventured to approach to say a few encouraging words to him. He stood in the furthest corner, but, as I approached, bellowed and made a precipitate rush at me; and though I retreated as quickly as I could, succeeded in catching my trouser-legs, which he grasped with one of his feet and tore, retreating immediately to the corner furthest away. This taught me caution for the present, though I had a hope still to be able to tame him.

He sat in his corner looking wickedly out of his grey eyes, and I never saw a more morose or more ill-tempered face than had this little beast.

The first thing was, of course, to attend to the wants of my captive. I sent for some of the forest-berries which these animals are known to prefer, and placed these and a cup of water within his reach. He was exceedingly shy, and would neither eat nor drink till I had removed to a considerable distance.

The second day found Joe, as I had named him, fiercer than the first. He rushed savagely at anyone who stood even for a moment near his cage, and seemed ready to tear us all to pieces. I threw him today some pineapple leaves, of which I noticed he ate only the white parts. There seemed no difficulty about his food, though he refused now, and continued during his short life to refuse, all food except such wild leaves and fruits as were gathered from his native woods for him.

The third day he was still morose and savage, bellowing when any person approached, and with retiring to a distant corner or rushing to attack. On the fourth day, while no one was near, the little rascal succeeded in forcing apart two of the bamboo rails which composed his cage, and made his escape. I came up just as his flight was discovered, and immediately got all the Negroes together for pursuit, determining to surround the wood and recapture my captive. Running into the house to get one of my guns, I was startled by an angry growl issuing from under my low bedstead. It was Master Joe, who lay there hid, but anxiously watching my movements. I instantly shut the windows, and called to my people to guard the door. When Joe saw the crowd of black faces he became furious, and, with his eyes glaring and every sign of rage in his little face and body, got out from beneath the bed. We shut the door at the same time and left him master of the premises, preferring to devise some plan for his easy capture rather than to expose ourselves to his terrible teeth.

How to take him was now a puzzling question. He had shown such strength and such rage already, that not even I cared to run the chance of being badly bitten in a hand-to-hand struggle. Meantime Joe stood in the middle of the room looking about for his enemies, and examining, with some surprise, the furniture. I watched with fear lest the ticking of my clock should strike his ear, and perhaps lead him to an assault upon that precious article. Indeed, I should have left Joe in possession, but for a fear that he would destroy the many articles of value or curiosity I had hung about the walls.

Finally, seeing him quite quiet, I despatched some fellows for a net, and, opening the door quickly, threw this over his head. Fortunately we succeeded at the first throw in fatally entangling the young monster, who roared frightfully, and struck and kicked in every direction under the net. I took hold of the back of his neck, two men seized his arms and another the legs, and thus held by four men this extraordinary little creature still proved most troublesome. We carried him as quickly as we could to the cage, which had been repaired, and there once more locked him in.

I never saw so furious a beast in my life as he was. He darted at everyone who came near, bit the bamboos of the house, glared at

us with venomous and sullen eyes, and in every motion showed a
temper thoroughly wicked and malicious.

As there was no change in this for two days thereafter, but
continual moroseness, I tried what starvation would do towards
breaking his spirit; also, it began to be troublesome to procure his
food from the woods, and I wanted him to become accustomed to
civilized food, which was placed before him. But he would touch
nothing of the kind; and as for temper, after starving him
twenty-four hours, all I gained was that he came slowly up and
took some berries out of my hand, immediately retreating to his
corner to eat them.

Daily attentions from me for a fortnight did not bring me any
further confidence from him than this. He always snarled at me,
and only when *very* hungry would he take even the choicest food
from my hands. At the end of this fortnight I came one day to
feed him, and found that he had gnawed a bamboo to pieces slyly
and again made his escape. Luckily he had but just gone; for, as I
looked round, I caught sight of Master Joe making off on all fours
and with great speed, across the little prairie for a clump of trees.

I called the men up and we gave chase. He saw us, and before
we could head him off made for another clump. This we surrounded. He did not ascend a tree, but stood defiantly at the
border of the wood. About 150 of us surrounded him. As we
moved up he began to yell, and made a sudden dash upon a poor
fellow who was in advance, who ran, tumbled down in affright,
and, by his fall, escaped, but also detained Joe sufficiently long
for the nets to be brought to bear upon him.

Four of us again bore him struggling into the village. This time
I would not trust him to the cage, but had a little light chain

fastened around his neck. This operation he resisted with all his might, and it took us quite an hour to securely chain the little fellow, whose strength was something marvellous.

Ten days after he was thus chained he died suddenly.

Reign of Terror

Lieutenant-Colonel J. H. Patterson

Early in human history men were frequently the victims of predatory animals. Nowadays this is rarely the case, but eighty years ago, when the Kenyan railway was being built (mainly with labour brought from India), work was seriously disrupted by two man-eating lions, whose depredations were so fearful that they even became the subject of a parliamentary statement by the British Prime Minister of the day.

After the first terrible attacks by the man-eaters, it was some months before the lions visited us again, though from time to time we heard of their depredations in other quarters. Not long afterwards, two men were carried off from the rail head, while another was taken from a place called Engomani, about ten miles away. Within a very short time, this latter place was again visited by the brutes, two more men being seized, one of whom was killed and eaten, and the other so badly mauled that he died within a few days. However, for the time being we at Tsavo enjoyed complete immunity from attack, and the coolies, believing that their dreaded foes had permanently deserted the district, resumed all their usual habits and occupations, and life in the camps returned to its normal routine.

At last we were suddenly startled out of this feeling of security. One dark night the familiar terror-stricken cries and screams awoke the camps, and we knew that the 'demons' had returned and had commenced a new list of victims. On this occasion a number of men had been sleeping outside their tents for the sake of coolness, thinking, of course, that the lions had gone for good, when suddenly in the middle of the night one of the brutes was discovered forcing its way through the *boma**. The alarm was at once given, and sticks, stones and firebrands were hurled in the direction of the intruder. All was of no avail, however, for the lion burst into the midst of the terrified group, seized an unfortunate wretch amid the cries and shrieks of his companions, and dragged him off through the thick thorn fence. He was joined outside by the second lion, and so daring had the two brutes become that they did not trouble to carry their victim any further away, but devoured him within thirty yards of the tent where he had been seized. Although several shots were fired in their direction by the *jemadar* of the gang to which the coolie belonged, they took no notice of these and did not attempt to move until their horrible meal was finished. The few scattered fragments that remained of the body I would not allow to be buried at once, hoping that the lions would return to the spot the following night; and on the chance of this I took up my station at nightfall in a convenient tree. Nothing occurred to break the monotony of my watch, however, except that I had a visit from a hyaena, and the next morning I learned that the two lions had attacked another camp about two miles from Tsavo – for by this time the camps were again scattered, as I had works in progress all up and down the line. There the man-eaters had been successful in obtaining a victim, whom, as in the previous instance, they devoured quite close to the camp. How they forced their way through the *bomas* without making a noise was, and still is, a mystery to me; I

* A protective barricade of very dense thorn bushes often erected round a camp or settlement in Africa.

should have thought it was next to impossible for an animal to get through at all. Yet they continually did so, and without a sound being heard.

After this occurrence, I sat up every night for over a week near likely camps, but all in vain. Either the lions saw me and then went elsewhere, or else I was unlucky, for they took man after man from different places without ever once giving me a chance of a shot at them. This constant night watching was most dreary and fatiguing work, but I felt that it was a duty that had to be undertaken, as the men naturally looked to me for protection. In the whole of my life I have never experienced anything more nerve-shaking than to hear the deep roars of these dreadful monsters growing gradually nearer and nearer, and to know that some one or other of us was doomed to be their victim before morning dawned. Once they reached the vicinity of the camps, the roars completely ceased, and we knew that they were stalking for their prey. Shouts would then pass from camp to camp, '*Khabar dar, bhaieon, shaitan ata*' ('Beware, brothers, the devil is coming'), but the warning cries would prove of no avail, and sooner or later agonizing shrieks would break the silence and another man would be missing from roll-call next morning.

I was naturally very disheartened at being foiled in this way night after night, and was soon at my wits' end to know what to do; it seemed as if the lions were really 'devils' and bore a charmed life. Tracking them through the jungle was a hopeless task; but as something had to be done to keep up the men's spirits, I spent many a weary day crawling on my hands and knees through the dense undergrowth of the exasperating wilderness around us. As a matter of fact, if I had come up with the lions on any of these expeditions it was much more likely that they would have added me to their list of victims than that I should have succeeded in killing either of them, as everything would have been in their favour. About this time, too, I had many helpers, and several officers – civil, naval and military – came to Tsavo from the coast and sat up night after night in order to get a shot at our daring foes. All of us, however, met with the same lack of success and the lions always seemed capable of avoiding the watchers, while succeeding at the same time in obtaining a victim.

I have a very vivid recollection of one particular night when the brutes seized a man from the railway station and brought him close to my camp to devour. I could plainly hear them crunching the bones, and the sound of their dreadful purring filled the air and rang in my ears for days afterwards. The terrible thing was to feel so helpless; it was useless to attempt to go out, as of course the poor fellow was dead, and in addition it was so pitch dark as to make it impossible to see anything. Some half a dozen workmen, who lived in a small enclosure close to mine, became so terrified on hearing the lions at their meal that they shouted and implored me to allow them to come inside my *boma*. This I willingly did, but soon afterwards I remembered that one man had been lying ill in their camp, and on making enquiry I found that they had callously left him behind alone. I immediately took some men with me to bring him to my *boma*, but on entering his tent I saw by the light of the lantern that the poor fellow was beyond need of safety. He had died of shock at being deserted by his companions.

From this time matters gradually became worse and worse. Hitherto, as a rule, only one of the man-eaters had made the attack and had done the foraging, while the other waited outside in the bush; but now they began to change their tactics, entering the *bomas* together and each seizing a victim. In this way two Swahili porters were killed during the last week of November, one being immediately carried off and devoured. The other was heard moaning for a long time, and when his terrified companions at last summoned up sufficient courage to go to his assistance, they found him stuck fast in the bushes of the *boma*, through which for once the lion had apparently been unable to drag him. He was still alive when I saw him next morning, but so terribly mauled that he died before he could be got to hospital.

Within a few days of this the two brutes made a most ferocious attack on the largest camp in the section, which for safety's sake was situated within a stone's throw of Tsavo Station and close to a Permanent Way Inspector's iron hut. Suddenly in the dead of night the two man-eaters burst in among the terrified workmen, and even from my *boma*, some distance away, I could plainly hear the panic-stricken shrieking of the coolies. Then followed cries of 'They've taken him; they've taken him', as the brutes carried off their unfortunate victim and began their horrible feast close beside the camp. The Inspector, Mr Dalgairns, fired over fifty shots in the direction in which he heard the lions, but they were not to be frightened and calmly lay there until their meal was finished. After examining the spot in the morning, we at once set out to follow the brutes, Mr Dalgairns feeling confident that he had wounded one of them, as there was a trail on the sand like that of the toes of a broken limb. After some careful stalking, we suddenly found ourselves in the vicinity of the lions, and were greeted with ominous growlings. Cautiously advancing and pushing the bushes aside, we saw in the gloom what we at first took to be a lion cub; closer inspection, however, showed it to be the remains of the unfortunate coolie, which the man-eaters had evidently abandoned at our approach. The legs, one arm and half the body had been eaten, and it was the stiff fingers of the other arm trailing along the sand which had left the marks we had taken to be the trail of a wounded lion. By this time the beasts had retired far into the thick jungle where it was impossible to follow them, so we had the remains of the coolie buried and once more returned home disappointed.

Now the bravest men in the world, much less the ordinary Indian coolie, will not stand constant terrors of this sort indefinitely. The whole district was by this time thoroughly panic-stricken, and I was not at all surprised, therefore, to find on my return to camp that same afternoon (December 1, 1898) that the men had all struck work and were waiting to speak to me. When I sent for them, they flocked to my *boma* in a body and stated that they would not remain at Tsavo any longer for anything or anybody; they had come from India on an agreement to work for the Government, not to supply food for either lions or 'devils'. No sooner had they delivered this ultimatum than a regular stampede took place. Some hundreds of them stopped the first passing train by throwing themselves on the rails in front of the engine, and then, swarming on to the trucks and throwing in their possessions anyhow, they fled from the accursed spot.

After this the railway works were completely stopped; and for the next three weeks practically nothing was done but build 'lion-proof' huts for those workmen who had had sufficient courage to remain. It was a strange and amusing sight to see these shelters perched on the top of water-tanks, roofs and girders – anywhere for safety – while some even went so far as to dig pits inside their tents, into which they descended at night, covering the top over with heavy logs of wood. Every good-sized tree in the camp had as many beds lashed on to it as its branches would bear – and sometimes more. I remember that one night when the camp was attacked, so many men swarmed on to one particular tree that down it came with a crash, hurling its terror-stricken load of shrieking coolies close to the very lions they were trying to avoid. Fortunately for them, a victim had already been secured, and the brutes were too busy devouring him to pay attention to anything else.

As I was leaving my *boma* soon after dawn on December 9, I saw a Swahili running excitedly towards me, shouting out 'Simba! Simba!' ('Lion! Lion!'), and every now and again looking behind him as he ran. On questioning him I found that the lions had tried to snatch a man from the camp by the river, but being foiled in this had seized and killed one of the donkeys, and were at that moment busy devouring it not far off. Now was my chance.

I rushed for the heavy rifle which Farquhar, one of my sports-man-visitors, had kindly left with me for use in case an opportunity such as this should arise, and led by the Swahili I started most carefully to stalk the lions, who, I devoutly hoped, were confining their attention strictly to their meal. I was getting on splendidly, and could just make out the outline of one of them through the dense bush, when unfortunately my guide snapped a rotten branch. The wily beast heard the noise, growled his defiance, and disappeared in a moment into a patch of even thicker jungle close by. In desperation at the thought of his escaping me once again, I crept hurriedly back to the camp, summoned the available workmen and told them to bring all the tom-toms, tin cans and other noisy instruments of any kind that could be found. As quickly as possible I posted them in a half-circle round the thicket, and gave the head *jemadar* instructions to start a simultaneous beating of the tom-toms and cans as soon as he judged that I had had time to get round to the other side. I then crept round by myself and soon found a good position and one which the lion was most likely to retreat past, as it was in the middle of a broad animal path leading straight from the place where he was concealed. I lay down behind a small ant-hill, and waited expectantly. Very soon I heard a tremendous din being raised by the advancing line of coolies, and almost immediately, to my intense joy, out into the open path stepped a huge maneless lion. It was the first occasion during all these trying months upon which I had had a fair chance at one of these brutes, and my satisfaction at the prospect of bagging him was unbounded.

Slowly he advanced along the path, stopping every few seconds to look round. I was only partially concealed from view, and if his attention had not been so fully occupied by the noise behind him, he must have observed me. As he was oblivious to my presence, however, I let him approach to within about fifteen yards of me, and then covered him with my rifle. The moment I moved to do this, he caught sight of me, and seemed much astonished at my sudden appearance, for he stuck his forefeet into the ground, threw himself back on his haunches and growled savagely. As I covered his brain with my rifle, I felt that at last I had him absolutely at my mercy, but . . . never trust an untried weapon! I pulled the trigger, and to my horror heard the dull snap that tells of a misfire.

Worse was to follow. I was so taken aback and disconcerted by this untoward accident that I entirely forgot to fire the left barrel, and lowering the rifle from my shoulder with the intention of re-loading, hoped I should be given time. Fortunately for me, the lion was so distracted by the terrific din and uproar of the coolies behind him that instead of springing on me, as might have been expected, he bounded aside into the jungle again. By this time I had collected my wits, and just as he jumped I let him have the left barrel. An answering angry growl told me that he had been hit; but nevertheless he succeeded once more in getting clear away, for although I tracked him for some little distance, I eventually lost his trail in a rocky patch of ground.

Bitterly did I anathematize the hour in which I had relied on a borrowed weapon, and in my disappointment and vexation, I abused owner, maker, and rifle with fine impartiality. On retracting the unexploded cartridge, I found that the needle had not struck home, the cap being only slightly dented; so that the whole fault did indeed lie with the rifle, which I later returned to Farquhar with polite compliments. Seriously, however, my continued ill-luck was most exasperating; and the result was that the Indians were more than ever confirmed in their belief that the lions were evil spirits, proof against mortal weapons. Certainly, they did seem to bear charmed lives.

After this dismal failure there was, of course, nothing to do but to return to camp. Before doing so, however, I proceeded to view the dead donkey, which I found to have been only slightly devoured at the quarters. It is a curious fact that lions always begin at the tail of their prey and eat upwards towards the head. As their meal had thus been interrupted evidently at the very beginning, I felt pretty sure that one or other of the brutes would return to the carcase at nightfall. Accordingly, as there was no tree of any kind close at hand, I had a staging erected some ten feet away from the body. This *machan* was about twelve feet high and was composed of four poles stuck into the ground and inclined towards each other at the top, where a plank was lashed to serve as a seat. Further, as the nights were still pitch dark, I had the donkey's carcase secured by strong wires to a neighbouring stump, so that the lions might not be able to drag it away before I could get a shot at them.

At sundown, therefore, I took up my position on my airy perch, and much to the disgust of my gun-bearer, Mahina, I decided to go alone. I would gladly have taken him with me, indeed, but he had a bad cough, and I was afraid lest he should make any involuntary noise or movement which might spoil all. Darkness fell almost immediately, and everything became extraordinarily still. The silence of an African jungle on a dark night needs to be experienced to be realized; it is most impressive, especially when one is absolutely alone and isolated from one's fellow creatures, as I was then. The solitude and stillness, and the purpose of my vigil, all had their effect on me, and from a condition of strained expectancy I gradually fell into a dreamy mood which harmonized well with my surroundings. Suddenly I was startled out of my reverie by the snapping of a twig: and, straining my ears for a further sound, I fancied I could hear the rustling of a large body forcing its way through the bush. 'The man-eater,' I thought to myself; 'surely tonight my luck will change and I shall bag one of the brutes.' Profound silence again succeeded; I sat on my eyrie like a statue, every nerve tense with excitement. Very soon, however, all doubt as to the presence of the lion was dispelled. A deep long-drawn sigh – sure sign of hunger – came up from the bushes, and the rustling commenced again as he cautiously advanced. In a moment or two a sudden stop, followed by an angry growl, told me that my presence had been noticed; and I began to fear that disappointment awaited me once more.

But no; matters quickly took an unexpected turn. The hunter became the hunted; and instead of either making off or coming for the bait prepared for him, the lion began stealthily to stalk *me*. For about two hours he horrified me by slowly creeping round and round my crazy structure, gradually edging his way nearer and nearer. Every moment I expected him to rush it; and the staging had not been constructed with an eye to such a possibility. If one of the rather flimsy poles should break, or if the lion could spring the twelve feet which separated me from the ground . . . the thought was scarcely a pleasant one. I began to feel distinctly 'creepy', and heartily repented my folly in having placed myself in such a dangerous position. I kept perfectly still, however, hardly daring even to blink my eyes: but the long-continued strain was telling on my nerves, and my feelings may be better imagined than described when about midnight suddenly something came flop and struck me on the back of the head. For a moment I was so terrified that I nearly fell off the plank, as I thought that the lion had sprung on me from behind. Regaining my senses in a second or two, I realized that I had been hit by nothing more formidable than an owl, which had doubtless mistaken me for the branch of a tree – not a very alarming thing to happen in ordinary circumstances, I admit, but coming at the time it did, it almost paralysed me. The involuntary start which I could not help giving was immediately answered by a sinister growl from below.

After this I again kept as still as I could, though absolutely trembling with excitement; and in a short while I heard the lion begin to creep stealthily towards me. I could barely make out his form as he crouched among the whitish undergrowth; but I saw enough for my purpose, and before he could come any nearer, I took careful aim and pulled the trigger. The sound of the shot was at once followed by a most terrific roar, and then I could hear him leaping about in all directions. I was no longer able to see him, however, as his first bound had taken him into the thick bush; but to make assurance doubly sure, I kept blazing away in the direction in which I heard him plunging about. At length came a series of mighty groans, gradually subsiding into deep sighs, and finally ceasing altogether; and I felt convinced that one of the 'devils' who had so long harried us would trouble us no more.

As soon as I ceased firing, a tumult of enquiring voices was borne across the dark jungle from the men in camp about a quarter of a mile away. I shouted back that I was safe and sound, and that one of the lions was dead: whereupon such a mighty cheer went up from all the camps as must have astonished the denizens of the jungle for miles around. Shortly I saw scores of lights twinkling through the bushes: every man in camp turned out, and with tom-toms beating and horns blowing came running to the scene. They surrounded my eyrie, and to my amazement prostrated themselves on the ground before me, saluting me with cries of '*Mabarak! Mabarak!*' which I believe means 'blessed one' or 'saviour'!

The news of the death of one of the notorious man-eaters soon spread far and wide over the country: telegrams of congratulations came pouring in, and scores of people flocked from up and down the railway to see the skin for themselves. From tip of nose to tip of tail, the lion had measured nine feet eight inches, and it had taken eight men to carry him back to camp.

It must not be imagined that with the death of this lion our troubles at Tsavo were at an end; his companion was still at large, and very soon began to make us unpleasantly aware of the fact. Only a few nights elapsed before he made an attempt to get at the Permanent Way Inspector, climbing up the steps of his bungalow and prowling round the verandah. The Inspector, hearing the noise and thinking it was a drunken coolie, shouted angrily, 'Go away!' but, fortunately for him, did not attempt to come out or to open the door. Thus disappointed in his attempt to obtain a meal of human flesh, the lion seized a couple of the Inspector's goats and devoured them there and then.

On hearing of this occurrence, I determined to sit up the next night near the Inspector's bungalow. Fortunately there was a vacant iron shanty close at hand with a convenient loophole in it for firing from; and outside this I placed three full-grown goats as bait, tying them to a half-length of rail, weighing about 250 lbs. The night passed uneventfully until just before daybreak, when at last the lion turned up, pounced on one of the goats and made off with it, at the same time dragging away the others, rail and all. I fired several shots in his direction, but it was pitch dark and quite impossible to see anything, so I only succeeded in hitting one of the goats. I often longed for a flashlight on such occasions.

Next morning I started off in pursuit and was joined by some others from the camp. I found that the trail of the goats and rail was easily followed, and we soon came up, about a quarter of a mile away, to where the lion was still busy at his meal. He was concealed in some thick bush and growled angrily on hearing our approach; finally, as we got closer, he suddenly made a charge, rushing through the bushes at a great pace. In an instant, every man of the party scrambled hastily up the nearest tree, with the exception of one of my assistants, Mr Winkler, who stood steadily by me throughout. The brute, however, did not press his charge home: and on throwing stones into the bushes where we had last seen him, we guessed by the silence that he had slunk off. We therefore advanced cautiously, and on getting up to the place discovered that he had indeed escaped us, leaving two of the goats scarcely touched.

Thinking that in all probability the lion would return as usual to finish his meal, I had a very strong scaffolding put up a few feet away from the dead goats, and took up my position on it before dark. On this occasion I brought my gun-bearer, Mahina, to take a turn at watching, as I was by this time worn out for want of sleep, having spent so many nights on the look-out. I was just dozing off comfortably when suddenly I felt my arm seized, and on looking up saw Mahina pointing in the direction of the goats. 'Sher!' ('Lion!') was all he whispered. I grasped my double smooth-bore, which I had charged with slug, and waited patiently. In a few moments I was rewarded, for as I watched the spot where I expected the lion to appear, there was a rustling among the bushes and I saw him stealthily emerge into the open and pass almost directly beneath us. I fired both barrels practically into his shoulder, and to my joy could see him go down under the force of the blow. Quickly I reached for the magazine rifle, but before I could use it, he was out of sight among the bushes, and I had to fire after him quite at random. Nevertheless, I was confident of getting him in the morning, and accordingly set out as soon as it was light. For over a mile there was no difficulty in following the blood-trail, and as he had rested several times I felt sure that he had been badly wounded. In the end, however, my hunt proved fruitless, for after a time the traces of blood ceased and the surface of the ground became rocky, so that I was no longer able to follow the spoor.

As it happened, there was no sign of our enemy for about ten days after this, and we began to hope that he had died of his wounds in the bush. All the same we still took every precaution at night, and it was fortunate that we did so, as otherwise at least one more victim would have been added to the list. For on the night of December 27, I was suddenly aroused by terrified shouts from my trolley men, who slept in a tree close outside my *boma*, to the effect that a lion was trying to get at them. It would have been madness to have gone out, as the moon was hidden by dense clouds and it was absolutely impossible to see anything more than a yard in front of me; so all I could do was to fire off a few rounds just to frighten the brute away. This apparently had the desired effect, for the men were not further molested that night; but the man-eater had evidently prowled about for some time, for we found in the morning that he had gone right into every one of the tents, and round the tree was a regular ring of his footmarks.

The following evening I took up my position in this same tree, in the hope that he would make another attempt. The night began badly, as while climbing up to my perch I very nearly put my hand on a venomous snake which was lying coiled round one of the branches. As may be imagined, I came down again very quickly, but one of my men managed to despatch it with a long pole. Fortunately the night was clear and cloudless, and the moon made everything almost as bright as day. I kept watch until about 2 a.m., when I roused Mahina to take his turn. For about an hour I slept peacefully with my back to the tree, and then woke suddenly with an uncanny feeling that something was wrong. Mahina, however, was on the alert, and had seen nothing; and although I looked carefully round us on all sides, I too could discover nothing unusual. Only half satisfied, I was about to lie back again, when I fancied I saw something move a little way off among the low bushes. On gazing intently at the spot for a few seconds, I found I was not mistaken. It was the man-eater, cautiously stalking us.

The ground was fairly open round our tree, with only a small bush every here and there; and from our position it was a most fascinating sight to watch this great brute stealing stealthily round us, taking advantage of every bit of cover as he came. His skill showed that he was an old hand at the terrible game of man-hunting: so I determined to run no undue risk of losing him this time. I accordingly waited until he got quite close – about twenty yards away – and then fired my ·303 at his chest. I heard the bullet strike him, but unfortunately it had no knock-down effect, for with a fierce growl he turned and made off with great long bounds. Before he disappeared from sight, however, I managed to have three more shots at him from the magazine rifle, and another growl told me that the last of these had also taken effect.

We awaited daylight with impatience, and at the first glimmer of dawn we set out to hunt him down. I took a native tracker with me, so that I was free to keep a good look-out, while Mahina followed immediately behind with a Martini carbine. Splashes of blood being plentiful, we were able to get along quickly; and we had not proceeded more than a quarter of a mile through the jungle when suddenly a fierce warning growl was heard right in front of us. Looking cautiously through the bushes, I could see the man-eater glaring out in our direction, and showing his tusks in an angry snarl. I at once took careful aim and fired. Instantly he sprang out and made a most determined charge down on us. I fired again and knocked him over; but in a second he was up once more and coming for me as fast as he could in his crippled condition. A third shot had no apparent effect, so I put out my hand for the Martini, hoping to stop him with it. To my dismay, however, it was not there. The terror of the sudden charge had proved too much for Mahina, and both he and the carbine were by this time well on their way up a tree. In the circumstances there was nothing to do but follow suit, which I did without loss of time: and but for the fact that one of my shots had broken a hind leg, the brute would most certainly have had me. Even as it was, I had barely time to swing myself up out of his reach before he arrived at the foot of the tree.

When the lion found he was too late, he started to limp back to the thicket; but by this time I had seized the carbine from Mahina, and the first shot I fired from it seemed to give him his quietus, for he fell over and lay motionless. Rather foolishly, I at once scrambled down from the tree and walked up towards him. To my surprise and no little alarm he jumped up and attempted another charge. This time, however, a Martini bullet in the chest and another in the head finished him for good and all; he dropped in his tracks not five yards away from me, and died gamely, biting savagely at a branch which had fallen to the ground.

Well had the two man-eaters of Tsavo earned all their fame: they had devoured between them no fewer than twenty-eight Indian coolies, in addition to scores of unfortunate African natives of whom no official record was kept.

Quest for the Horned Horse

Sir Harry Johnston

We do not yet know all Nature's secrets! It is still possible that unknown creatures or others considered long extinct may yet survive. After all, the coelacanth, thought to be extinct for many millions of years, was dredged up alive and kicking – for he was known as Old Four-legs – from the Indian Ocean, while seventy years ago the scientific world was greatly surprised by the discovery of an animal until then unknown to zoologists: the okapi, cousin of the giraffe.

I remember having encountered in my childhood – say in the 1860's – a book about strange beasts in Central Africa which was based on information derived from early Dutch and Portuguese works. The publication of this book was more or less incited at the time by du Chaillu's discovery of the gorilla and other strange creatures on the west coast of Africa, and its purport was to show that there were in all probability other wonderful things yet to be discovered in the Central African forests. Amongst these suggested wonders was a recurrence of the myth of the unicorn. Passages from the works of the aforesaid Dutch and Portuguese writers were quoted to show that a strange, horselike animal, of striking markings in black and white, existed in the depths of these equatorial forests. The accounts agreed in saying that the body of the animal was horselike, but details as to its horn or horns were very vague. The compiler of the book (the late Philip Gosse, I think) believed that these stories pointed to the existence of a horned horse in Central Africa.

Somehow these stories – which may have had a slight substratum of truth – lingered in my memory, and were revived at the time H. M. Stanley published his account of the Emin Pasha expedition, *In Darkest Africa*. A note* in an appendix of this book states that the Congo Dwarfs knew an animal of horselike appearance which existed in their forests and which they caught in pitfalls. The occurrence of anything like a horse or ass – animals so partial to treeless, grassy plains – in the depths of the mightiest forest of the world seemed to me so strange that I determined to make further enquiries on the subject whenever fate should lead me in the direction of the great Congo Forest. Fate was very kind to me in the matter. In the first place, soon after arriving in Uganda my intervention was necessary to prevent a too-enterprising German carrying off by force a troop of Congo Dwarfs to perform at the Paris Exhibition. These little men had been kidnapped on Congo Free State territory. The Belgian authorities very properly objected, and as the German impresario had fled with his Dwarfs to British territory, they asked me to rescue the little men from his clutches and send them back to their homes. This was done, and in so doing, and in leading them back to the forests where they dwelt, I obtained much information from them on the subject of the horselike creature which they called the 'okapi'. They described this creature as being like a zebra, but having the upper part of its body a dark brown. The feet, however, they said, had more than one hoof.

* Stanley's brief note, which was to lead Johnston to his momentous discovery, ran thus: 'The Wambuttu knew a donkey and called it "atti". They say they sometimes catch them in pits. What they can find to eat is a wonder. They eat leaves.' Sir Harry recorded that the pygmies pronounced the animal's name 'o'api', Stanley evidently having misheard the word. – A.C.J.

When we reached Belgian territory, on the west side of the Semliki River, our enquiries were renewed. The Belgian officers at once said they knew the okapi perfectly well, having frequently seen its dead body brought in by natives for eating. They stated that the natives were very fond of wearing the more gaudy portions of its skin; and calling forward several of their native militia, they made the men show all the bandoliers, waist-belts, and other parts of their equipment made out of the striped skin of the okapi. They described the animal as a creature of the horse tribe, but with large, ass-like ears, a slender muzzle, and more than one hoof. For a time I thought we were on the track of the three-toed horse, the hipparion (a long-extinct species considered ancestrally related to the horse). Provided with guides, we entered the awesome depths of the Congo Forest. For several days we searched for the okapi, but in vain. We were shown its supposed tracks by the natives, but as these were footprints of a cloven-hoofed animal, while we expected to see the spoor of a horse, we believed the natives to be deceiving us, and to be merely leading us after some forest eland. The atmosphere of the forest was almost unbreathable with its Turkish-bath heat, its reeking moisture, and its powerful smell of decaying, rotting vegetation. We seemed in fact to be transported back to Miocene times, to an age and a climate scarcely suitable for the modern type of real humanity. Severe attacks of fever prostrated not only the Europeans, but all the black men of the party, and we were obliged to give up the search and return to the grasslands with such fragments of the skin as I had been able to purchase from the natives. Seeing my disappointment, the Belgian officers very kindly promised to use their best efforts to procure a perfect skin of the okapi.

Some months afterwards, the promise was kept by Mr Karl Eriksson, a Swedish officer in the service of the Congo Free State, who obtained from a native soldier the body of a recently killed okapi. He had the skin removed with much care, and sent it to me accompanied by the skull of the dead animal, and a smaller skull which he had obtained separately. The skin and skulls were forwarded to London, where they arrived after considerable delay. The British Museum entrusted the setting up of the okapi to Mr Rowland Ward of Piccadilly, and from the mounted skin and other data I eventually made various drawings, though the coloured drawing was in the main done in Africa from the skin, whilst this was fresh and still retained some indication of the animal's form. The colours of the hair were brighter before the skin made its journey to London. This coloured drawing originally differed in some particulars from the appearance of the okapi as set up by Mr Rowland Ward. Until the okapi has been photographed alive or dead, and its exact shape in the flesh is thus known, it is difficult to say which of the two versions of my water-colour drawing is the more correct – that published in the 'Proceedings of the Zoological Society' (which was done in Africa) and the later, revised version of the same painting. In the first version I have given the animal a very stout, horselike build: in the second, based on Mr Rowland Ward's restoration, I have given a more giraffe-like form to the mysterious okapi.

The size of the okapi is that of a large stag. It stands relatively higher in the legs than any member of the ox tribe; otherwise I should compare its size to that of an ox. Like the giraffe, this creature has only two hoofs, and no remains whatever of the other digits, which are represented outwardly in the deer, oxen and in most antelopes by the two little 'false hoofs' on either side of the third and fourth toes.

The coloration of the okapi is quite extraordinary. The cheeks and jaws are yellowish white, contrasting abruptly with the dark-coloured neck. The forehead is a deep red chestnut; the large broad ears are of the same tint, fringed, however, with jet black. The forehead ranges between vinous red and black in tint, and a black line follows the bridge of the nose down to the nostrils. The muzzle is sepia-coloured, but there is a faint rim or moustache of reddish yellow hair round the upper lip. The neck, shoulders, barrel, and back range in tone from sepia and jet black to rich vinous red. The belly is blackish, except just under the knees. The tail is bright chestnut red, with a small black tuft. The hindquarters, hind and fore legs are either snowy white or pale cream-colour, touched here and there with orange. They are boldly marked, however, with purple-black stripes and splodges, which give that zebra-like appearance to the limbs of the okapi that caused the first imperfect account of it to indicate the discovery of a new striped horse. The soft parts of the animal being as yet unknown, it cannot be stated positively that the okapi possesses a prehensile tongue like the giraffe, but the long and flexible lips would seem to atone for the very weak front teeth. It is probably by the lips and tongue that the creature gathers the leaves on which it feeds, for according to the accounts of the natives it lives entirely on foliage and small twigs. Like all living ruminants (except the camel), it has no front teeth in the upper jaw. The molars are very like those of the giraffe.

My first examination of the skull and skin of the okapi cause me to name it tentatively *Helladotherium*. The *Helladotherium* was a giraffe-like animal that existed in the Tertiary Epoch in Greece, Asia Minor, and India. In India the *Helladotherium* attained a very great size, but the Greek specimens were not quite as large as the modern giraffe. The *Helladotherium* was hornless, like the okapi, and in another point it resembled this animal, because the neck was not disproportionately long, and the fore and hind limbs were nearly equal in length. The okapi bears on the frontal and nasal bones three slight prominences, which may be the commencement of horn-cores. These are covered outwardly with little twists of hair. From the shape of the skull, which is straight and not arched, Professor Ray Lankester argues that the okapi has never developed horns. Though the okapi bears certain superficial resemblances to the *Helladotherium*, it is probable, on the whole, that it comes nearest in relationship to the giraffe. Being, however, sufficiently different from both, it has been constituted by Professor Lankester a separate genus, to which he has given the name *Okapia*.

So far as is yet known, the existing range of the okapi is confined to the northern part of the Congo Forest, near the Semliki River. The okapi is found in the little territory of Mboga, which is an outlying portion of the Uganda Protectorate. It is also found in the adjoining province of the Congo Free State. This same forest, I believe, conceals other wonders besides the okapi, not yet brought to light, including enormous gorillas. I have seen photographs of these huge apes, taken from dead animals which have been killed by the natives and brought in to the Belgians. A careful search might reveal several other strange additions to the world's mammalian fauna.

Quite recently fossil remains of giraffe-like animals have been found in Lower Egypt, as well as in Arabia, India, Greece, Asia Minor, and Southern Europe. It is probable that the okapi and giraffe are the last two surviving forms of this group in tropical Africa. The giraffe has escaped extermination from the attacks of carnivorous animals by developing keen sight, wary habits, and a size of enormous bulk. The giraffe, unlike the okapi, prefers relatively open country, dotted with low acacia trees, on which it feeds. Towering up above these trees, the giraffe with its large eyes can scan the surrounding country from an altitude of twenty feet above the ground, and in this way during the daytime, and possibly on nights when they are not too dark, can detect the approach of a troop of lions, the only creature besides man which can do it any harm. Man, of course, has done his level best to exterminate the mammoth, the Ur ox, the quagga, the dodo, and the auk. But for the presence of man, the giraffe might have been one of the lords of the earth. The defenceless okapi, however, only survived by slinking into the densest parts of the Congo Forest, where the lion never penetrates, and where the leopard takes to a tree life and lives on monkeys. The only human enemies of the okapi hitherto have been the Congo Dwarfs and a few Bantu Negroes who dwell on the fringe of the Congo Forest. How much longer the okapi will survive now that the natives possess guns and collectors are on the search for this extraordinary animal, it is impossible to say. Let us earnestly hope that the British and Belgian governments will combine to save the okapi.

Snake Man

Alan Wykes

Constantine Ionides was one of the world's most famous herpetologists. His quest was a particularly dangerous one. He supplied zoos and serum-making laboratories with poisonous snakes, caught at great risk to himself – in fact, he was bitten no fewer than thirteen times. Here is a 'typical' working day in his life, which ended in 1967.

At a little after eight in the morning a messenger arrived in a state of considerable agitation. His news was that his wife, who had been helping with the clearing of fallen mango leaves, had uncovered a spitting cobra while raking the ground and had been spat at in both eyes and blinded; also, high in the mango tree beside which the cobra lurked, a green mamba had been observed curled on a branch in the sun. We first of all set off in the Bedford truck to the village in question, where Ionides treated the woman's eyes with a solution of permanganate of potash squirted from a fountain-pen filler. Her sight would come back in an hour or two, he said, though her eyes would be painful for a few days.

We now proceeded a short distance through heavy banana and pineapple growth to where a tall mango tree stood in the centre of a space fifty or so yards across. Here, it seemed, was the venue of our immediate quest.

Not far from the tree stood a three-feet-high cone-shaped stack of branches, twigs, leaves, straw and grass. This was the heap the woman had been raking when the cobra had attacked her. We had, of course, no evidence that the snake was still there, and as no one had been posted to keep watch it seemed highly probable that it had had plenty of opportunity to go on its way unseen; but Ionides thought it likely that the cobra was still somewhere underneath the muck. Before we began turning it over, however, he demanded to be shown the mamba that was alleged to be in the tree. Unfortunately, if it was still there at all, it was too high to be seen through the heavy foliage, and Ionides decided to concentrate on getting the cobra first. 'The disturbance and vibration of feet down here is going to affect him first anyway, if he's still there, so let's see what we can find.'

He armed me with one of the short wooden sticks with the Y-notch at the end and told me to put on a pair of the rubber-set goggles – which he also wore. 'Now walk slowly round and round the heap,' he added, and keep a distance of eight feet or so from it. While I'm dismantling the heap I want you to keep a very careful watch and tell me if you see anything that looks like a snake. He may be black, brown, red, grey or pink. Walk softly, and, if I give you any orders, carry them out without hesitation.'

He began very carefully to dismantle the heap of rubbish with his forked stick, spreading out the leaves and twigs over a much wider area, prodding gently, and from time to time shifting his stance so that he got a good circumambient view. I too was walking slowly around at my prescribed distance, changing from time to time from a clockwise to a widdershins direction and peering with (I hope) a keen eye at every inch of the slowly flattening heap. I carried my stick like a lance and felt myself to be quite a daring dog. (Eight feet is a good distance from a snake to feel daring at.)

Quite suddenly I saw Ionides make a lunge with his stick. 'Keep your distance, but move round to my side,' he called; and when I'd done this he added, 'Now, if you look along the stick you'll see our cobra thrashing about in there. I've got him pinned down, but nothing like near enough to his head. He's got both striking and spitting power at the moment. I want you to un-cover him a little more, and, if you can, put your stick on his neck.'

This, I need scarcely say, was not easily done. I could in fact see very little of the cobra thrashing about. I carefully thrust aside a few more leafy branches without noticing any more than a vague movement; but suddenly, as I lifted off a few lengths of straw, he became visible in a far from vague way. His head swung up through the scattered rubbish and I had a splendid sight of a cobra with hood expanded spitting a long jet of venom directly at Ionides' left eye. His marksmanship, as I saw for myself in a moment, was remarkably accurate; but for a few seconds I was far too anxious to aid the situation by getting his head pinned down to do more than overhear the impressive flow of invective Ionides was directing at him in exchange for the venom. Numer-ous times before, I had seen Ionides in precisely similar circum-stances pin down the head of a mamba or cobra while one of the Africans fixed the body – so quickly and effortlessly that it was difficult to believe that there was any skill at all involved; but doing the job myself – that, not altogether surprisingly, revealed somewhat jitteringly that there was, and that I didn't possess any of it. The cobra spat again – at me this time; but the venom fell a bit short. I made a few fierce lunges with my stick, all of them wildly inaccurate, began to feel panic, moved in near with some nonsensical notion of getting to grips with the snake to counteract my panic, and heard Ionides say sharply, 'Stop.'

Eagerly I stopped. 'I fear not,' he said courteously; 'your methods are a little too impatient. You're angering the cobra and there may be distressing results. Drop your stick on the ground exactly where it is; then come and take mine over.'

I did this, and as his stick was transferred from his grip to mine I noticed the stream of venom still running down his left goggle; I also noticed, with considerable trepidation, that the strength of the cobra beneath the stick was very powerful. Though forcibly held immobile at my point of contact with it, it seemed to have vigour and to spare in the bits that were lashing about, and this transmitted itself in a faint but unmistakable vibration to my hands. It still spat away angrily, though with weakening ejections now.

Immediately Ionides picked up the stick I'd dropped on the ground the situation – not unnaturally – changed. I could see exactly how I would go about the job and almost called to him to let me make another attempt. Wisdom prevailed, however, and I held on, somewhat ruefully, to the allotted task that had been more than half completed for me. All the same, it now seemed perfectly obvious to me that if the snake had got his neck into *that* position while I had been trying to pin down his neck I could scarcely have failed; for he had conveniently ducked his head beneath the rubbish and had come so close to, and parallel with, the ground that he seemed to be practically asking for it. (It was only later that I recalled that while I was having my chance of fixing him he had done exactly this, several times, but that I'd simply been too clumsy to cope with the opportunity.) Anyway, fixed he was within five seconds of Ionides taking over; and as he squatted down to grip the snake's head with the tongs he chose to enlighten me on the ability of the cobra to spread a hood. 'The cervical ribs are elongated,' he explained, 'so that when spread they flatten the neck and expand it into a hood. Now if you'd be so kind as to hand me one of those bags we'll incarcerate him.' He paused, then added with mild derision, 'No doubt you'll be able to turn the bag inside out for me.' I'd seen this done a good many times too, but I didn't accomplish it without a certain amount of fumbling. I did, however, accomplish it, and even got a good grip on the bag with the tongs and got the bagged snake into the box and nailed the lid down. 'Not bad,' I said with somewhat glowing self-gratification.

'As a snake-catcher,' Ionides said with bland charm, 'you make a good writer. Now: to business. Allegedly, if you recall, there's a green mamba at the top of that tree. This time I think you'd better stay on the ground.'

He moved towards the tree. The villagers, who all this time had been watching the capture of the cobra with their usual display of alarm mingled with high-pressure giggles, moved in round us and Ionides bellowed at them to stand back. They scampered away and hid among the trees and bamboos, their faces peering from behind boles and leaves with a coyness I found faintly reminiscent of the chorus in a spectacular but un-inspired Drury Lane musical of the 'thirties, 'Song of the Drum'. Only one of the elders – a man with broken teeth and a skull-cap embroidered with gold thread – stayed to offer an indication of where the mamba had been seen. Though voluble, his informa-tion appeared to be pretty useless by now, for although I could see Ionides examining with intense care the indicated topmost branches on one side of the tree, it was clear from his frequent head shakings that the mamba must have moved elsewhere. Since the tree was an isolated one, though, presumably the snake must still be ensconced somewhere in the foliage unless it had descended and escaped across the ground – an unlikely happening in view of the general chaos after the blinding of the woman.

Several times before I had witnessed the capture of a mamba in a mango or cashew tree. On each occasion Rashedi and Kingukuti, two of Ionides' men, had nimbly ascended the tree with their grab-sticks and with infinite patience had eventually got the two pincer-grips on the snake and brought it unhurriedly down to the lower branches until it was within reach of Ionides, who remained on the ground wielding a third grab-stick. Each capture naturally posed different problems; but the principal one, after the snake had been gripped, was always for the 'boys' to descend through the heavy foliage, passing the sticks adroitly through interstices in the branches, without damaging, or releasing the pincer-grips' hold on the snake – which would of course be vigorously lashing out and curling its tail round innumerable branches in its efforts to escape. It had always seemed to me a splendid 'moment of truth' when the mamba, magnificent in its anger, had finally been lowered to the ground and was being released from the pinioning grips and grasped by Ionides' hand through a thin cotton bag.

But all these captures had involved three men; this time, apparently, Ionides proposed to ascend the tree alone and attempt the capture single-handed. He was standing back now, looking upward, the tattered brim of his hat rolled back and held with one hand, a 'Crown Bird' between his lips. 'Not much hope of spotting it from down here,' he said. 'I must go up. I don't care for climbing trees very much. Heights don't agree with me. However, that's not the fault of the snake. I'll take the extending grab-stick if you'll be so kind as to hand it to me.' I gave him the stick and he thanked me and, with his head cocked on one side and the familiar satyric smile, added, 'I advise you not to stand directly under the tree; if I should inadvertently knock the snake down it might fall on you; then you won't even be a good writer, let alone a bad snake-catcher.'

I estimated the tree to be a good hundred feet high. About ten feet up its bole divided into three almost symmetrical branches, and above that there was a cool leafless tunnel ascending for perhaps another twenty feet to the thick foliage that reached to the top. I paced out the spread of the tree and found it to be about twenty-three feet across. Somewhere in that extensive foliage a green mamba lay curled along a branch. I watched intently as Ionides hitched himself fleetly up into the lower branches and leant his grab-stick against a convenient support while he made a rapid survey. No sign of the snake, apparently, for he moved round in turn to the remaining two principal branches, and then climbed on upward, very slowly, through the leafless tunnel until he was almost completely concealed from me in the upper foliage.

As a matter of interest, I was timing this whole operation. It was now nine-ten a.m. exactly, and for the next ten minutes I heard and saw nothing at all but the faint rustle and movement of leaves. Then Ionides began to descend and I saw his legs emerge among the lower branches. 'He's there all right,' he called softly. 'Well out on a limb at the top. My dear boy, if you have prayers, prepare to pray them now. I already feel twinges of vertigo.'

With that he disappeared upward once more, having taken the grab-stick from its resting-place. 'Mind over matter,' I called up, with some intention of encouragement, and heard him swear softly.

He had of course other problems beside his acrophobia. The snake could scarcely now be unaware of his approach. Unable to ascend farther, or to move laterally to another tree, it could escape only downward, and if the fear of capture turned its natural nervousness into aggression Ionides was in an impossible position to escape. Also, the snake had every advantage of evasive movement. As I had observed for myself, it was difficult enough for Rashedi and Kingukuti, who were as nimble as monkeys and as correspondingly fearless of heights, to capture an arboreal mamba with two sticks. I failed to see how, if at all, Ionides was going to succeed with one and bring the snake down as well. I nervously moved outward to a wide perimeter and continued my crick-necked gazing upward.

A disturbance of the branches showed me where Ionides was. He was about six feet short of the top of the tree, and I could see that he was lying almost horizontally along a none-too-stout limb. Of the snake I could see nothing; but after a suspenseful interlude in which I thought I observed Ionides' eyes close as if the ground might be blurring below him, I watched what I had thought to be a thickened extremity of a branch detach itself and glide upward. The sun caught the bloom on the mamba's skin and I saw Ionides turn and manoeuvre the grab-stick back towards the interior of the tree in anticipation of the snake's escapist tactics.

At that moment, though, one of his worn plimsoll soles slipped a little, and he had to make a lunge to prevent himself falling. Those were an uncomfortable five seconds and I thought, 'Surely to God he'll leave the damned thing now and get down while he can.' Needless to say, he didn't. At nine thirty-seven the snake had apparently moved down a little, and I saw Ionides manoeuvring the grab-stick once again. All his movements were slow and extremely cautious. Once, I had another glimpse of the snake, and it appeared to be within a very few feet of Ionides' head. Then there was a quick, elaborate, and partially concealed series of movements and a triumphant cry from him.

It was ten-three then. But the operation was far from over. He had snapped the pincer-grip of the grab-stick fast on a very happily chosen spot a couple of inches behind the mamba's head. The difficulty of working the stick and the snake downward through the close foliage, however, proved to be too great, and after ten minutes of frustrated attempts at doing so he decided to grip the snake's neck in one hand and abandon the stick altogether. 'I'm dropping the stick,' he called. 'Mind your head, but catch it if you can. Those sticks are very light aluminium and easily distorted.' The stick came clattering down and I managed to catch it.

Then began what must have been for him an interminable journey downward. With only one hand to assist himself, and a five-foot mamba lashing furiously about his arm and body, and with, as he told me afterwards, a discomforting feeling of insecurity due to frequent and rapid attacks of giddiness, it can hardly have seemed brief. But at ten thirty-seven he had reached the junction of the branches ten feet above the ground. His shirt and slacks were ripped into tatters by the abrasions of the descent and his skin was bleeding in several places. Hastily I scrabbled up the heap of refuse in which we'd caught the cobra and piled it at the base of the tree. It would be impossible for him to shin down a vertical trunk with one hand, and I wanted to break his jump so that his leg wouldn't suffer any damage.

'Okay,' I told him, 'jump now.'

He jumped, very lightly, landed in the heap with relaxed knees, and scarcely toppled at all. He still held the mamba firmly in his right hand. Its body was coiled remorselessly round his shoulder and arm, and its tongue was darting furiously in and out. It was ten forty-five then, and we bagged the snake quickly.

Operation Oryx

M. H. Woodford

During the past fifty years no fewer than forty species of mammals alone have been exterminated. Many others are threatened and the only hope for some of these animals lies in captive breeding in zoos, with the ultimate aim of restocking the native habitat. The well-known expedition described here pioneered the way for many other projects, and creatures as varied as the Hawaiian goose and Przewalski's horse are being successfully rescued through captive breeding.

The Arabian oryx is a medium-sized antelope, weighing about 250 pounds and standing forty inches high at the shoulders. Its coat is pure white, with chocolate-coloured legs and face markings, and both males and females have long, straight horns. In fact, the oryx is among the animals thought by some to be the legendary unicorn, for when seen from certain angles it appears to have only one horn. The animal has great powers of strength, endurance, and bravery and many Bedouin believe that by killing and eating it, some of these attributes will pass to the successful hunter. The consumption of oryx flesh is also supposed to rejuvenate the senile, cure stomach aches, heal fractures, and expel embedded bullets! These beliefs have caused the oryx to be named 'Doctor of the Arabs' by some of the tribesmen of Arabia.

In the past, the Arabian oryx ranged throughout the greater part of the Middle East. In 1800, oryx were still to be found in Sinai, southern Palestine, Jordan, Iraq, and almost all of the Arabian peninsula. During the next 100 years, however, the range of this spectacular antelope diminished rapidly, and by the out-

break of the First World War there were very few survivors outside Saudi Arabia. Human activity in the deserts then increased
rapidly, and it was this factor, coupled with the ensuing wide
distribution of fire-arms, which brought about the extinction of
the animal outside Saudi Arabia. The last remaining 'unicorns'
took refuge in the 1930's in the Nafud desert in northern Saudi
Arabia and in the Southern Wilderness of the Rub al Khali, or
Empty Quarter, in the south. These two groups were isolated
from one another.

In the late 1930's, the Arabian princes obtained access to oil
revenues, which enabled them to purchase cars, petrol and
automatic weapons. Then, copying the example of the oil company employees, they set out to hunt the rather scanty wildlife of
the desert.

Unfortunately for them, these fleet antelopes prefer to live on
the *jol*, or gravel desert, where their speed and endurance stand
them in good stead against enemies on foot or camel-riders. But
the *jol* is also ideal for high-speed driving; it is flat, and only
rarely intersected by *wadis*, or dry water courses, where the sand
is soft. With the coming of cars and lorries to the desert, oryx and
gazelle were driven down and slaughtered in hundreds by hunting
parties composed of up to 300 vehicles. Repeating shot-guns as
well as rifles were used, and often the terrified animals were
simply chased until they were exhausted, when their throats
were cut by members of the royal retinue. In the last ten years,
the richer sheikhs have even added light aircraft to their hunting
parties.

In January 1961, the Fauna Preservation Society heard that a
member of the ruling family of Qatar, a small oil-rich state on the

Persian Gulf, had led a motorized hunting party some 600 miles across the Rub al Khali; the party had then killed a large number of oryx in their last refuge in the desolate *wadis* just inside the north-eastern corner of the Eastern Aden Protectorate. Formal protests were made to the Qataris, and plans were made immediately to launch a rescue operation. For a variety of reasons it was not possible for the expedition to leave until the spring of 1962 and in the meantime, in spite of high-level protests, the Qataris carried out two more raids in the same area in December 1961 and January 1962. Each time they found and killed a number of oryx.

Our expedition consisted of seven Europeans, from Britain, Aden, and Kenya, and was led by Major Ian Grimwood, Chief Game Ranger of Kenya. For reconnaissance, the team was equipped with a Piper Cruiser aircraft lent by the East African Wildlife Society. We assembled in Mukalla in mid-April, and set out in a convoy manned and provided by the local Arab military unit, the Hadhrami Bedouin Legion, a colourful force commanded by Lt-Colonel J. W. Gray. Our convoy of Land Rovers and Bedford 3-tonners wound its way laboriously north-west into the fertile Wadi Do'an. We then followed the ancient incense routes until we came to the white Legion-occupied fort overlooking the well at Al Abr in the country of the Saar.

We lingered at the fort only long enough to inspect some pre-Islamic rock carvings, among which we were able to distinguish representations of the Arabian ostrich, the wolf, and the oryx. We left at dawn so as to have time to cross the soft sand of some of the southernmost dunes of the Rub al Khali before the sun made the sand too hot to support our vehicles.

From Al Abr we motored in a north-easterly direction along the length of the gravel plains of the northern deserts, stopping only for a few hours at night to pitch our camp on the sand among the scorpions and camel spiders. We passed the Legion forts at Thamud and Sanau and after seven days of driving in temperatures which reached 120 degrees Fahrenheit by day, we reached our destination. This was the Wadi Mitan, an area of gravel-desert *jol* lying between the sand seas of Saudi Arabia to the north and the mountains of the Mahra country to the south. We were 120 miles from the well at Sanau and an equal distance from the only other source of fresh water at Habarut. We were in oryx country at last!

As we progressed eastwards, so the stories told us by the Bedouin were of more recent sightings. At Sanau fort we had enlisted the aid of two members of the élite corps of Desert Guards, the trackers and guides for the Hadhrami Bedouin Legion. These two men, Tomatum and Mabkhut Bin Hassanah, promised us that we should catch oryx if we could find tracks not less than forty-eight hours old. They indicated that we should have to search an area of about six thousand square miles. So with high hopes we pitched our tents and set up the radio homing beacon for the aircraft.

We prepared the catching vehicle, a thirty-hundredweight truck. In the roof of the cab we cut a turret so that a man could stand on the passenger seat with his head and shoulders projecting through the roof. From this vantage point we hoped it would be possible to slip a noose of cotton rope, attached to a long aluminium pole, over the head of a galloping oryx.

The steppe country of the Wadi Mitan is uninhabited in

summer, for the Bedouin, driven south by the heat, move with their families and camels to the wells at Sanau and Habarut. The northern deserts are left at this time of year to the wolf, the desert cat, the gazelle, and, we hoped, the oryx.

Our guides told us that our best plan was to travel north up the *wadi* to the point where it disappears into the dunes of the Ramlat Mitan and Saudi Arabia. Here, in this jumble of grey gravel plains, soft yellow *wadi* bottoms with their sparse vegetation, red and yellow incipient sand dunes, and rocky gorges, we searched for days for the fresh tracks of an oryx driven by the daily increasing heat of the sun from the dunes on to the *jol*.

We saw the tracks left by the sand tyres of the Qatari hunting vehicles which harassed the oryx in this area in January. We crossed the ancient camel road which disappeared beneath an enormous sand dune and which is said to lead to the legendary city of Ophir, buried somewhere in the wastes of the Empty Quarter. After a week of fruitless searching we suddenly came upon fresh oryx tracks; we had followed them for about twenty-five miles when our guides told us that we were getting close to the animal. We then moved forward at about five m.p.h. with Tomatum or Mabkhut sitting on the bonnet of the Land Rover. This we did early in the morning and during the evening when the low sun cast a tiny shadow on the almost invisible hoofmarks.

And then, a few moments after a warning from Tomatum, we saw an oryx. It got to its feet from where it had been lying in the shade of an acacia bush, stretched, and set out across the flat stony wastes. The catching truck set out in pursuit and within a few minutes we were all sitting on one of the rarest animals in the world. The capture had proved easy. The oryx ran straight and did not jink. His top speed was about thirty-five m.p.h. and he was overhauled and noosed before he became exhausted. Following a mile or so behind the catching party was one of the Hadhrami Bedouin Legion's 3-tonners loaded with our escort of Legionnaires and two oryx crates. After the oryx, which proved to be an old bull, had been injected with a drug to ward off the effects of the shock of his capture, he was put in a crate and transported slowly across the desert back to the fort at Sanau where a stall had been prepared for him.

We spent the next fourteen days searching. Our pilot, accompanied by Tomatum as navigator (because our homing beacon had broken down), flew many abortive sorties. All he saw were Qatari tracks and occasional gazelle. Then suddenly we came on the fresh tracks of oryx moving south towards our camp in the Wadi Mitan. At once we started to follow them and after tracking in the blinding sunlight for fifty-eight miles we caught up with three oryx resting from the midday heat in a little area of shade under an overhanging rock. Once again the catching vehicle raced out across the gravel and soon the noose had been slipped neatly over the rapier-like horns of a fine female oryx. Leaving this most valuable captive behind in its crate on the *jol*, the truck tore after the other two. This time the chase was rather more protracted because the vehicle became stuck in the soft sand of the *wadi* bed. Finally, however, both were successfully caught.

During this last chase Major Grimwood, who was manipulating the catching poles, was thrown against the edge of the turret and broke two ribs.

Shortly after the capture of these last two oryx, both of which were bulls, one of them died. The subsequent post-mortem revealed the presence of a ·303 bullet which must have been fired some weeks previously by the Qatari raiders.

We now had our hands full back at the fort in Sanau. Three oryx , two bulls and a cow, had to be fed and to do this a Land Rover had to scour the surrounding gypsum hills for suitable vegetation. Meanwhile, back in the Wadi Mitan, the catching teams continued their efforts to locate further specimens. But luck had left us. We had caught all the animals we had seen, and although we saw signs of a total of eleven oryx, it was evident that the remainder, harried so often by motorized hunters, had withdrawn eastward in the direction of Mugshin in Dhofar.

On May 24th an RAF Beverley flew up from Aden on a ration run to the fort at Sanau. It had been arranged that we should load our crated oryx into the empty aircraft for the return flight to Aden.

We left Sanau at 4.15 in the morning, just as the sun was stretching out long fingers of yellow light over the gravel steppes; five hours later we were dripping with sweat as we transferred our precious cargo from the Beverley to an RAF Transport Command Britannia at Aden's Khormaksar Airport. The final leg of the oryx's long journey to their 'place of greater safety' in Kenya was soon under way and the same afternoon we landed at Nairobi Airport. Customs formalities were waived and the crates were quickly loaded on to Game Department lorries. These carried the somewhat bewildered trio to a game farm just outside Nairobi; there they were released in specially prepared pens equipped with infra-red lamps against the cold, damp Nairobi weather.

The oryx have now been moved to Isiolo, in the Northern

Frontier District of Kenya, where the climate is more suitable. They will stay in Isiolo until it has been decided where this breeding nucleus of Arabian oryx shall be located. The ultimate aim of the Fauna Preservation Society is to return some specimens to Arabia when adequate arrangements have been made to ensure their protection. In the meantime, it is likely that the raids from Qatar will continue, for the prevailing philosophy in Arabia towards wildlife is: 'If I don't kill them today, someone else will tomorrow.'

First Catch Your Goose

Peter Scott and James Fisher

The wonders of bird migration have never been completely and satis-factorily explained. Here two of the most distinguished modern ornitholo-gists show something of the important scientific value of ringing birds, both to assess their numbers and to plot their migration routes.

Just before a calm October sunrise the first wild geese lifted from the sandbanks of a Scottish firth and headed inland towards their feeding grounds. There were twenty geese in the skein; and they flew high over a village, over a railway, over two main roads and three miles of farm lands, before they came to the familiar stubble-fields where they had been feeding each day for nearly a week. They began to glide down and to circle over the oat-stubble. It seemed that they were not, after all, the first geese to leave the firth, for already half a dozen were there ahead of them. They hardly seemed to notice that those half-dozen were strangely still, nor could they have known that underneath the feathers were bodies of wood-wool. So they landed beside the decoys, and stood for a while looking at them. The lack of movement made them feel slightly uncomfortable, but some of their number began to feed. Fifty more geese were already circling over the field, and the distant roar of goose voices indicated that more were on the way. Above the wood on the hill behind was a great skein of five hundred, and as it reached the familiar fields the long lines of its V-formation broke; the geese came tumbling down like autumn leaves in a gale. Nearer the ground they re-

formed into a tight flock, which swept backwards and forwards
in the low orange sunlight over the thick cluster of geese on the
ground. At each sweep more geese dropped down on fast-flapping
wings, and the crowd on the ground became a solid blue-grey
patch on the yellow stubble. Still more skeins were coming over
the wood, tumbling down, circling and settling, and the chorus
of their calling rose and fell like waves breaking on the shore.
More than a thousand were down now, and the original six still
ones were swamped and unnoticed by the crowd of moving,
feeding, quarrelling, preening geese.

None of them had noticed the little camouflaged box on wheels
which stood in the corner of the field close to the hedge. None of
them knew that four human beings were sitting inside it, watching through narrow shuttered windows, gauging the exact position of the flock through binoculars which wobbled with excitement. Stuck in to the stubble straw were markers – white-tipped
goose tail-feathers; and the thickest part of the flock was within
the square they formed. Long nets lay folded and hidden under a
thin layer of straw and grass, the rockets which were to propel
them lay in the little holes which had been dug for them, equally
well hidden, and connected to the hide by 150 yards of wire flex.
For once, after days of preparation and misfortune, everything
had gone right for the goose catchers.

The flight had been a fast one, flock following flock before the
first ones had had time to disperse across the field. The geese had
pitched in the right place, no suspicion of the nets or decoys had
caused them to flare, or to swing wide before settling, no un-
timely shepherd or rabbit-catcher or aeroplane had appeared to
disturb them, and now they were feeding right in the catching

area – now was the time. 'Start the cameras – one, two, three, four, five, FIRE!' With a swish the rockets leap out and carry the nets over a part of the flock. It's a catch, a big catch, with more than a hundred geese under the nets.

A jeep drives on to the field, the party from the hide runs out and the marking of the geese begins. As each bird is taken out of the net it is brought to the ringer, who slips a numbered and addressed aluminium ring on to its leg and closes the ring with pliers. The details are written down in a notebook. Then the white tail is dipped into a bucket of dye and finally the goose is put into one of the compartments of the 'keeping-cage' – a device of hessian and bamboo which provides a row of 'stalls' in which the geese can wait until the last of their number has been marked. The keeping-cages have no bottoms, so that the geese are sitting on the ground, and half an hour later, when all have been ringed and dyed, the keeping-cages are lifted off so that all the birds fly away simultaneously as a flock.

For geese this is important, because family ties are strong throughout the winter. If the geese were liberated singly the families would be broken up, and also geese are more vulnerable when alone than when flying in a flock. After a catch the released geese form up into a V and fly off towards the estuary.

These rocket nets were invented and developed by the Severn Wildfowl Trust in 1948 (although a comparable method using small cannons to propel the net was developed soon afterwards, and quite independently, in America). During the winter of 1950-51 the Trust's netting team caught and ringed no less than 634 pinkfeet, mostly in Scotland. In subsequent winters we have caught even more.

Apart from the scientific value of the results, the actual netting is immensely exciting. How often we have sat breathlessly in the trailer-hide as the first geese prepared to settle. The precise point at which the first bird puts down its feet seems, at that moment, to be the most important thing in the world, the only thing that matters. If they pitch wrong there is bitter anxiety and frustration, but if they pitch right, then there are golden moments as more and more geese settle and the grey patch thickens on the yellow stubble. And all the while the breathless tension rises. Will they thicken in the right place? Will they see the wire or the nets? Is this going to be the big catch of which we have dreamed, and for which we have been preparing and waiting so long?

It was only natural that, while making those first Scottish catches in October 1950, our minds should turn to the possibility of following the marked birds to their breeding grounds in the Arctic, and catching and marking more during the flightless period in late summer, when the adults moult their wing feathers and the young are still unable to fly. This we thought might lead to all sorts of new and interesting conclusions, not only about the age and migration of pinkfeet, but also about their family affinities, their local movements, their attachment to particular nesting sites and feeding grounds and, most important of all, about their numbers. For when a substantial part of a population is marked, and that population is sampled again later, the proportion of birds in the second sample which already carry rings can lead the sampler to a mathematical estimate, within calculable limits of probability, of the size of the total population.

Why should such an estimate be important? First there is the conception that all new scientific knowledge is important whether or not it can be directed towards the material benefit of mankind. The study of birds only rarely has significance in the field of economics, but mankind would be the poorer without a capacity to be curious about the living creatures which share his world, and poorer still without the creatures themselves. Yet many species have already been exterminated as a direct result of man's greed and thoughtlessness. Such a danger threatens various kinds of ducks and geese. It is important, therefore, to find out which species are threatened and which are safe, how acute is the danger, what factors affect their status, whether they are increasing or decreasing and by how much. We must know these things before we can preserve the stocks of wild ducks and geese for future generations to enjoy, whether as naturalists or sportsmen or both.

These are the reasons why we think estimates of total population are important and why we undertook this programme of marking pinkfeet on a large scale, which set us off on our wild-goose chase from Scotland to the stark fells of Iceland – where we marked no fewer than 1,151 pinkfooted geese, rounding them up on horseback into catching-pens, a method made possible by their flightless state.

Strange Ride

Charles Waterton

Waterton, who lived from 1782 to 1865, was a pioneer in helping to change men's attitude to nature and in arousing their interest in the subject. He realized that the only true way of getting to know wild creatures was to study them on the spot. To this end he made four expeditions to unexplored South America, frequently risking his life in the process. He turned his estate in Yorkshire into a wildlife sanctuary and was probably the first naturalist to mark birds for recognition purposes.

I had long wished to examine the native haunts of the cayman, but as the River Demerara did not afford a specimen of the large kind, I was obliged to go to the River Essequibo to look for one.

I got the canoe ready, and went down in it to Georgetown, where, having put in the necessary articles for the expedition, not forgetting a couple of large shark-hooks with chains attached to them, and a coil of strong new rope, I hoisted a little sail which I had got made on purpose, and at six o'clock in the morning shaped our course for the River Essequibo. I had put a pair of shoes on to prevent the tar at the bottom of the canoe from sticking to my feet. The sun was flaming hot, and from eleven o'clock till two beat perpendicularly upon the top of my feet, betwixt the shoes and the trousers. Not feeling it disagreeable, or being in the least aware of painful consequences, as I had been barefoot for months, I neglected to put on a pair of short stockings which I had with me. I did not reflect that sitting still in one place, with your feet exposed to the sun, was very different from being exposed to the sun while in motion.

We went ashore in the Essequibo about three o'clock in the afternoon, to choose a place for the night's residence, to collect firewood, and to set the fish-hooks. It was then that I first began to find my legs very painful: they soon became much inflamed and red and blistered; and it required considerable caution not to burst the blisters, otherwise sores would have ensued. I immediately got into the hammock, and there passed a painful and sleepless night, and for two days after I was disabled from walking.

About midnight, as I was lying awake and in great pain, I heard the Indian say, 'Massa, massa, you no hear tiger?' I listened attentively, and heard the softly sounding tread of his feet as he approached us. The moon had gone down, but every now and then we could get a glance of him by the light of our fire. He was the jaguar, for I could see the spots of his body. Had I wished to have fired at him I was not able to take a sure aim, for I was in such pain that I could not turn myself in my hammock. The Indian would have fired, but I would not allow him to do so, as I wanted to see a little more of our new visitor, for it is not every day or night that the traveller is favoured with an undisturbed sight of the jaguar in his own forests.

Whenever the fire got low the jaguar came a little nearer, and when the Indian renewed it he retired abruptly. Sometimes he would come within twenty yards, and then we had a view of him sitting on his hind-legs like a dog; sometimes he moved slowly to and fro, and at other times we could hear him mend his pace, as if impatient. At last the Indian, not relishing the idea of having such company in the neighbourhood, could contain himself no longer, and set up a most tremendous yell. The jaguar bounded off like a racehorse, and returned no more. It appeared by the print of his feet the next morning that he was a full-grown jaguar.

In two days after this we got to the first falls in the Essequibo. There was a superb barrier of rocks quite across the river. In the rainy season these rocks are for the most part under water, but it being now dry weather we had a fine view of them, while the water from the river above them rushed through the different openings in majestic grandeur. Here, on a little hill jutting out into the river, stands the house of Mrs Peterson, the last house of people of colour up this river. I hired a Negro from her and a coloured man who pretended that they knew the haunts of the cayman and understood everything about taking him. We were a day in passing these falls and rapids, celebrated for the pacou, the richest and most delicious fish in Guiana. The coloured man was now in his element: he stood in the head of the canoe, and with his bow and arrow shot the pacou as they were swimming in the stream. The arrow had scarcely left the bow before he had plunged head-long into the river and seized the fish as it was struggling with it. He dived and swam like an otter, and rarely missed the fish he aimed at.

Did my pen, gentle reader, possess descriptive powers, I would here give thee an idea of the enchanting scenery of the Essequibo; but that not being the case, thou must be contented with a moderate and well-intended attempt.

Nothing could be more lovely than the appearance of the forest on each side of this noble river. Hills rose on hills in fine gradation, all covered with trees of gigantic height and size. Here their leaves were of a lively purple, and there of the deepest green. Sometimes the caracara extended its scarlet blossoms from branch to branch, and gave the tree the appearance as though it had been hung with garlands.

This delightful scenery of the Essequibo made the soul overflow with joy, and caused you to rove in fancy through fairyland; till, on turning an angle of the river, you were recalled to more sober reflections on seeing the once grand and towering mora now dead and ragged in its topmost branches, while its aged trunk, undermined by the rushing torrent, hung as though in sorrow over the river, which ere long would receive it and sweep it away for ever.

During the day the trade-wind blew a gentle and refreshing breeze, which died away as the night set in, and then the river was as smooth as glass.

The moon was within three days of being full, so that we did not regret the loss of the sun, which set in all its splendour. Scarce had he sunk behind the western hills when the goatsuckers sent forth their soft and plaintive cries; some often repeating 'Who are you – who, who, who are you?' and others 'Willy, willy, willy come go.'

The Indian and Daddy Quashi often shook their head at this, and said they were bringing talk from Yabahou, who is the Evil Spirit of the Essequibo. It was delightful to sit on the branch of a fallen tree near the water's edge and listen to these harmless birds as they repeated their evening song; and watch the owls and vampires as they every now and then passed up and down the river.

The next day, about noon, as we were proceeding onwards, we heard the campanero tolling in the depth of the forest. Though I should not then have stopped to dissect even a rare bird, having a greater object in view, still I could not resist the opportunity offered of acquiring the campanero. The place where he was tolling was low and swampy, and my legs not having quite recovered from the effects of the sun, I sent the Indian to shoot the campanero. He got up to the tree, which he described as very high, with a naked top, and situated in a swamp. He fired at the bird, but either missed it or did not wound it sufficiently to bring it down. This was the only opportunity I had of getting a campanero during this expedition. We had never heard one toll before this morning, and never heard one after.

About an hour before sunset we reached the place which the two men who had joined us at the falls pointed out as a proper one to find a cayman. There was a large creek close by and a sandbank gently sloping to the water. Just within the forest, on this bank, we cleared a place of brushwood, suspended the hammocks from the trees, and then picked up enough of decayed wood for fuel.

The Indian found a large land-tortoise, and this, with plenty of fresh fish which we had in the canoe, afforded a supper not to be despised.

The tigers had kept up a continual roaring every night since we had entered the Essequibo. The sound was awfully fine. Sometimes it was in the immediate neighbourhood; at other times it was far off, and echoed amongst the hills like distant thunder.

It may, perhaps, not be amiss to observe here that when the word tiger is used it does not mean the Bengal tiger. It means the jaguar, whose skin is beautifully spotted, and not striped like that of the tiger in the East. It is, in fact, the tiger of the new world, and receiving the name of tiger from the discoverers of South

America it has kept it ever since. It is a cruel, strong and dangerous beast, but not so courageous as the Bengal tiger.

We now baited a shark-hook with a large fish, and put it upon a board about a yard long and one foot broad which we had brought on purpose. This board was carried out in the canoe, about forty yards into the river. By means of a string long enough to reach the bottom of the river, and at the end of which string was fastened a stone, the board was kept, as it were, at anchor. One end of the new rope I had bought in town was reeved through the chain of the shark-hook and the other end fastened to a tree on the sandbank.

It was now an hour after sunset. The sky was cloudless, and the moon shone beautifully bright. There was not a breath of wind in the heavens, and the river seemed like a large plain of quicksilver. Every now and then a huge fish would strike and plunge in the water; then the owls and goat-suckers would continue their lamentations, and the sound of these was lost in the prowling tiger's growl. Then all was still again and silent as midnight.

The caymen were now upon the stir, and at intervals their noise could be distinguished amid that of the jaguar, the owls, the goat-suckers and frogs. It was a singular and awful sound. It was like a suppressed sigh bursting forth all of a sudden, and so loud that you might hear it above a mile off. First one emitted this horrible noise, and then another answered him; and on looking at the countenances of the people round me I could plainly see that they expected to have a cayman that night.

We were at supper when the Indian, who seemed to have had one eye on the turtle-pot and the other on the bait in the river, said he saw the cayman coming.

Upon looking towards the place there appeared something on the water like a black log of wood. It was so unlike anything alive that I doubted if it were a cayman; but the Indian smiled and said he was sure it was one, for he remembered seeing a cayman some years ago when he was in the Essequibo.

At last it gradually approached the bait, and the board began to move. The moon shone so bright that we could distinctly see him open his huge jaws and take in the bait. We pulled the rope. He immediately let drop the bait; and then we saw his black head retreating from the board to the distance of a few yards; and there it remained quite motionless.

He did not seem inclined to advance again; and so we finished our supper. In about an hour's time he again put himself in motion, and took hold of the bait. But probably suspecting that he had to deal with knaves and cheats, he held it in his mouth but did not swallow it. We pulled the rope again, but with no better success than the first time.

He retreated as usual, and came back again in about an hour. We paid him every attention till three o'clock in the morning, when, worn out with disappointment, we went to the hammocks, turned in and fell asleep.

When day broke we found that he had contrived to get the bait from the hook, though we had tied it on with string. We had now no more hopes of taking a cayman till the return of night. The Indian took off into the woods and brought back a noble supply of game. The rest of us went into the canoe and proceeded up the river to shoot fish. We got even more than we could use.

As we approached the shallows we could see the large sting-rays moving at the bottom. The coloured man never failed to hit them with his arrow. The weather was delightful. There was scarcely a cloud to intercept the sun's rays.

I saw several scarlet aras, anhingas and ducks, but could not get a shot at them. The parrots crossed the river in innumerable quantities, always flying in pairs. Here, too, I saw the sun-bird, called tirana by the Spaniards in the Oroonoque, and shot one of them. The black and white scarlet-headed finch was very common here. I could never see this bird in the Demerara, nor hear of its being there.

We at last came to a large sandbank, probably two miles in circumference. As we approached it we could see two or three hundred fresh-water turtle on the edge of the bank. Ere we could get near enough to let fly an arrow at them they had all sunk into the river and appeared no more.

We went on the sandbank to look for their nests, as this was the breeding-season. The coloured man showed us how to find them. Wherever a portion of the sand seemed smoother than the rest there was sure to be a turtle's nest. On digging down with our hands about nine inches deep we found from twenty to thirty white eggs; in less than an hour we got above two hundred. Those which had a little black spot or two on the shell we ate the same day, as it was a sign that they were not fresh, and of course would not keep; those which had no speck were put into dry sand, and were good some weeks after.

At midnight two of our people went to this sandbank while the rest stayed to watch the cayman. The turtle had advanced on to the sand to lay their eggs, and the men got betwixt them and the water; they brought off half a dozen very fine and well-fed turtle. The egg-shell of the fresh-water turtle is not hard like that of the land-tortoise, but appears like white parchment, and gives way to the pressure of the fingers; but it is very tough, and does not break. On this sandbank, close to the forest, we found several guana's nests; but they had never more than fourteen eggs apiece. Thus passed the day in exercise and knowledge, till the sun's declining orb reminded us it was time to return to the place from whence we had set out.

The second night's attempt upon the cayman was a repetition of the first, quite unsuccessful. We went a-fishing the day after, had excellent sport, and returned to experience a third night's disappointment. On the fourth evening, about four o'clock, we began to erect a stage amongst the trees close to the water's edge. From this we intended to shoot an arrow into the cayman: at the end of this arrow was to be attached a string which would be tied to the rope, and as soon as the cayman was struck we were to have the canoe ready and pursue him in the river.

While we were busy in preparing the stage a tiger began to roar. We judged by the sound that he was not above a quarter of a mile from us, and that he was close to the side of the river. Unfortunately the Indian said it was not a jaguar that was roaring, but a couguar. The couguar is of a pale, brownish-red colour, and not as large as the jaguar. As there was nothing particular in this animal I thought it better to attend to the apparatus for catching the cayman than to go in quest of the couguar. The people, however, went in the canoe to the place where the couguar was roaring. On arriving near the spot they saw it was not a couguar, but an immense jaguar, standing on the trunk of an aged mora-tree which bended over the river; he growled and showed his teeth as they approached; the coloured man fired at him with a ball, but probably missed him, and the tiger instantly descended and took off into the woods. I went to the place before dark, and we searched the forest for about half a mile in the direction he had fled, but we could see no traces of him or any marks of blood; so I concluded that fear had prevented the man from taking steady aim.

We spent best part of the fourth night in trying for the cayman, but all to no purpose. I was now convinced that something was materially wrong. We ought to have been successful, considering our vigilance and attention, and that we had repeatedly seen the cayman. It was useless to tarry here any longer; moreover, the coloured man began to take airs, and fancied that I could not do without him. I never admit of this in any expedition where I am commander; and so I convinced the man, to his sorrow, that I could do without him, for I paid him what I had agreed to give him, which amounted to eight dollars, and ordered him back in his own curial to Mrs Peterson's, on the hill at the first falls. I then asked the Negro if there were any Indian settlements in the neighbourhood; he said he knew of one, a day and a half off. We went in quest of it, and about one o'clock the next day the Negro showed us the creek where it was.

The entrance was so concealed by thick bushes that a stranger would have passed it without knowing it to be a creek. In going up it we found it dark, winding, and intricate beyond any creek that I had ever seen before. When Orpheus came back with his young wife from Styx his path must have been similar to this, for Ovid says it was

'Arduus, obliquus, caligine densus opaca',

and this creek was exactly so.

When we had got about two-thirds up it we met the Indians going a-fishing. I saw by the way their things were packed in the curial that they did not intend to return for some days. However, on telling them what we wanted, and by promising handsome presents of powder, shot and hooks, they dropped their expedition and invited us up to the settlement they had just left, and where we laid in a provision of cassava.

They gave us for dinner boiled ant-bear and red monkey: two dishes unknown even at Beauvilliers in Paris or at a London city feast. The monkey was very good indeed, but the ant-bear had been kept beyond its time: it stunk as our venison does in England; and so, after tasting it, I preferred dining entirely on monkey. After resting here we went back to the river. The Indians, three in number, accompanied us in their own curial, and, on entering the river, pointed to a place a little way above well calculated to harbour a cayman. The water was deep and still, and flanked by an immense sandbank; there was also a little shallow creek close by.

On this sandbank, near the forest, the people made a shelter for the night. My own was already made, for I always take with me a painted sheet about twelve feet by ten. This thrown over a pole, supported betwixt two trees, makes a capital roof with very little trouble.

We showed one of the Indians the shark-hook. He shook his head and laughed at it, and said it would not do. When he was a boy he had seen his father catch the caymen, and on the morrow he would make something that would answer.

In the meantime we set the shark-hook, but it availed us naught: a cayman came and took it, but would not swallow it.

Seeing it was useless to attend the shark-hook any longer, we left it for the night and returned to our hammocks.

Ere I fell asleep a reflection or two broke in upon me. I considered that as far as the judgement of civilized man went, everything had been procured and done to ensure success. We had hooks and lines and baits and patience; we had spent nights in watching, had seen the cayman come and take the bait, and after our expectations had been wound up to the highest pitch all ended in disappointment. Probably this poor wild man of the woods would succeed by means of a very simple process, and thus prove to his more civilized brother that, notwithstanding books and schools, there is a vast deal of knowledge to be picked up at every step, whichever way we turn ourselves.

In the morning, as usual, we found the bait gone from the shark-hook. The Indians went into the forest to hunt, and we took the canoe to shoot fish and get another supply of turtle's eggs, which we found in great abundance on this shallow sandbank.

We went to the little shallow creek, and shot some young caymen about two feet long. It was astonishing to see what spite and rage these little things showed when the arrow struck them; they turned round and bit it: and snapped at us when we went into the water to take them up. Daddy Quashi boiled one of them for his dinner, and found it very sweet and tender. I do not see why it should not be as good as frog or veal.

The day was now declining apace, and the Indian had made his instrument to take the cayman. It was very simple. There were four pieces of tough, hard wood a foot long, and about as thick as your little finger, and barbed at both ends; they were tied round the end of the rope in such a manner that if you conceive the rope to be an arrow, these four sticks would form the arrow's head; so that one end of the four united sticks answered to the point of the arrowhead, while the other end of the sticks expanded at equal distances round the rope. Now it is evident that, if the cayman swallowed this (the other end of the rope, which was thirty yards long, being fastened to a tree), the more he pulled the faster the barbs would stick into his stomach. This wooden hook, if you may so call it, was well-baited with the flesh of the acouri, and the entrails were twisted round the rope for about a foot above it.

Nearly a mile from where we had our hammocks the sandbank was steep and abrupt, and the river very still and deep; there the Indian pricked a stick into the sand. It was two feet long, and on its extremity was fixed the machine: it hung suspended about a foot from the water, and the end of the rope was made fast to a stake driven well into the sand.

The Indian then took the empty shell of a land-tortoise and gave it some heavy blows with an axe. I asked why he did that. He said it was to let the cayman hear that something was going on. In fact, the Indian meant it as the cayman's dinner-bell.

Having done this we went back to the hammocks, not intending to visit it again till morning. During the night the jaguars roared and grumbled in the forest as though the world was going wrong with them, and at intervals we could hear the distant cayman. The roaring of the jaguars was awful, but it was music to the dismal noise of these hideous and malicious reptiles.

About half-past five in the morning the Indian stole off silently to take a look at the bait. On arriving at the place he set up a tremendous shout. We all jumped out of our hammocks and ran to him. The Indians got there before me, for they had no clothes to put on, and I lost two minutes in looking for my trousers and in slipping into them.

We found the cayman ten feet and a half long fast to the end of the rope. Nothing now remained to do but to get him out of the water without injuring his scales: 'hoc opus, hic labor.' We mustered strong: there were three Indians from the creek, there was my own Indian Yan, Daddy Quashi, the Negro from Mrs Peterson's, James, Mr R. Edmonstone's man, whom I was instructing to preserve birds, and lastly myself.

I informed the Indians that it was my intention to draw him quietly out of the water and then secure him. They looked and stared at each other, and said I might do it myself, but they would have no hand in it; the cayman would worry some of us. On saying this, 'consedere duces', they squatted on their hams with the most perfect indifference.

The Indians of these wilds have never been subject to the least restraint, and I knew enough of them to be aware that if I tried to force them against their will they would take off and leave me and my presents unheeded, and never return.

Daddy Quashi was for applying to our guns, as usual, considering them our best and safest friends. I immediately offered to knock him down for his cowardice, and he shrunk back, begging that I would be cautious, and not get myself worried, and apologizing for his own want of resolution. My Indian was now in conversation with the others, and they asked if I would allow them to shoot a dozen arrows into him, and thus disable him. This would have ruined all. I had come above three hundred miles on purpose to get a cayman uninjured, and not to carry back a mutilated specimen. I rejected their proposition with firmness, and darted a disdainful eye upon the Indians.

Daddy Quashi was again beginning to remonstrate and I chased him on the sandbank for a quarter of a mile. He told me afterwards he thought he should have dropped down dead with fright, for he was firmly persuaded if I had caught him I should have bundled him into the cayman's jaws. Here, then, we stood in silence like a calm before a thunderstorm. 'Hoc res summa loco. Scinditur in contraria vulgus.' They wanted to kill him, and I wanted to take him alive.

I now walked up and down the sand, revolving a dozen projects in my head. The canoe was at a considerable distance, and I ordered the people to bring it round to the place where we were. The mast was eight feet long, and not much thicker than my wrist. I took it out of the canoe and wrapped the sail round the end of it. Now it appeared clear to me that, if I went down upon one knee and held the mast in the same position as the soldier holds his bayonet when rushing to the charge, I could force it down the cayman's throat should he come open-mouthed at me. When this was told to the Indians they brightened up, and said they would help me to pull him out of the river.

'Brave squad!' said I to myself. ' "Audax omnia perpeti", now that you have got me betwixt yourselves and danger.' I then mustered all hands for the last time before the battle. We were four South American savages, two Negroes from Africa, a creole from Trinidad, and myself a white man from Yorkshire. In fact, a little tower of Babel group, in dress, no dress, address, and language.

Daddy Quashi hung in the rear. I showed him a large Spanish

knife which I always carried in the waistband of my trousers: it spoke volumes to him, and he shrugged up his shoulders in absolute despair. The sun was just peeping over the high forests on the eastern hills, as if coming to look on and bid us act with becoming fortitude. I placed all the people at the end of the rope, and ordered them to pull till the cayman appeared on the surface of the water, and then, should he plunge, to slacken the rope and let him go again into the deep.

I now took the mast of the canoe in my hand (the sail being tied round the end of the mast) and sunk down upon one knee, about four yards from the water's edge, determining to thrust it down his throat in case he gave me an opportunity.

I certainly felt somewhat uncomfortable in this situation, and I thought of Cerberus on the other side of the Styx ferry. The people pulled the cayman to the surface; he plunged furiously as soon as he arrived in these upper regions, and immediately went below again on their slackening the rope. I saw enough not to fall in love at first sight. I now told them we would run all risks and have him on land immediately. They pulled again, and out he came – 'monstrum horrendum, informe'. This was an interesting moment. I kept my position firmly, with my eye fixed steadfast on him.

By the time the cayman was within two yards of me I saw he was in a state of fear and perturbation. I instantly dropped the mast, sprung up and jumped on his back, turning half round as I vaulted, so that I gained my seat with my face in the right position. I immediately seized his fore-legs, and by main force twisted them on his back: thus they served me for a bridle.

He now seemed to have recovered from his surprise, and

probably fancying himself in hostile company he began to plunge furiously, and lashed the sand with his long and powerful tail. I was out of reach of the strokes of it by being near his head. He continued to plunge and strike and made my seat very uncomfortable. It must have been a fine sight for an unoccupied spectator.

The people roared out in triumph, and were so vociferous that it was some time before they heard me tell them to pull me and my beast of burden farther inland. I was apprehensive the rope might break, and then there would have been every chance of going down to the regions under the water with the cayman. That would have been more perilous than Arion's marine morning ride:

'Delphini insidens vada caerula sulcat Arion.'

The people now dragged us above forty yards on the sand: it was the first and last time I was ever on a cayman's back. Should it be asked how I managed to keep my seat, I would answer, I hunted some years with Lord Darlington's fox-hounds.

After repeated attempts to regain his liberty the cayman gave in and became tranquil through exhaustion. I now managed to tie up his jaws and firmly secured his fore-feet in the position I had held them. We had now another severe struggle for superiority, but he was soon overcome and again remained quiet. While some of the people were pressing upon his head and shoulders I threw myself on his tail, and by keeping it down to the sand prevented him from kicking up another dust. He was finally conveyed to the canoe, and then to the place where we had suspended our hammocks. There I cut his throat; and after breakfast was over commenced the dissection.

Mammoth Mystery

Bernard Heuvelmans

The sudden disappearance of the mammoths, close kindred of the elephants, is a mystery that has for long interested naturalists. But did all these contemporaries of early man disappear – or could some have survived much longer than is thought?

The Yukaghir tribe, whose territory in the Soviet Union stretches beyond the Arctic Circle all along the Arctic Ocean from the Lena delta to beyond the Kolyma, relate this legend: the creation of the mammoth was a blunder of the Superior Being. In creating such an enormous animal, the Creator did not take into consideration the size of the earth and its resources. One earth could not stand the weight of the mammoth and its vegetation was not sufficient to feed the mammoth race. In swampy or sandy places the mammoth sank into the ground and disappeared under the earth, where he froze during the winter. Often in the hole over him water gathered in a lake. In this way the mammoth gradually disappeared from the earth's surface. This is why now whole carcases of the animal are to be found in the frozen soil.

Both among the Yakuts and the Ostiaks, who are Mongols, and among the Koriaks, who are a Siberian race of whites who have settled on the shores of the Sea of Okhotsk, there are legends about a sort of giant rat called *mamantu* or 'that-which-lives-beneath-the-ground', from which word 'mammoth' is derived. It cannot survive the light of day. The moment it comes into the light it is struck dead. Its wanderings underground are the cause of earthquakes. Again, in Mongolia and Manchuria the mammoth's ghost appears as a gigantic mole called *tai-shu* in Chinese classics written before the beginning of the Christian era. It is a hairy monster with tiny eyes and a short tail; and it digs enormous tunnels in the snow with its two teeth shaped like picks . . .

Legends though these are, it is a fact that many mammoths have been found intact in the permafrost of Far Siberia and from time to time have come to the surface. The trade in mammoth ivory was very ancient: it was mentioned in Chinese chronicles more than 2,000 years ago. Pliny the Elder had heard of it from a pupil of Aristotle, who reported that ivory was extracted from the ground. As early as the ninth century the Arabs entered the trade, buying their ivory at a market on the Volga. Mammoth ivory was certainly sold in Europe from this time, but as it came from merchants from the south no one was surprised.

Then in 1611 an English traveller called Josias Logan exhibited in London an elephant's tusk that he had brought back from Russia. Everyone 'knew' that elephants were only found in Africa and India. It was true that their remains had been dug up in Europe, but these were thought to have been left by Hannibal's armies. Yet Logan seemed to be an honest man. He said that he had obtained his astonishing trophy from a Samoyed, near the mouth of the Pechora, which flows into the Barents Sea in the Arctic.

Later in the same century, in 1692, a Dutch diplomat called Evert Ysbrants Ides went to China on Peter the Great's behalf to make a peace treaty with the Emperor. But incidentally he brought back reports that the people of Siberia believed that 'there were Elephants in this country before the Deluge, when this Climate was warmer, and that their drowned bodies floating on the surface of the water of that Flood, were at last wash'd and forced into Subterranean Cavities: But that after this Noachian Deluge, the Air which was before warm was changed to cold, and that these Bones have lain frozen in the Earth ever since, and so are preserved from putrefaction till they thaw, and come to light; which is no very unreasonable conjecture.'

Peter the Great's curiosity was aroused by Ides's reports and he sent a German naturalist, Dr D. G. Messerschmidt, to explore Siberia and try to solve the question of the incredible burrowing elephants. Either by good luck or because mammoth's carcases were extraordinarily common, Messerschmidt happened to hear that one of these beasts had just emerged from the melting ice of the Indigirka river. In 1724, a Russian soldier had arrived in time to examine the remains, already largely putrefied and eaten by wolves. There was little left but the head, while there was also found a huge strip of rotten skin, covered with hairs and sticking out of a sand dune.

However, at the beginning of the nineteenth century, a mammoth appeared in flesh and blood to a Siberian-Tungus chief called Ossip Shumakhoff. The beast was embedded in a block of melting ice somewhere in the Lena delta and only a distorted picture of it was visible through its glassy case. Ossip fled in superstitious terror, but curiosity overcame his fear and he came back from time to time to see if it was still there. Two years after he had first seen it, one of the tusks emerged from the ice, and he was much tempted by the value of the ivory, but still terrified that the mammoth might come right out of the ice after its long sleep, for he had heard tales of people who had died from the mere sight of the monster. Indeed it preyed on his mind to such an extent that he fell ill and thought he was dying. Fortunately there was a Russian merchant called Boltunoff in the village. He saw a chance of profitable business and managed to make Ossip forget his fears and take him to the mammoth. In 1804 they went and violated its 'tomb', and found the beast now quite free of its shell; at first Ossip nearly died of fear, but soon he was helping Boltunoff to remove the tusks, and the shrewd Russian merchant immediately bought them for the miserable sum of 50 roubles.

Boltunoff also made a crude sketch of the beast which eventually came into the hands of Johann Friedrich Blumenbach of Göttingen University. This *mammont* did not look much like an elephant – its trunk had no doubt been ripped off by hungry wolves; the pressure of the ice had strangely twisted its tusks; its ears had come off, and as a result of decomposition Boltunoff had mistaken the ear-holes for eye-sockets! However, Blumenbach had no difficulty in recognizing what he had called *Elephas primigenius*, for, on the basis of certain bones he had discovered, he had long been of the opinion that a species of elephant had existed in Europe. In addition, Boltunoff's sketch of one of the molars left no doubt that Ossip's beast was the mammoth, and no legendary creature such as a giant mole!

Meanwhile, a Russian botanist called Professor Adams had got wind of the rumours that a mammoth had been found preserved whole, and set off to see for himself. When he arrived he found wolves, arctic foxes, wolverines and even Yakuts, who had heard there was a stock of meat for their dogs, had all been there before him. Apart from the skeleton, from which one foot was missing, there was not much left of the beast: an ear covered with silky hair, an eye, the brain, some tendons, and the lower part of the legs. Three-quarters of the skin had been preserved. It was dark grey and covered with a reddish woolly fleece, with scattered black hairs like horsehair which on the neck were as much as 27 inches long. Adams set about collecting these relics. His native guides helped him to remove the skin which was almost an inch thick in places and needed ten men to lift it. Then they carefully swept the ground and collected 37 pounds of hair. Everything was packed up with infinite care and sent to St Petersburg, where the skeleton was scrupulously remounted. The curators of the 'Cabinet of Rarities' founded by Peter the Great had bought it from Professor Adams for 8,000 roubles – 160 times as much as poor Ossip got for his precious tusks. It may still be seen in the Zoological Museum in Leningrad. The skin had lost all its hair on the journey, but it was now known for certain that the *mammont* was a hairy elephant, though many details about its appearance were still a mystery.

At least a score more frozen mammoths were discovered in northern Siberia between the Ob and the Bering Strait, the most recent being in 1935 (Wrangel Island) and 1948 (Taimyr Peninsula), and there is no reason why many more should not come to light as erosion gnaws away ceaselessly in the subsoil at layers of clay which cover the beds of fossil ice where the hairy giants sleep.

In April 1901 the Imperial Academy of Science of St Petersburg learnt from the governor of Yakutsk that a mammoth in a perfect state of preservation was imprisoned in a melting glacier on the banks of the Berezovka, a tributary of the Kolyma which flows through eastern Yakutsk. The Tsar offered 16,000 roubles to the Academy, who hastened to send off an expedition under Dr Otto Herz, Curator of the Academy's Zoological Department, an entomologist whom one might expect to chase nothing larger than butterflies. This time wolves and other scavengers had not been able to eat all the carcase. Only the head emerged from the ice and had begun to thaw; and only the trunk, the chief delicacy, had been eaten. But bacteria were already hard at work, and an appalling stench arose from the putrefying meat.

To cut up a carcase which would gradually turn into an ever fouler cesspit was certainly a task to make any but the most devoted scientist blench. Besides Dr Herz, the expedition included D. P. Sevastianov, a geologist from Yurievsk University, a Cossack called Innokenti Iavlovski, who had already been to the place, and a young German taxidermist, E. W. Pfizenmayer. This thirty-six-year-old Swabian who had always dreamt of excavating prehistoric monsters found his wish coming true with a vengeance. He was able to dissect the animal and study the smallest details of its anatomy. As he had several more opportunities later, his work on the mammoth eventually became the world's greatest authority.

As a result we now have an excellent idea both of the habits and exact appearance of the Siberian mammoth (*Elephas berezovkius*). It was covered all over its body with a reddish-yellow woolly fleece and also with long black hairs like horsehair, between 1 foot and 2 feet 3 inches in length, which hung from its cheeks, lower jaw, shoulders, flanks and abdomen, making a sort of overcoat which reached almost to the ground. The colour of the wool has faded with time and the beast was probably mainly reddish-black. It had a short tail, under the root of which was a flap of skin which protected its anus from the cold. The Indian elephant has a similar flap which probably acts as a protection against insects. This common feature shows the close relationship between the two species. The mammoth's thick skin was lined with a layer of fat about $3\frac{1}{2}$ inches thick, and on the crown of its head and on its withers it had two fatty humps, which, like the camel's, served as a reserve of food.

Its concave forehead and small ears remind one of the Indian elephant, and here we must say something about the size of the mammoth. In *Le Petit Larousse Illustré* you will find under *Mammouth* a picture of a man looking at a reconstruction of the hairy elephant. From their relative sizes the animal seems to be about twenty feet high at the withers. No mammoth was ever so enormous. True, there are various species of mammoth; there was once a giant North American species (*Elephas imperator*) which was a little over 13 feet high. Fraas's German mammoth (*E. fraasi*) was no doubt some 18 inches taller, but the Siberian mammoth was not even 10 feet high. It was a little smaller than the Indian elephant, which sometimes reaches that height, while the African elephant may be as much as 12 feet high at the withers. All the same, the Siberian mammoth's humps and its shaggy coat must have made it an impressive mountain of fur.

Why did the mammoth become extinct? Did a sudden wave of cold destroy the vegetation, leading to the starvation of the species? Did a drastic climatic change lead to extinction for another reason? As in the case of living elephants, the mammoth had no sebaceous or sweat-glands. Without these, without a constant flow of sebum and sweat to oil the hair and keep the fleece waterproof, the mammoth's thick fur would be no protection against cold and damp. Snow and icy rain would be able to penetrate its thick coat, soaking it through and through until it became a wretched cloak of ice, frozen to its skin. Or is the explanation contained in the Yukaghir traditions? – When the hordes of mammoths followed the last of the retreating glaciers, they were gradually led to the north-east. When they inadvertently ventured on to the marshy plains of north Siberia did their own weight make them sink into the icy mud? – where they have been preserved ever since.

But are we certain that the mammoth *is* extinct? After all, the okapi remained unknown to science until 1900, hidden in the forests of the Congo – so is it not possible that mammoths have survived in the Siberian taiga? I think it is more than possible.

The taiga is the largest forest in the world: it covers nearly three million square miles, more than thirty times the area of Great Britain, and about three-quarters of the area of the United States of America. This vast forest is largely unexplored, or little explored. Herds of hundreds or even thousands of mammoths could easily live there without running the least risk of being seen by man. In fact the extraordinary thing is that some of these mammoths sometimes *are* reported to have been seen by the Ostiaks and Yakuts who live in the forests.

There is also a more circumstantial account of an adventure which is supposed to have occurred to a Russian hunter in 1918. This is his story, told to the French chargé d'affaires in Vladivostok: The second year that I was exploring the taiga, I was very much struck to notice tracks of a huge animal, I say huge tracks, for they were a long way larger than any of those I had often seen of animals I knew well. It was autumn. There had been a few big snowstorms, followed by heavy rain. It wasn't freezing yet, the snow had melted, and there were thick layers of mud in the clearings. It was in one of these big clearings, partly taken up by a lake, that I was staggered to see a huge footprint pressed deeply into the mud. It must have been about 2 feet across the widest part and about 18 inches the other way, that's to say the spoor wasn't round but oval. There were four tracks, the tracks of four feet, the first two about twelve feet from the second pair, which were a little bigger in size. Then the track suddenly turned east and went into the forest of middling sized elms. Where it went in I saw a huge heap of dung; I had a good look at it and saw it was made up of vegetable matter.

Some ten feet up, just where the animal had gone into the forest, I saw a row of broken branches, made, I don't doubt, by the monster's enormous head as it forced its way into the place where it had decided to go, regardless of what was in its path.

I followed the tracks for days and days. Sometimes I could see where the animal had stopped in some grassy clearing and then had gone on forever eastward.

Then, one day, I saw another track, almost exactly the same. It came from the north and crossed the first one. It looked to me from the way they had trampled about all over the place for several hundred yards, as if they had been excited or upset at their meeting. Then the two animals set out marching eastwards, both tracks mingling and ploughing up the earth together.

I followed them for days and days thinking that perhaps I

should never see them, and also a bit afraid, for indeed I didn't feel I was big enough to face such beasts alone. I had a good hunting gun, but only with five ball-cartridges left, hardly enough with which to attack such enormous game. All the same I followed the trail as fast as possible, and thought from the freshness of the tracks that I was gaining on the beasts. Meanwhile it was growing bitterly cold, and I had no way of getting warm in the evening except by drinking scalding tea and building a shelter of leaves and branches which keeps in the warmth of a wood fire for a long time.

One afternoon it was clear enough from the tracks that the animals weren't far off. The wind was in my face, which was good for approaching them without them knowing I was there. All of a sudden I saw one of the animals quite clearly, and now I must admit I really was afraid. It had stopped among some young saplings. It was a huge elephant with big white tusks, very curved; it was a dark chestnut colour as far as I could see. It had fairly long hair on the hindquarters, but it seemed shorter on the front. I must say I had no idea that there were such big elephants. It had huge legs and moved very slowly. I've only seen elephants in pictures, but I must say that even from this distance (we were about 300 yards apart) I could never have believed any beast could be so big. The second beast was around, I saw it only a few times among the trees: it seemed to be the same size.

When evening came, the hunter who told this story reluctantly left his hiding-place, because he could no longer bear the cold. Next morning when he returned, the beasts had gone. Winter had set in and the weather was too bitter for him to go on tracking them. It was time for him to find a sheltered place to settle for the winter, and in any case he had not the ammunition to open war on the beasts.

This hunter was an illiterate peasant, too ignorant to know that what he had actually seen were mammoths – or indeed the sort of person who would have made up such a story. Moreover, the best evidence, to my mind, of the truth of the story, is that the hunter says he met the mammoths in the forest: in the past it is the tundra, the barren, treeless region that was looked upon as the habitat of the mammoth, but it is in the vast taiga that the mammoths could have survived.

Let me conclude with evidence from a much earlier date of the possibility of the mammoth's survival into historic times. At the end of the sixteenth century the Stroganoff family, who owned salt-mines in Siberia, were concerned because they were being pillaged by brigands. They therefore decided to send Don Cossacks to set things to rights, and despatched them on this police mission under Yermak Timofeyevich in 1580. These Cossacks took their task so much to heart that they eventually conquered the whole of Siberia. They split into small bands, living on what they could pillage, and went down rivers, explored vast tracts of quite unknown country on their own account, set up towns and called upon Russian workers and their families to help them. After some sixty years of continual fighting with the native tribes, these Cossacks, or rather their successors, reached the Sea of Okhotsk on the Pacific Ocean. They had crossed the whole of Asia, rather like the Huns and the Mongols, but in a different direction. Right at the beginning Timofeyevich reported that beyond the Ural mountains he met 'a large hairy elephant'. According to the natives it was part of the wealth of the Kingdom of Sibir, valued as food and known as 'mountain of meat'. This happened at a time when even the Slav world had never heard of the mammoth.

A Journey to the Kuldur

Ivan Aramilev

Nowadays, because pressure of human population has reduced the animals' habitat, the practice of wild game ranching is spreading, for often native wild ungulates provide more protein than domestic cattle reared in alien conditions. In the Soviet Union, for example, extensive farming of elk and red deer is carried out. This episode is about the search for a new red deer stag to sire a herd on a collective farm.

The last stag in the herd succumbed. He was a magnificent, powerful beast and held out for a long time, but finally illness overcame him too. Twelve does were left behind.

They stood about in silence with drooping heads. I left the farm for a meeting, in the company of Dimitry Ivanich, the president of the kolkhoz – the collective farm.

'It's a disaster, zootechnologist,' said the president. 'An absolute disaster!'

He said no more and I could guess what he left unsaid. He was thinking of the great pains we had taken to set up a farm for breeding red deer. The antlers from our farm were sent not only to Moscow but also as far afield as China. We were written up in the papers and awarded certificates of merit. And now our fame and prosperity hung on a thread.

The members of the kolkhoz had assembled in the administrative building. I saw worried faces and expected reproaches. Soon someone would say: 'What are you employed for, honoured comrade? You haven't saved our animals. How shall we punish you?'

But curiously enough they all tried to console me. No one so much as mentioned the possibility of judging and punishing anyone. Quite the contrary. Everyone explained his own plan for saving the farm. But the more they talked, the more clearly everyone realized that there was no solution.

The last person to speak was Yerofey the hunter. He was a thin man of medium height and his reddish hair was perpetually towsled. He was about thirty but looked considerably older. His first wife had died eight years ago. When he became a widower Yerofey began to drink heavily, behaving scandalously and getting into all kinds of trouble. This spring he had suddenly come to his senses, stopped drinking and, to everyone's surprise, married Natalya Cheremnich, a pretty, vivacious girl.

A real Siberian, Yerofey adopted an independent point of view at our meetings; he loved to hear the sound of his own voice and today again he spoke at length without making any practical suggestions.

It was impossible to buy a stag suitable for breeding purposes, nor was it possible to capture one in the neighbouring districts of the taiga; for that a trip to the salt-marsh on the upper reaches of the Kuldur (a tributary of the River Amur) was necessary. The founder of the farm, Pavel Michailovich Shabanov, and his son had captured the original animals there. Old Shabanov had caught a cold and died the year before. One of his sons was serving in the Red Army, the other was working in the city and apart from them nobody else knew the way to the remote salt-marsh which the wild red deer visited for the salt.

The men took out their tobacco pouches and rolled cigarettes. Dimitry Ivanich looked at Yerofey:

'What exactly is your proposal then? To slaughter the does and close the farm down?'

'What nonsense you do talk,' said Yerofey. 'Give me a companion and I'll be the first to go. Even if I walk myself footsore and the snakes in the taiga eat me, I'll still go. When it's for the common good, there's nothing more to be said. But who will go with me?'

Dimitry Ivanich lowered his eyes.

'That's the whole trouble; nobody can show you the way.'

There was a general silence. Clouds of blue smoke rose above the table. The women had gone out into the road. There was more room, but the atmosphere inside the hut was even gloomier.

'Listen, farmers, there is somebody here who could go to the salt-marsh,' said Dimitry suddenly. 'There is one, by God!'

'Who is it?' we all asked as if with one voice.

'Vandaga the hunter.'

'That's right,' said Yerofey impulsively. 'The old man used to go hunting there. How on earth could I have forgotten?'

Now a discussion began. Vandaga was not a member of the kolkhoz. A chance wind had blown him to our village. He was here today and gone tomorrow. What did a kolkhoz farm matter to a rolling stone like him? How could we keep him with us?

I had already heard something about Vandaga. His mother was a Nanai, his father a Udege (both numerically small East Asiatic races); he was a real son of the taiga. As a young man he he had left his tribe and crossed over to the right bank of the Amur. In his search for fortune, he traversed the Great and Little Khingans and the coastal district. He shot sable, looked for medicinal roots, collected sea-slugs, killed musk-deer, gathered fungi and lichen. He nearly became rich in the process. He settled in Manchuria near the River Tudachese.

There he was visited by misfortune. Maurauding Tunguse attacked his little cottage, killed his wife and son and plundered his property. He himself was wounded in the fight with the Tunguse and only just escaped with his life. Since then he had been an itinerant visitor to various Russian settlements and was widely known as a brilliant hunter.

A better guide could not have been found in the whole of the Amur territory. The question was: would he be willing to lead a member of the kolkhoz to the Kuldur?

Dimitry Ivanich went off to look for Vandaga. We stayed behind and waited. No one spoke and their very silence told me how excited the kolkhoz members were. Half an hour went by, then a whole hour. It was so full of smoke in the hut that you could scarcely breathe. You could hear the steady roar of the river and the twittering of the birds in the birch trees.

The president dashed in, looking cheerful.

'It's all in order,' he shouted almost before he had crossed the threshold. 'Now we must make the arrangements. I appoint you,' he said to me, 'leader of the expedition. Yerofey will be your assistant.'

Fearing that Vandaga might reconsider his decision we decided to set out on the very same day. We would ride through the taiga on our way to the salt-marsh and return with our captive on a raft.

Uncle Karpucha the stableman led three Walachians out into the road. They were decrepit old hacks which were no longer any use for work on the kolkhoz.

'If you manage to capture a stag,' said the president, 'I give you permission to shoot these old jades. It is out of the question to sail through the rapids with them. Don't forget to bring their hides back.'

Yerofey and I cleaned our guns, filled the cartridges and stuffed the saddle-bags with biscuit. Men and women helped us with the preparations. Some brought cigarettes and pipe-tobacco, others flints. Danilo the farm manager appeared with the very same net with which Pavel Shabanov had once caught the red deer.

Vandaga came up to me with his dog Chady. Our guide had a sunburnt oval face, a small flattened nose and lively dark-brown eyes. His cheek bones were rather prominent. His long black hair was plaited in a pigtail. A Berdan gun was slung over his shoulder.

Vandaga greeted me, addressing me, for some reason best known to himself, as commissar. It turned out that the old man was actually delighted by the idea of the trip. He had not been in distant parts for over a year. After being in one place for much longer than usual, he wanted to stretch his legs again.

He inspected my clothes, enquired whether my boots were not too tight, what the saddle-bags were filled with and how many cartridges I was taking with me.

I was moved by his paternal solicitude. I replied that everything appeared to be in order and asked whether we would actually manage to capture a stag. Vandaga was surprised:

'Why not catch? Animals have many habits. We arrive at salt-marsh, stay there for short while and catch one.'

Axes, saws, cooking-pots and a tent were loaded and roped down. The horses were saddled. Vandaga, who was lean and sinewy, stroked Gnedka and swung lightly into the saddle. They brought me a pot-bellied reddish Walach with bandy legs called Machtak. Yerofey slung his Winchester over his shoulder with a swaggering air and mounted his shaggy horse Skorochod.

Dimitry Ivanich handed me a double-barrelled shotgun.

'May you come back safely,' he said. 'But don't return empty-handed.'

We set out. The kolkhoz members accompanied us, laughing and joking. Vandaga's dog Chady ran behind us. It was a warm day without a breath of wind and a fine mist lay over the river.

I went hunting with Vandaga to shoot some game for supper. The hollows were full of last year's tall grass. An almost imperceptible wind stirred the larches and young oak trees. Twice Chady put up capercailzie, but we did not get a chance to shoot. The brushwood crackled beneath our feet and the birds had very acute hearing.

By evening we had penetrated far into the taiga. Yerofey lit a fire and put up our tent. The horses were tied up and left to graze in the clearing.

Slightly depressed by our bad luck we emerged on to a slope in less dense forest. There was no grass here; only moss and sandhills.

'Look, bear been here not long ago,' Vandaga pointed to the paw marks in the sand which were as big as a Siberian loaf of bread. Other animals had left their tracks behind as well as the bear.

'You understand what sort of people been here?'

I shook my head.

'Young boar been here,' whispered Vandaga. 'Is somewhere quite close. Must walk softly and look everywhere.'

Vandaga interpreted nature in human terms: the bear, the elk, the ant, the juniper bush, the sun, the water – they were all 'people' in his language.

We took care not to tread on the dry twigs. The sun had disappeared behind the mountains, the shadows of the trees fell in the clearings. Quiet reigned in the forest. Chady darted about, sniffed the earth and disappeared into a clump of rosemary.

Vandaga signalled to me. We stood in silence for a few minutes. Then all of a sudden Chady barked. Vandaga ran to the left, I made straight for the sound of the dog's voice.

A young dirty-brown wild boar stood with its back to a larch. Chady flew at him like a bullet; it was impossible to shoot. I waited, with my gun at the ready. The boar gnashed his tusks, hurled himself on Chady and showed me his flank. I pulled the trigger and the boar fell forward over the roots of a tree. Vandaga crept out of the bushes and laughed.

'You shoot good, commissar.'

Chady licked the blood off the dead beast. We drove the dog away, tied the boar's feet together with a strap, ran a pole through beneath the knots and carried our bag back to camp. The light of the fire glimmered between the trunks of the stone-pines and we felt as if we were nearly at the lighted windows of our own homes.

Yerofey greeted us joyfully: 'So you've bagged a young boar? Splendid. We'll enjoy the meat, then it'll be all the more fun to continue our journey.'

I took off my boots and sat down on a fallen tree. Yerofey skinned the boar. Vandaga put its trotters in the glowing embers, until they were charred all over. Then he cut them up with a knife and sucked out the hot marrow. They must have tasted delicious, because the old man's face glowed with pleasure.

Yerofey roasted a hind leg and told us how he had decoyed red deer here the year before with a horn made of birch wood. According to him tigers also hunted red deer by imitating their cries.

'Once I uttered a cry with the horn and listened,' said Yerofey. 'An old stag answered. His call was astonishingly clear and slightly different from the red deer's usual cry, although it was very similar. I called – he answered. I stalked towards him through the undergrowth and he came nearer, too. We met in a clearing. When I saw what I had been calling, ice-cold shudders ran down my spine. "What am I going to do now?" I wondered. It was no use running away; the tiger was much faster than I. I was doubly furious because this filthy beast was playing tricks and behaving like a stag. There was no excuse for that. I levelled my Winchester and shot him between the eyes. The very first shot bowled him over.'

I know that you cannot believe every word a hunter says. Besides, Yerofey had a fund of tall stories and I had my doubts whether the tiger had really behaved like that. Nevertheless, Vandaga confirmed Yerofey's story.

'Tiger always trick red deer so. When look for doe, stag quite crazy. Then he have no idea what sort of people calling in the taiga.'

Vandaga took a piece of wood from the fire and lit his pipe. I scrutinized his weather-beaten beardless face. How old was he really?

'Many years, commissar, many years,' he laughed and bared

his close-set yellowish teeth. 'I do not like to count. I live, live, death comes – then die. Why count years?'

'Don't judge him by his years,' said Yerofey. 'A Nanai lives in the forest, sleeps on the earth, lets the moon warm his back and fears neither heat nor cold. A long span of life is his portion. His eyes are keen, his hearing is acute. He can even smell wild animals. Yes, he scents them out, just you ask him!'

Vandaga complained that the taiga was becoming impoverished and that the animals were disappearing. In the past he used to kill dozens of sable in a single winter along the tributaries of the Amur. The skins were cheap. To buy an iron cooking-pot the men of the taiga paid the traders as many sable skins as the pot would hold. They would pay a whole armful of skins for a Winchester rifle and cartridges. Now the hunting was bad – less animals, more men.

The old hunter told us about his encounters with tigers. Once he set out in winter to inspect his traps. He had five cartridges loaded with shot in his pocket. In an open clearing he saw a tiger, his mate and two cubs in the act of disembowelling a deer.

The wild beasts were intent on their meal and his skis made no sound in the soft snow so that Vandaga was able to approach within forty paces. To take on four tigers when all he had was a Berdan and five cartridges was naturally very dangerous. Yet it never entered Vandaga's head to beat a retreat.

With his first shot he bagged the tiger. The tigress turned and attacked the hunter, hissing furiously. The copper cartridge case had jammed in the breech of Vandaga's gun. One second lost in reloading and he had to kill the second animal when it was almost upon him. The tigress collapsed almost at his feet. When it tried to struggle to its feet again, he sank his Udege knife into its shoulder blade.

The young tigers watched in terror, then they arched their tails and made off. Vandaga brought one of them down with another shot, but did not bother about the surviving cub.

'You are a brave man, but you won't escape the tiger's teeth,' prophesied Yerofey. 'With age your eyes will get weaker, you'll miss your shots and it will be all over.'

'As it is decreed,' said Vandaga softly. 'Perhaps I'll finish him off, perhaps he get me. I not afraid. Have dog and Berdan.'

I asked Vandaga how many tigers he had actually killed during his years spent wandering in the taiga. The old man did not answer at first. He muttered something unintelligible and began to count on his fingers. He had great difficulty in working it out. This is where our sportsmen often make themselves look ridiculous. They write down when and where they shot a snipe, woodcock, or teal and often the description of such a shoot does not even fill a whole page. Vandaga, on the other hand, was quite indifferent about all his past exploits; he only remembered the most important events of his hunting life. After lengthy reflection and muttering to himself, the old man laughed self-consciously.

'I not remember, commissar.'

I questioned him in such a way as to form some idea of the truth and then counted his trophies of the chase. He had been hunting for over forty-six years. Every year he shot one or two tigers, in good years five or six adult animals and a like number of cubs. I took an average and multiplied it by forty-five.*

* Only about sixty Siberian tigers are estimated to survive in the Soviet Far East. – A. C. J.

If a Frenchman or an Englishman goes to India or Africa and shoots five lions or tigers with the help of native hunters and beaters, he's a hero. Articles are written about him in the newspapers, the newsreels feature him and hunting clubs are named after him.

Vandaga recalled that his relatives had expelled him from the tribe. The Nanai call the tiger *amba*, the Udege *kutymafa*. In olden times the two tribes hardly ever hunted this wild beast, which they revered as sacred.

Tigers lived close to human settlements, ate a good half of the musk-deer and deer caught in the traps, carried off dogs and robbed the stocks of frozen fish. As a young lad Vandaga was scared of aiming his gun at a striped cat, for he believed that a hunter would be visited by misfortune as a punishment for attacking a tiger. But once, after the first snows, a tiger broke into the nomads' camp at dawn and carried off Vandaga's favourite dog. Then he saw red and followed the wild beast's tracks. The tiger was cowardly; when he heard the footsteps of a human being, he left his prey and hid.

The young hunter stood by the body of his dog for a long time, crying and cursing. His grief drove him to make a bold decision. He put his loaded gun down beside the dog with a cord attached to the trigger and went back to camp. 'If the tiger is a sacred animal,' he reasoned, 'the gun will not fire when he touches the cord tied to the trigger with his chest. But if it fires, the tiger is a forest thief who must be destroyed.'

All night long Vandaga dreamed that the tiger had broken his gun in a rage. What would he go hunting with then?

In the morning he was almost beside himself with excitement

when he visited the spot where his loaded weapon was tied to the dog. The tiger lay stretched out in the snow.

That was how Vandaga grew out of the tribal superstitions. He was no longer afraid of tigers and began to poison them with strychnine which he bought from the Koreans, as well as shooting them with a gun.

The elders condemned Vandaga because he had violated the traditions handed down by their forebears. Everyone shunned him. No matter which nomads' camp he visited, no one spoke to him and none of the girls would become his wife. That was why he began a new life on the other side of the Amur.

Yerofey kept watch; Vandaga lay down to sleep. The sunset glow still shone on the mountains but down below the darkness had enveloped the clearings and the night birds were crying in the forest.

The next morning I was awakened by the call of a lynx which miaowed somewhere quite near and then was silent. I lifted the flap of the tent. Chady had jumped up ready to plunge into the thicket.

'Down,' I ordered. 'The leader of the expedition forbids hunting today.'

The dog lay down reluctantly, gave me a glance out of the corner of one eye and wagged his tail. I let him come up to me and scratched his head.

In the cool of the morning the forest wore a festive look. Sunbeams played on the trunks of the fir trees; dewdrops trembled on the birch leaves. I fanned the camp fire and woke Yerofey and Vandaga. One of them was supposed to be on watch, but they were both snoring.

After breakfast, we swung into the saddle again and rode along a path which had not been used for some considerable time. We could still see the yellowish marks of signs blazed on the trees with an axe. We waded through a rocky stream and rode up-river on the left bank.

The path disappeared; scrub barred the way. Small branches scratched the horses' flanks and the saddle-bags. Yerofey jumped down and led Skorochod by the bridle. He chopped away bushes and birch saplings with his axe but he soon wearied of this occupation and swung into the saddle again.

The horses could scarcely force their way through the trees. But now the pine forest came to an end. The surrounding scene was gloomy. Firs and silver firs were covered with grey-green moss and reddish mould and they looked as though they were sunk in deep sleep.

The day was overcast and well suited to this particular forest. Soon we branched off from the stream, then we turned towards its bed again. Perhaps we had lost our way? Vandaga only laughed.

'Keep going. I know the way like back of hand.'

Yerofey suggested that we made for the mountains, because it was drier on the slopes and the wood was less dense there.

'There no good,' answered Vandaga. 'There trees fall, stones fall, horses can't walk at all. Here little brushwood, marsh not thawed: keep going.'

Whether it was true or not, we had to agree. Only Vandaga's practised eyes could find the way in this wilderness.

'How many more hours is it to the pass?' asked Yerofey.

'I not know hours. In the evening we there.'

'Curse this route,' moaned Yerofey. 'It's the devil's own hunting ground. Let's rest for a while.'

I fell in with this suggestion.

Yerofey fetched dry wood for a fire. Vandaga drew water from a pool and hung the kettle from a tripod. I spread the tent out like a tablecloth and we sat down to lunch. The horses stuck their heads into the trees and chewed twigs. The poor creatures had nothing to munch, for all that grew at their feet was moss and lichen. Vandaga fed the horses biscuits.

'It's not right to give those old hacks bread,' scolded Yerofey. 'Perhaps we'll go hungry ourselves.'

'Why you make fuss?' replied the old man gently. 'We will shoot various people, then is meat to cook and we live.'

We rested for an hour or so and rode on westwards. As Vandaga had foretold the taiga actually did begin to grow more open towards evening. The ground was firmer and the conifers were mingled with deciduous trees. In the clearing stood the heads of last year's tall grasses whose stems were so closely intertwined that the horses could scarcely force a way through with their chests.

Something dark slithered over a fallen tree and hid in the grass. At first I thought it was a shadow, for there were tatters of ashen grey cloud sailing through the sky and casting their shadows on the taiga below. But Chady dashed off to one side, barking, and we stopped.

'A sable!' shouted Yerofey. 'Mother of God!'

Now I could see the sable too. He scuttled up to the top of an elm and looked down at the dog. Yerofey ran towards the tree and raised his Winchester. A shot rang out, not very loud, and the sable fell.

Chady took it by the throat and carried it to his master. Vandaga said something under his breath and Chady put the animal down in the grass. With a self-satisfied laugh Yerofey picked up his bag. Vandaga went to him and tore the long hairs from the sable's back; they came away easily. Underneath the dark yellow woolly hair was visible.

'You big idiot,' yelled Vandaga furiously. 'If you take it to fur merchants they not accept it. Everyone call you idiot, idiot.'

Yerofey tried to justify himself. Old animals wore their winter coats until the spring was almost over. He thought that this was an old sable and that its fur could be used. He wanted to give it to his young bride as a present.

Vandaga became even more angry.

'The taiga's being ruined by dolts like you. You think everything permitted: in the taiga, no law, no chief. When eyes sees bird or wild beast, always shoot, shoot! Present for wife. Who wants bad present? You stupid devil.'

Suddenly Yerofey weakened and went pale.

'Perhaps I made a slight mistake,' he confessed. 'It's been the same ever since I was a child: if I see a sable I lose my reason. I'm a very excitable person.'

Vandaga would not be pacified. They went on quarrelling for a long time before they finally stopped. Yerofey suddenly exhibited an unusual appetite for work. He tightened up the saddlebags and girths, and wiped the horses' sweating chests.

'Another time I won't stand by and watch,' Vandaga began again. 'Have to cut your throat a little.'

Yerofey gave Vandaga a challenging look and tossed the sable on the grass. Then I intervened and reprimanded them both. I

pointed out that when three men set out on a communal enterprise they must not quarrel. I elaborated on this theme and spoke
of friendship as the noble sentiment which binds men together
and enables them to triumph over hardship. Apparently I was a
bit too verbose, because Yerofey thought he saw an ally in me.

'The old man's quite crazy,' he said, winking at me. 'He bawls
me out as if the sable was his blood-brother. As if one animal
more or less would make any difference in the taiga!'

'You've gone too far yourself,' I raged and forgot all the fine
words I had just said about friendship on a great venture like ours.
'Vandaga is right. You must beg his pardon.'

Yerofey looked at me darkly: 'I've admitted that I was in the
wrong. What more do you want of me? Have I got to fall on my
knees or something?'

I made a pacifying gesture: 'That's enough!'

We crossed a fairly high mountain ridge and rode down the
slopes into the valley on the far side. A vast expanse of dark blue
sky arched above us; there was not a breath of wind and the grass
shone gold in the sun. The landscape was much gayer and
brighter. It smelt of flowers and the horses stepped out more
briskly as if they were glad to have the damp deserted taiga behind them.

On the bank of a river we took off the horses' saddles. They
cropped the fresh grass greedily. Yerofey pitched the tent in a
forest glade. Vandaga showed us a remarkable mass of broken
rock which overhung the river like a lofty wall. We climbed up it,
holding on to projecting bits of rock, rosemary and briar bushes,
and finally struggled to the top. The marshy district along the
river, which was covered with pine woods, blended with the

horizon; the hills and the rounded spurs of the mountain chain were bathed in yellow light.

'There grow stone-pines, there birches,' Vandaga pointed to light and dark patches in the taiga. 'Behind mountain River Sutar. I caught sable there and built hut. Very good place.'

We sat on a stone.

'Ah, precipice,' said Vandaga delightedly. 'Good precipice. Here come many different people. I shot elk and reindeer here.'

He told us how the animals escaped from wolves and hunting dogs here. They fled straight to this precipice and fought off their enemies with feet and antlers. Neither wolves nor hounds could find a chink in their armour here.

When the red deer was exhausted, he lay down on the edge of the precipice. What was the usual outcome of these struggles? The harassed stag either missed his footing and fell to his death or he leapt forward and tore his enemy to pieces. Hunters call these precipices 'sanctuaries', because this is where the deer finds refuge in time of trouble.

When Vandaga first hunted here, his dog Buschma went off after a red deer and disappeared. For three whole days he looked for the dog, blowing his horn and firing shots in the hope that Buschma would answer and come back. But still he did not come. Vandaga grew used to the idea that a tiger had eaten the dog.

When he reached this spot, he could not believe his eyes; there lay Buschma on his stomach, barking at a stag which was scarcely able to stand, although he was equally exhausted.

Yerofey called to us from below; it was time for supper. Climbing down a precipice is more like crawling than walking. Although it was so steep that a man could scarcely cling to it, a narrow path wound from the foot of the crag to the top. The trails of red deer, elks and their fresh droppings could be seen on the moss and between the stones.

'It's not easy for the wild beasts to climb up here,' I remarked.

'They fly up like bullets,' laughed Vandaga, 'but go down very slowly. Look: path first right, then left; always zigzag. Red deer think that out to make going down easier. Sable go here too.' He plucked a tuft of sable hairs from a bush and rolled them into a tiny ball between finger and thumb. 'Here many sable! But impossible to hunt,' he sighed. 'I hunt him with Chady, but sable hide in cleft in rock. Can't fetch him out with fire, dog or bullet. One time sable die in cleft in rock, but not come out. No doubt about it, sable very thick-skulled people.'

At the foot of the rock-face lay bleaching bones and skulls, and yellow-grey fur was festooned on the bushes like spiders' webs. This was the cemetery of the red deer and elks which had fallen headlong from their sanctuary and then been devoured by the wolves.

We spent the night by the camp fire. For a long time I could not go to sleep. The air was clear and cool. The moon rose above the forest. The tops of the trees were clearly visible in the moonlight, but below the topmost branches of the fir trees it was pitch-dark. I lay on my back and looked at the dark green sky.

Vandaga and Yerofey took turns to guard the horses, for there were wild beasts in the neighbourhood. We often heard, quite close to us, the growl of a bear, the miaow of a lynx, the frightened call of a roebuck or the hideous moan of the glutton. The horses snorted and pressed closer to the fire.

It was morning and the sun was rising behind the mountains.

The trees, bathed in the bright morning light, seemed half asleep. Hawks circled above the mountains.

We saddled the horses and set out. The mountains were left behind and to one side. The dense thickets reappeared. Dark-coloured game tracks led through the moss. Notches cut by axes were visible on the pines and spruces. Twigs shaped like arrows showed where a man unknown to us had passed.

'I go here,' recalled Vandaga. 'Straight path to the salt-marsh.'

'It's a beautiful wilderness,' said Yerofey who was accustomed to hunting in the inhabited part of the taiga near villages and rivers. 'What on earth sent you to this deserted spot?'

'A hunter can go anywhere,' answered Vandaga. 'Where going easy, nothing to shoot. Where going difficult, much to shoot. You grow rich and eat plenty.'

We walked in Indian file, leading the horses by their bridles. There was still sheet ice under the moss in places. The riderless horses frequently slipped and fell.

I looked at my watch: the time was passing slowly. At last the wood began to grow less dense. The sun had warmed the soil here. The horses stuck in a marsh. Several times we had to take off their packs and carry them ourselves. Yerofey pulled a bad-tempered face. He growled that it was senseless to go so far without a rest. In fact we were in about as much of a hurry as if we were visiting our mothers-in-law.

'Go just a little, little more,' urged Vandaga soothingly. 'Soon we see valleys of Kuldur. Must have a little more patience.'

In two hours' time we reached the top of the pass. It had grown hot. The air seemed petrified in the burning glare. Our hearts beat faster. I looked down into the plain below.

The taiga unfolded before us like a sea in which the dark gorges of the smaller rivers and the valleys of the Oldoga, the Sobolina and the Kuldur were clearly visible. Light-coloured jagged mountains shimmered in the haze in the distance. We had almost reached the salt-marsh.

'We go down slope,' said Vandaga. 'Will find spring without name; leads to Kuldur.'

We had eaten all the meat from our wild boar. Vandaga advised us to lay in a supply of meat here, because we dared not make a noise or shoot in the area where we hoped to capture our stag. Yerofey looked down pessimistically: 'It doesn't smell of edible game here. Are we supposed to shoot jays? They'll only blow our stomachs up.'

Vandaga looked at Yerofey as if he was a temperamental child, shook his head and laughed.

When we had taken a short rest, we descended into a dense pine forest. The gorge grew wider and next to the tiny stream wound a barely perceptible game track which we followed first on one side of the bank, then on the other. Then we turned aside, crossed a moor and reached a plain dotted with hummocks and scattered pines. We halted briefly to rest the horses. They flicked their tails joyfully and chewed the grass which was as high as their bellies. Vandaga plucked a stem of this grass and explained:

'It's called aga. Stays green all winter under snow. Frost not harm it, never grows yellow. Is quite fresh fodder for various people. Young pigs and red deer come here to eat.'

Chady suddenly found a trail and dashed off.

'Wait little, little while,' whispered Vandaga. 'Chady find some sort of people.'

About fifty paces away a roebuck shot up and leapt over the hummock and away with astonishing ease and grace. Yerofey fired first, then Vandaga. Roebuck and dog vanished out of sight.

Yerofey cursed his Winchester. Its trigger was too heavy and as a result he missed frequently.

'Is it possible I miss too?' asked Vandaga, his eyes wide open with astonishment. 'What's wrong here?'

'So you missed too?' laughed Yerofey. 'Yet you boasted "I shoot tiger in ear". You're lucky my trigger was too heavy. Otherwise I'd show you how to shoot a running buck.'

We followed the roebuck's tracks and saw red spots on the grass.

'Look,' laughed Vandaga. 'Is hit. Chady catch him, bite his throat. Must look for him round here.'

Yerofey stayed with the horses. I accompanied Vandaga in pursuit of the bloody trail into the wilderness of last year's dry grass. It was a yard high and many traces were visible there. Dozens of deer had traversed it that morning. Vandaga shook his head worriedly, because he had lost the trail of the wounded roebuck. Apparently the wound must have been a minor one. The tracks crossed and merged, and the dog could not get his bearings at all.

Vandaga took out a flint, something to strike it on and a wick, lit it and set fire to the grass. The flames crept in all directions. My eyes were swimming and my heart was pounding.

'Have you gone crazy?' I cried. 'You're frightening the animals and we're going to be roasted alive.'

'Grass not burn long,' replied the old man calmly. 'Further on, marsh, wet moss; wind blow in that direction, you nothing to fear. After fire young grass grow well, animals say thank you to hunter.'

The fire raged over an enormous area. Clouds of black smoke billowed above the smouldering grass. We stood on a hummock. Chady barked from somewhere in the smoke. Vandaga bent double and ran towards the dog. I could scarcely follow him.

It turned out that Chady had found the roebuck and started to tear it open. He had already begun to gorge himself on the entrails when he was frightened by the smoke. He smelled the danger and began to bark. We cut the roebuck up and returned to our horses. Yerofey was amazed:

'What's this, did you find the buck?'

'I never lose nothing,' replied Vandaga proudly. 'Heaven forbid, lose bag!'

Yerofey cut the meat into small pieces, salted it and packed it in the sack. We went round the moor and after crossing a rocky slope reached a forest of young stone-pines. The clearings in the forest were gaily decked with the blue and violet flowers of the Siberian speedwell, the pointed-leaved hellebore and ferns like ostrich feathers. Most of the trees were encircled by Amur vines.

The forest was heady with scents and there was dry warm earth underfoot. New game tracks were continually branching off from the path we were following.

The face of the taiga had altered. The monotonous gloom of the pine forests had ceased. On both sides of the path Amur lime trees, Manchurian walnuts, ash and maples rustled as if greeting the travellers. Yerofey's stirrup was broken. While waiting for him to sew up the strap again, we unloaded the horses and fed them. I stood in front of an elm with a fat squat trunk and gnarled branches. I was fascinated by its bluish bark, bathed in sunlight and wreathed with grape vines. It was an enormous tree: I had never seen such a giant.

I fetched paper and coloured pencils from the saddle-bag. Vandaga bent down and looked over my shoulder. Soon the tree's outlines, the sunbeams and the green of the leaves appeared on the paper. Vandaga breathed deeply, clicked his tongue and shook his head. Then he interrupted me firmly:

'We must go on. Many different people in salt-marsh. You paint there. Here not necessary to paint!'

He dragged me away and announced that we would see many more beautiful trees which I could sketch in my book. I finished my sketch in a hurry. We swung into the saddle again and rode through a sunny valley sheltered from the wind by mountains. We were surrounded by trees which I had never seen in those parts before: the Daurian birch, satinwoods, the Chinese paper-mulberry, wild cherries, lilacs, maples with green bark and elms with leaves as small as willows.

Now we descended at a trot. Before us lay a large clearing carpeted with yellow flowers. In a few minutes we stopped on the granite banks of the Kuldur. The water rippled and splashed. A small sandbank bordered with green bushes and luxuriant clumps of grass was faintly visible through the steam rising from some springs.

Vandaga pointed proudly: 'There it is, the hot salt-marsh!'

Three-quarters of a mile from the hot salt springs we pitched our tent, washed our clothes in the river, bathed and collected a supply of wood. The horses were tied up with long ropes which enabled them to crop the grass near our camp.

'Rest, eat meat, drink tea,' said Vandaga, but went off himself to inspect the approaches to the salt-marsh. He soon returned looking worried and gloomy: 'Very bad luck, commissar. No fresh tracks. Red deer not visit salt-marsh for long time.'

Yerofey intervened: it had rained during the last few days, the tracks were washed out, so there was no need to worry.

'You got head?' asked Vandaga angrily. 'Go so many years in taiga with gun and understand nothing. What sort of hunter are you?'

He took us to the sandbank and stirred the dry droppings with his foot: 'You see that? Red deer leave that long time ago.'

Yerofey said nothing.

'Nevertheless we must wait,' I said. 'Perhaps they have not come for several days, but today or tomorrow they will be here again.'

In the approach to the main spring of the salt-marsh we dug a deep pit, stretched the net over it and covered the trap with grass and branches. Vandaga built the hide in which we would wait for the animals.

At night Yerofey kept watch over the horses. I went to the salt-marsh with Vandaga. Chady lay in the grass next to his master. I expressed the fear that the dog might bark on seeing the red deer and frighten them away from the trap.

'He understand everything,' said Vandaga soothingly. 'He only bark when necessary.'

What could I do? The old man had his whims. Night came. The ripple of the streams was barely audible. In the distance a wolf bitch howled, answered by an old male wolf. Then, quite close by, a fox yelped; he had a thin, whimpering voice and seemed to me to be upset about something. Perhaps a hostile animal had ventured into his territory and he was trying to drive it away by barking and fighting.

At midnight a wind got up which made the trees rustle. On the ground a twig snapped suspiciously. Then the gusts suddenly died down and it was quiet in the woods again. I was listening to a noise behind us. It sounded as if a man was walking barefoot through the grass, then stopped and sighed. But I knew how deceptive nocturnal sounds were in the taiga.

Chady growled. I heard Vandaga's angry whisper, a blow and a muffled whimper. The old man was keeping his dog quiet. So much for the intelligent animal who only barks when necessary, I thought!

The dawn was coming. The white granite cliffs on the banks of the Kuldur were visible again. The nuthatches were already singing and the other birds were beginning to wake up.

We walked through the damp grass. Not far from the spring we came across a red deer which had been torn to pieces several days ago. Head, legs and spine had been gnawed absolutely bare.

'Look there,' said Vandaga, catching sight of some giant footprints in the clay soil of the bank. 'Tiger passed here.'

We exchanged glances in silence.

'Tiger kill red deer, eat little, little, go to sleep,' reasoned Vandaga. 'Then wolves come, eat rest.'

We circled the spot several times and came upon some brandnew tiger tracks which led to the beast's lair in the salt-marsh. Ice-cold shivers ran down my spine when I thought of the noise in the night and the dog's growl. Perhaps Vandaga only took Chady with him because he was counting on the chance of meeting a tiger? The tiger had sneaked up and lain down only ten paces from our hiding-place. That was why Chady had snarled.

Now everything was clear. The robber was scaring the red deer, elks and roebuck away from the salt-marsh. Salt is a delicacy to all four-footed game and they came here from far and wide to lick it. But when a tiger was lurking in the vicinity, the animals gave up their favourite delicacy.

We went to our camp and held a council of war. Vandaga's opinion was that we should hunt the tiger first: 'We must make tiger kaput, commissar. Then red deer will come to salt-marsh and we catch him.'

Yerofey's courage dropped at once.

'We mustn't do anything silly, brother,' he mumbled. 'A tiger is no hare. By the time we have tracked him down and got him in our sights, one or even two weeks will have passed. Then our supplies will run out and we'll begin to shoot roes. In that way we'll frighten the red deer away for good.'

'And what do you advise then?'

'Going back home.'

I shamed Yerofey.

'And what will they think about us in the kolkhoz then?'

'All right, then we'll be stuck here until Assumption Day (15th August),' growled Yerofey.

The struggle continued until evening. Presumably Yerofey was missing his young bride badly, because he tried hard to convince us of the senselessness of our plan. His presumption annoyed me, and I ordered Yerofey to be quiet. After all, I pointed out, I was the leader of the expedition and I approved Vandaga's plan.

If Yerofey wanted to leave us, well and good. We two would catch the red deer together.

'All right,' agreed Yerofey gloomily. 'I give in, but nothing will come of all this.'

The weather changed suddenly. It drizzled and our tent was not thick. Vandaga built a roomy shelter of bark and twigs and we moved into our new quarters. We drank tea and ate roast venison.

The rain poured down incessantly. Torrents of water roared down the ravines. The Kuldur overflowed its banks and flooded the meadows near the forest. Vandaga removed the net from the trap and walked up and down in gloomy silence.

It rained for three days with only brief intervals. When the sky cleared, I went for walks along the river. Giant stone-pines and larches with their dark needles gleaming after the rain stood out above the young green saplings like cliffs at sea. I sat near the river on a black poplar which had been uprooted by the wind. An Asiatic water-wagtail flew by; I saw the penduline titmouse and ortolans; a jay called – and then all was quiet again in the rain-swept forest.

Raindrops fell from the trees. One could almost see the grasses grow after their liberal watering of the last few days. When we arrived I had seen nothing but sedge and wormwood with feather-like stems. But today various species of rhododendrons were in bloom, the Siberian speedwell with its lanceolate leaves unfolded its buds and was covered with violet and blue flowers.

To my left an industrious tree-creeper was working on an old larch tree. This tiny bird, which can be found in the remotest woods near rivers, climbs rapidly up the trunk and pecks at the bark with its thin sharp beak. It is most amusing when it comes down tail-first and yet hardly touches the tree with its claws.

A nuthatch was at work close to the tree-creeper. His beak was like a short chisel with which he pecked the bark first on one side then on the other. His little head was wagging away like a pendulum.

A solitary kingfisher was catching small fish from the sandbank. He sat in the water with his vivid blue plumage and consumed his prey. Either the birds could not see me or they were unafraid of me.

Sometimes the clouds lifted completely and the sun appeared. Bars of light fell on the grass at my feet. Mist rose from the hummocks. I unbuttoned my collar, took off my cap and inhaled the sweetish scent of the stone-pines. 'Patience,' I said to myself. 'You must have patience.'

To pass the time I took out my sketch book and drew. The hours flew by. Then new rain clouds began to appear from the upper reaches of the river. Birds and insects fell silent. It poured again and I went back to our camp. The horses greeted me with a low whinny. Machtak tossed his head, as much as to say: 'Give me some biscuit.'

Chady stood at the entrance to the shelter and wagged his tail in friendly fashion. He was a strange dog. Every day I gave him bones and tried to make friends with him. He licked my hands and rubbed against me, but that was all. On no account would he go walking with me in the taiga unless Vandaga was there.

That evening Vandaga said: 'Smoke from camp fire go straight up: rain soon finish.'

'Thank Heavens,' cried Yerofey. 'I'm just about dying of boredom in this hole.'

We finished our pipes and went to sleep. The next morning it really had cleared up. There was a rainbow above the forest in which orange and red predominated.

I went with Vandaga to reconnoitre the salt-marsh. We passed the springs and penetrated deep into the thicket of elders and black alder bushes. Suddenly Chady's hair stood on end. The dog looked around fearfully. Vandaga released the safety catch of his Berdan and sent the dog off ahead. He put one foot ahead of the other in the grass with the care of a setter on the trail of a sitting bird.

I cocked my gun and raised it to my shoulder. Behind the bushes we could hear growling and crackling in the brushwood. We parted the bushes cautiously and stepped out into the clearing. In front of us lay an elk which had just been disembowelled by a tiger.

'Tiger frightened, run, run!' said Vandaga. 'Now is far away. At night tiger come again, eat elk. We must hide: watch, listen, shoot.'

We returned to the shelter. A sunny day of radiant beauty began; the birds were twittering everywhere and rejoicing in the warmth. I could not stop thinking about the tiger: would we be able to kill him?

Before sunset Yerofey handed me his Winchester. He claimed that I dare not fire at the tiger with my double-barrelled gun, although I had cartridges with heavy charges. Vandaga advised me to keep my own gun: 'Has large bullets, can knock tiger over.'

This time Chady stayed behind near the shelter, on the lead. We also left Yerofey behind, so that our camp was guarded, and went off to our hide. We were counting on the beast coming down to the river over the slope. We sat down in the bushes, with our faces turned towards the river. Vandaga was ten paces away from me. The flies buzzed around the elk's corpse. There was a smell of resin, moisture and decaying moss.

A pale moon stood above the mountains. The colours in the sky grew denser yet paler. The night was clear. The wind had died down and there was only a gentle rustling to be heard. We waited. I have no idea how many hours passed. The moon was already high in the sky but the silence of the forest still surrounded me. I listened and hugged my gun.

At sunrise we heard the same snarl as the day before. The tiger was approaching the elk's body and parting the bushes. At first his mighty shadow appeared in the clearing, then his heavy clumsy body became visible. He stalked round the clearing, yawned and apparently smelt man, because he raised his head and listened.

I was paralysed. I felt an unbearable weight on my shoulders as if someone was trying to push me into the earth. Perhaps it was only my imagination but I thought that I could distinguish the animal's strong smell which reminded me of the sweat of an old dirty cat. Vandaga and I shot almost simultaneously. The tiger fell, but was on its feet again at once and leapt at me. I still had a cartridge in my left barrel. I shot at almost point-blank range. The bullet should have blown the tiger's head off but that was not what happened. In my panic at the beast's proximity I missed. The tiger knocked me into the grass.

What else happened? I can only remember a flash of light above me and the crack of a shot in my ears. The tiger collapsed. I jumped to my feet and saw . . . Yerofey. He was standing almost next to me and his Winchester was smoking.

'So you two wanted to kill the tiger on your own?' he said triumphantly. 'There he is, you heroes.'

Vandaga came up, covered in confusion. The old man had been let down by his Berdan: an exploded cartridge case had jammed in the chamber. While he was trying to reload the gun, Yerofey had intervened. He told us that he had simply been unable to stay in the shelter any longer.

'My heart was heavy. I had no peace. Suddenly some misfortune will befall them, I thought, and here am I watching the horses so that gluttons don't get them. That's the way it was. Just look what a giant he is! I'd say he weighed fifteen poods.* Just imagine that one can kill a brute like that with one bullet. But there's no escape from my Winchester; I let him have it in the ear and it was all over!'

He was fully conscious of his own importance and let us know it: without him Vandaga and I would have perished. I hastened to thank him and shook hands with him to cut short his flow of oratory. His merit was recognized and he was satisfied. Vandaga bent over the body and examined the wounds.

'Tiger dead. Three bullets hit him. Yerofey shoot well, I shoot well, commissar shoot well. So many bullets hit him, but he still live. Merciful God, what strong people tigers are!'

I looked round. It seemed to me as if it was much freer and more pleasant in the forest now. I could breathe more easily.

---

* A pood is a Russian weight equal to about 36 lb. A male tiger can weigh anything between four and five hundred pounds and measure up to about $9\frac{1}{2}$ feet in length. – A.C.J.

Even the midges and flies no longer bothered me after our victory over the tiger.

'Well done, friends,' I said. 'Now we still have to capture the red deer.'

'Want to smoke a bit,' laughed Vandaga happily. 'Tiger dead, no work; now can rest and talk. Now we are allowed.'

He sat on the tiger and filled his pipe. He lit up and took deep puffs. His eyes were veiled by his eyelashes, his face was motionless and only the lips sucking at the mouthpiece moved a little. The tobacco in the bowl of his pipe kept glowing and then dying down again as he smoked. I looked at Vandaga and wondered whether the old man would be frightened if the tiger moved under him and tried to get to its feet again?

I remembered such an occasion. A fully grown tiger had been killed in the vicinity of a village. It was fetched with a horse, placed on a sledge, and lashed on with a rope so that it could not roll off on the slopes. The old hunter sat in front and drove the horse. En route the tiger came to its senses again, roared, and began to tear at the rope with which it was tied to the sledge. The horse bolted. The old man sat paralysed with fear because he had not so much as an axe in the sledge to hit the tiger with. His terrified son ran behind the sledge, but could not shoot; he might have hit his father or the horse instead of the tiger. So the father charged into the village with the roaring tiger. The horse was covered with sweat. He shot into his familiar farmyard and nearly dashed himself against the wall. Then the old man came to his senses and climbed down from the driving seat. He grabbed his cudgel and shattered the tiger's skull.

I told Vandaga about this to see whether he would look frightened.

'Well then,' he answered, 'tiger come alive, I jump to one side, shoot again: gun always loaded.'

I asked Vandaga if he had never been frightened once while out hunting. He explained that his most terrifying memory was not meeting a tiger. About twenty years ago he had built a log cabin in the taiga in which he kept skins, dead game and hunting supplies. In the cold season he also slept there. There was no lock for it. When Vandaga went out hunting he barred the door with a stake. Occasionally a hunter entered the cabin in his absence, drank tea, loaded his cartridges and went on his way. No one robbed the hunting cabin.

In the autumn Vandaga was once out late in the forest. His dog was on the track of a sable and kept him waiting so long that he returned to his cabin alone in the twilight. He came closer and saw that the door was open and the stake lay on the ground. In great surprise Vandaga stood on the threshold and asked: 'Who is there?'

No one answered, but his ears caught a sound. A floorboard creaked. There was someone in the cabin. Vandaga lit a piece of birch bark and, torch in hand, stepped inside. Next to the stove stood two gluttons – wolverines – showing their fangs. Everything in the hut was broken and chewed up.

'I was terribly afraid that time,' recalled Vandaga and nodded his head. 'I thought: they not gluttons, but bad spirits come to destroy cabin and take skins.'

One glutton leapt at him, but he whipped round, dashed out and bolted the door with the stake. He was trembling all over and could not control his hands when he tried to change the cartridges loaded with shot for a bullet.

Then his dog came back and Vandaga felt a little easier in his mind. During the night the gluttons were busy trying to undermine the wall. Vandaga breathed a sigh of relief. They were not evil spirits, for would a spirit dig holes under a log cabin? He would be more likely to disappear by changing himself into a bird or a beetle.

In the morning Vandaga knocked the window in (a piece of deer-membrane), pushed his gun through the opening and shot the gluttons.

Vandaga and Yerofey skinned the tiger. The old man hummed a song whose words were unintelligible to me, but I knew what he was singing about: one more tiger, enemy of deer and men, killed, commissar brings striped skin and white moustache of wild beast into village, all the people will rejoice and praise the successful hunters.

The sun had risen. A faint bluish mist lay over river and plain. One could just hear the rustle of the stone-pines in the morning breeze. For a whole week we rested in the shelter. The weather was fine, but we had nothing to do, because the red deer did not visit the salt-marsh. The days grew warmer and the young grass was already over three feet high.

Our stock of meat had run out. Vandaga snared hazel-hens, Yerofey fashioned a fish trap which he set in shallow backwaters. He produced a fish every morning.

One morning the old man came back from his reconnaissance trip bursting with excitement. I feared the worst – had he stumbled on fresh tiger tracks again?

'Red deer come to salt-marsh,' he announced. 'A doe, a stag and one youngster. Our affair very good, commissar.'

We rejoiced and discussed the news animatedly. Yerofey prepared a splendid lunch in honour of the occasion, consisting of an enormous Siberian salmon seasoned with garlic. Night came. I checked the trap with Vandaga. We stretched the net between stakes and moved into the hide.

At first the dark night was absolutely still; but after a time I heard the noise of animals. They had come at last. They were cropping the juicy ranunculus, which grows there, licking the pebbles and nibbling at the salt deposits in the soil. But what sort of animals could they be? Elks perhaps? I scarcely dared to move. Vandaga, who could see better in the dark than I could, already knew what was to be done.

Then something surprising happened: the animals, which must have been frightened for some reason, dashed to the precipice as fast as their legs would carry them. One fell into the net. We could hear snorting, thrashing and kicking in the pit.

Vandaga lit a torch of birch bark. A doe which could not have been more than two years old was struggling in the meshes of the net. By the light of the flame I could see the terror in her big black eyes.

'Why you go in trap?' said Vandaga angrily to the doe. 'Are you blind? We no use for you at all.' He reached for his knife to cut her throat, but I held him back and said: 'Let her go!'

The old man disagreed. 'Must kill her, commissar.'

'Set her free at once!' I ordered. The old man gave in, stuck the torch in the fork of a bough and pulled the doe's head out of the meshes. The freed animal shot away like a whirlwind.

I chuckled, without knowing why. We stood silently smoking there in the nocturnal stillness, then we returned to the shelter.

'You do very bad thing, commissar,' Vandaga reproached me. 'Doe now go in taiga and tell all people: "In salt-marsh is trap." How you not understand?'

I repressed a laugh with difficulty: 'Animals cannot speak. You are wrong, my friend. I know that for certain.'

The old man was convinced that the insects, the birds and all the other animals had their own language and warned each other of danger.

'Crow sit on fir-tree, see hunter with gun. Crow caw faintly, faintly – racoon* run, roebuck run, red deer run! Many different people in taiga understand crow, all people hide from hunter.'

For once the old hunter was wrong, for the next night the deer came to the salt-marsh again. One of them stopped in front of the trap. Vandaga shouted 'Uch, uch!' The animal jumped and fell into the net covering the pit. We ran up with ropes and tied its feet together. At last we had what we wanted: a wonderful specimen of a stag. He was a ten-pointer with a massive chest. He was already carrying his reddish-brown summer coat with slate-coloured woolly hair. He struggled against his bonds and his whole body trembled.

'Lie still,' Vandaga advised him. 'We do you no harm. Not cut throat. You go on visit to does.'

The old man was convinced that the animal understood him.

Delighted with the success of our mission we rolled dry logs to the river-bank and made a raft. We took the stag to the raft on a drag-net and laid him safe and sound in the stern. Yerofey had

---

* Vandaga must have meant the racoon-like dog (*Nyctereutes procyonoides*), not the real racoon which of course exists in North America. – A.C.J.

covered the logs with grass so that the prisoner would lie comfortably.

Chady jumped on to the raft; with hair on end he growled at the stag. Vandaga had only to threaten his dog with one finger: Chady curled up, but he never took his watchful eyes off the animal.

We could go. The horses came down to the bank, looking at us and swishing their tails. We had grown used to them and now we had to shoot them. I ordered Yerofey to do it. He raised his Winchester and aimed at Skorochod. I closed my eyes tightly. For a long time there was no shot and Yerofey coughed suspiciously. When I opened my eyes again, I saw Yerofey standing there with lowered gun.

'I can't do it,' he said. 'You shoot them.'

'Not necessary shoot these people,' said Vandaga gently. 'We make big raft, all people lie on raft, fetch to kolkhoz.'

Skorochod put his front legs in the water and uttered a long-drawn out whinny. Machtak and Gnedko answered him. If one were to believe Vandaga, one could imagine that the horses were calling to each other: 'Look, our masters are setting out for home. They ought not to leave us in this wilderness where there are so many wild beasts.'

'Wretched old nags!' groaned Yerofey. 'We'll have trouble with them. They've got to be fed and watered on the way back. But it's a pity to shoot them all the same.'

'Raft only swim badly length of four suns,' Vandaga reassured us. 'Then river flow calmly, swim very well.'

Once more the whine of our saws and the crash of our axes filled the forest. We built a new raft, long and narrow, which we

covered with twigs, moss and grass. We carried the stag to it and
tied the horses up tightly.

Vandaga made a sail out of the tent. At noon we pushed off.
The stag gazed at us with mournful eyes. The raft swirled along
in the current, the green banks rushed rapidly by. Then the
current grew stronger and the water boiled against the rocks.
We took down the sail and slowed the raft down with oars and
poles to stop it being shattered against the rocky cliffs.

Mountains were still visible on both sides of the river, game
paths wound along the slopes like black bands in the moss.
Somewhere ahead of us my ear caught an indefinable noise.
Vandaga craned his neck forward: 'Whirlpool, commissar, don't
be afraid.'

We sailed into the whirlpool caused by the confluence of two
rivers. The water, for which there was no room on the river bed,
was forced up into huge bubbles and shot from one bank to the
other. The water was boiling furiously in this cauldron and was
covered with white foam.

The raft was tipped up sideways and then dived down from
the wave tops into the troughs between. The logs gave and the
lashings groaned. We were covered in spray. The horses fell over
and Chady whimpered anxiously. At last we were swept out of the
whirlpool into a wide calm stretch of water.

Yerofey was pale and there was fear in his eyes. Vandaga wiped
his face with his arm. I asked if there were many more whirlpools
like that ahead of us.

'Will be whirlpools, rapids come,' laughed the old man softly.
'It's nothing, commissar, I make raft well.'

From on board the raft it seemed as if we were stationary and the banks were rushing past. Steep hillocks with cloud shadows on their slopes approached us, in the valleys blue, yellow and cherry-red predominated in turn. Streams flowed down from the hills into the river. The sun glowed red in the sky. It was pleasant to sit on the raft and feel the sun's beneficent warmth at the same time as the refreshing chill of the water.

At twilight we tied up to the bank. We hobbled the horses and let them crop in a forest glade. Vandaga and Yerofey looked after the stag. They gave him water to drink from a vessel made of birch wood, fed him grass and heavily salted biscuit. He took the water but refused to eat. He pushed the food out on to the raft with his tongue. I was worried by the animal's stubbornness: I hoped he would not die of hunger after all.

Vandaga reassured me: 'Stag not die on way home. For two suns can fast, even three, but fourth sun eat everything. He no fool, he understand: we good people, not stab him with knife – will eat.'

We ate our evening meal by the camp fire. Chady had finished his share and was taking a walk. From the thicket into which he had plunged came long-drawn-out cries which sounded like the call of a water-rail. Suddenly they stopped and we heard Chady's bark.

I loaded my gun, Vandaga followed me carrying an axe. An enormous snake was hissing in the middle of the clearing with Chady dancing around it. I raised my gun but Vandaga pushed me aside and chopped off its head with his axe.

We carried the snake to our camp. Yerofey laughed contemptuously: 'Imagine grown-ups bothering with such a disgusting creature.' He could not bear snakes and grunted: 'A useless animal. Neither fish, flesh, fowl nor good red herring. It makes you sick just to look at him.'

Vandaga threw dry wood on to the camp fire which flared up brightly. It was as light as day in the clearing. I slit the snake's stomach open with a knife and we found a mouse and a bluish snub-nosed nuthatch in its stomach. The snake had only recently swallowed the two animals.

'Good heavens, this filthy reptile has eaten a bird,' exclaimed Yerofey. 'How on earth does he catch a nuthatch? I suppose he must have swallowed a dead bird.'

'Miki eat nothing dead,' said Vandaga. 'She go softly, softly through the grass. You walk past, hear nothing. Mice, jays, nuthatches sleep a little. Miki come, swallow all up. During day Miki lie in sun like tree. Nuthatch think: nothing living there, play close, sit on Miki's head. Then Miki open mouth and swallow.'

'Have you seen that yourself or did your uncle tell you about it?' asked Yerofey.

Vandaga was silent. He was as guileless and naive as a child and had probably never told a lie in his life. He was always annoyed when someone doubted his word. I had to make amends for Yerofey's tactlessness and supported Vandaga vigorously. Yerofey crept shamefacedly into our hut of willow twigs and was snoring within a few minutes. Vandaga went fishing on the river. Chady followed him like a shadow.

The camp fire burnt down and the sky grew lighter. Soon the sun would rise and all living creatures rejoice. The ducks would make their morning flight over the river, the flowers would awake from their sleep, open their calyxes and unfold their dew-laden petals.

I looked at the mountain ridges which bordered the river in the mist, listened to the nocturnal sounds in the forest, the fish jumping near the sandbank, and thought how wonderful was life on this fruitful earth which renewed itself every year. How pleasant it would be not to grow old, to roam through the forests with a gun, discover new regions, swim in foaming rivers and sleep at night near the camp fire in the cool dewy grass – for centuries.

The horses had eaten their fill; they came back to the camp fire and fell asleep standing up. Vandaga returned with a wicker basket full of fish. He made up the fire again and settled down to making fish soup. I wanted to tell Vandaga what a splendid comrade he was and that from now on we would be good friends and go hunting together, but sleep overcame me and I fell on to the grass as if I was falling into a ravine from a steep slope.

At sunrise we pushed off from the bank. The river grew broader, the rapids and the straight reaches between two curves were calmer. In the backwaters we put up gleaming silver mergansers and teal; kingfishers and stormy petrels flew up from the gravel and high above in the sky eagles circled.

When the ducks flew over our raft, I shot at them; sometimes I managed to bring down one or two. While Chady leapt into the water to retrieve them, we stopped the raft with a pole. The dog climbed aboard again and gave the bird to his master. He could see that Vandaga had not fired, but he absolutely refused to deliver the bag to me.

'Stupid dog,' I said and scratched his wet back. 'It's all the same, birds go into the common cook pot. Why do you behave like that?'

At last the stag began to eat grass and swallow biscuits moistened with water from the bucket. A load was off our minds. Even Vandaga laughed, looking on happily and clicking his tongue. Yerofey was quite beside himself and began to dance on the raft.

We stayed alongside the bank for a whole day. Yerofey took it into his head to go hunting and shot a young elk. Chady followed the wounded animal and disappeared. From time to time Vandaga fired into the air to call the dog back. Perhaps Chady had met wolves and been torn to pieces?

Yerofey urged us to carry on. I asked Vandaga what he thought.

'Must wait a little,' said the old man. 'Without Chady I can't go hunting any more.'

'The kolkhoz will give you a dog,' Yerofey interrupted him. 'We have too many dogs. You can pick out any one you like.'

Vandaga gave Yerofey a hostile look: 'Chady alone worth many dogs. Dogs are different. Chady never leave me in lurch. I not leave him in lurch.'

'You must be attached to each other!' said Yerofey excitedly. 'If we were just on a trip somewhere, we could wait. But supposing the stag dies suddenly? The kolkhoz farmers will thrash us because of your dog.'

I said nothing. Vandaga lowered his eyes. Even he understood the risk was too great.

'Off we go,' I ordered. Without a word Vandaga loaded the horses on to the raft, set the sail, lit his pipe and took his place by the rudder. He did not argue with me but I knew that he was terribly upset. I was sorry for him, I looked at his bowed back and thought what wonderful self-control he had.

We had floated about a quarter of a mile when Vandaga leapt to his feet like a jack-in-the-box.

'Hey, commissar!' he shouted. 'Look there!'

Chady was running along the bank. We could hear his hoarse angry bark. We rowed to a sandbank and the missing passenger embarked. His flanks were distended; presumably he had caught up with the wounded elk and made a hearty breakfast.

'You miserable brute!' shouted Yerofey. 'We wait here and he stuffs his belly full.'

The dog snuggled against his master. There was a gleam of joy in Vandaga's dark eyes but the dog must be made to pay for his crime. 'You very bad dog,' said the old man and wagged his finger at Chady. 'Stag must go to kolkhoz fast, commissar in hurry. Yerofey want to see young wife. You understand that?'

Chady's tail barely moved. Vandaga took a hazel switch and gave the dog two blows across his back. Chady lay down and whimpered hypocritically.

'Remember that,' advised Yerofey. 'You ought to have your ribs broken for behaving like that!'

Vandaga threw the switch away, stroked the dog and said something to him in his own tongue. Chady looked dejected and blinked guiltily.

Now the raft carried us further over glittering water. Bright red and yellow butterflies with dark spots on their wings fluttered round us and settled on the logs. They looked at us with their black protruding eyes as if they wanted to ask: 'What sort of people are you? Where are you going and where do you come from?'

I took them in the palm of my hand and let them fly away again after I had kept them captive for a while. They rose into the air and flew across to the bank.

In a straight quietly-flowing stretch of river a small boat, a dug-out made from a poplar, came out from the riverside bushes to meet us. A long trident lay in the stern. An old Udege stood in the boat, rowing with a double-bladed paddle. He exchanged greetings with Vandaga.

'Sorodä'!

'Sorodä'!

Apparently this corresponded to our 'Good morning' or 'God be with you'. The Udege came nearer. He was Macha, a fisherman and hunter, who was an old friend of Vandaga's. They gossiped for a while, then with a sudden movement Macha steered his boat into the rapids bubbling in front of us. The little boat danced on the waves. Macha put down his paddle, took up his trident, jabbed it into the water and took out a large fish. Then he stuck his trident into the river bottom, thus keeping his boat stationary. As we slipped past him, he threw the fish over on to the raft: 'That's my present. Eat, comrades.'

Vandaga made some reply, Yerofey and I waved our hands. Our raft was carried away by the current. The Udege stood up in his boat and watched us.

'Thank heavens!' said Yerofey. 'At last we're in inhabited territory again. We'll soon be home again. Natalya has waited long enough for me.'

Gone now were the rapids partially jammed with driftwood. We sailed on all night without a break. The stag was eating out of Yerofey's hand. There was not a breath of wind and the sail hung limply against the mast. The raft was only moving slowly. We could no longer touch bottom with the pole and were forced to use the oars again.

About midnight, mayflies, whose larvae lived temporarily in the water, rose out of the river. Today these little water bugs had become winged creatures of pale blue with transparent wings and three tail bristles. They fluttered above the water like snow-flakes, flying in all directions. Their life only lasts for one day. They rise out of the water into our bright sunny world to multiply and die.

Millions of mayflies were zooming up and down the water. They settled on the raft and everything, including the stag's antlers, was covered with them like the petals of the most exotic flowers. We sat motionless, captivated by the sight. Vandaga stopped rowing.

'Oh, how many new people appear,' he whispered dreamily. 'One sun and all dead.'

For about twenty minutes it was like floating through a snowstorm. Then the mayflies disappeared but the low-pitched buzzing of their wings lingered in our ears for a long time.

Towards noon we neared our home village. Yerofey spread the tiger skin out on the starboard side so that everyone would see his trophy of the chase.

'Why boast and make a bazaar of the raft?' I asked.

'Let them look. Why should we be ashamed? After all, the skin was not stolen,' answered Yerofey.

An incorrigible fellow!

They had spotted our raft in the village. The children were the first to meet us.

'They're bringing a stag, a stag,' they shouted at the top of their voices. 'And they've killed a tiger!'

The members of the kolkhoz ran up. Dimitri Ivanich and Danilo arrived with a big lorry.

'Little father!' exclaimed the president. 'Even the old hacks are safe and sound. Devil take it, they've even put on weight, we could take them straight to market. And we were in such a state, you were away so long. We thought perhaps something had happened.'

We undid the stag, laid it in the lorry and drove to the farm. Nil Demyanich, the keeper, opened the gate. Cautiously we led the wild stag into the herd. The does, frightened by the noise, pressed against the fence. Dimitri Ivanich stood by the gate with his hand on the latch and could not stop smiling. The stag stood up, trembling all over. The does looked at him and snorted. He went to the water trough and drank long and avidly.

Behind the fence I could hear cheerful whispering: 'Now everything's in order. Not even Pavel Michailovich brought such a fine specimen.'

Dimitri Ivanich shut the gate and enfolded me in his bearlike embrace: 'Thank you,' he said and kissed me on the forehead. 'Many thanks.'

'You must thank him,' I pointed to Vandaga. 'If it hadn't been for him we would have come back empty-handed.'

'In the name of all the members of the kolkhoz, our most humble thanks,' he said feelingly, embracing Vandaga. 'We shall not forget your services, dear friend.'

We were not left in peace for long. The banquet was ready and we were taken into the dining-room. Yerofey had already shaved and put on his Sunday best. He told the breathless audience about our expedition. He elaborated quite a bit on our adventures in the taiga, especially the encounter with the tiger. The cunning rogue said nothing about shooting the sable and what Vandaga had said to him about it.

There were piroschkis stuffed with fish, meat and cabbage, stewed pork and large reddish-brown cakes on the table. Bottles of wine were opened and everyone's glass was filled. There was a great deal of noise; Vandaga alone said nothing. Yerofey talked louder than anyone, Natalya sat next to him and looked at him lovingly. The president called for a moment's silence. Everyone stopped talking as he raised his glass: 'We drink to bravery, comrades. We drink too to the good of the people who have fulfilled a difficult mission.'

Then they drank the healths of myself, Vandaga and Yerofey in turn. Even Chady, who had guarded us, was remembered and of course the prosperity of the farm and the healthy offspring from the stag.

I would have dearly liked to raise my glass to the nocturnal quiet of the taiga, to the summer sun, the smoke of the camp fire and many other things which one experiences on such an expedition to unknown places. But I was afraid of making myself look ridiculous and did not say what was on the tip of my tongue.

Vandaga's cheeks were flushed with wine, his eyes shone. He whispered: 'I like you very much, Nikolai Vassilyevich. In the autumn we must go into mountains, shoot tiger, shoot wild boar. With two of us good hunting.'

'Yes, yes,' I replied, 'we must definitely go.'

I had the idea of persuading Vandaga to take over the cattle farm, for he understood the animals' minds better than anyone else. If he looked after the farm, everything would be in tiptop order. But how could I pin him down to one place, when he had always been used to roving?

'Listen, friend,' I said to him softly. 'How would you like to become head of the farm? We'll build you a cabin and you can live in peace.'

The old man was silent. His eyes narrowed and his lips moved as they did in his usual conversations with himself. Then he leant back in his chair and gave me a warm-hearted look.

'Thanks, commissar. I grown a bit old. Eyes see badly, feet hurt at night. Soon have to give up hunting. I think about farm. I thank you.'

I shook his hand warmly.

On the Trail of the Brontosaurus and Co.

Fulahn

The survival of supposedly extinct animals and the existence of 'new' ones has continued to arouse speculation and curiosity. Just as men try to probe the secrets of the universe, so would they like to probe the secrets of the far-distant past. This Nature Quest, if successful, would lead us back to days long before human existence!

A big-game hunting expedition now – 1927 – engaged in Central Africa under the leadership of Lieutenant-Colonel H. F. Fenn, D.S.O. intends to film gorillas in the as-yet-unpenetrated depths of the Belgian Congo: it hopes to secure a full-grown male gorilla for the Natural History Museum in London.

That capture in itself would provide enough adventure for most folks to go on with. There are few seasoned big-game hunters whose hearts would not go pit-a-pat were they to get the great chance of coming face to face with a full-grown gorilla. 'But,' says Colonel Fenn, 'the most thrilling part of our expedition will be our attempt to solve the long-existing problem of certain unknown species of animals which the natives say live in unexplored areas.'

That is putting it modestly; for Colonel Fenn has met a hunter who has told him what every big-game hunter worth the name has heard. That there is a monster in Lake Edward – a mysterious beast called the irizima; and irizima means 'The-thing-that-may-not-be-spoken-of'.

This mystery animal, the irizima, is said by some to be like a gigantic hippopotamus with the horns of a rhinoceros upon its head. Not long ago a madcap fellow trekked up from the Cape and plunged into the Congo forests to catch it. He declared that he saw it crashing through the reeds of a swamp, and that it was the brontosaurus – a huge marsh animal, ten times as big as the biggest elephant. In the Cape Town clubs they called him a liar; but a famous American scientific institute guessed better, and sent out an expedition to capture this 'brontosaurus'. It was never caught. Mishaps dogged the expedition and spoiled all chance of capturing the mystery monster.

Others declare the irizima to be a marsh monster with a hippo's legs, an elephant's trunk, a lizard's head, and an aardvaark's tail. No less a personage than Lewanika, King of the Barotse, saw the beast in the marshes of his land, and set a special warrior watch to capture it. 'A monster,' says he in his official report to the British Government, 'with a head like a snake, making a huge track in the reeds as large as a full-sized waggon would make were its wheels removed.' He speaks, of course, of the old Boer trek-waggon, a big, lumbering concern pulled by twenty or more oxen.

Under the name of the 'lau', perhaps the same animal has been seen, not only by black hunters, but by white men as well, in the great swamps of the Nile valleys below Malakal to Rejaf, and in the region of Lake No to Shambe.

This may be a different mystery beast, for it is said to be like a gigantic cobra, striped dark brown and yellow, covered with thick, wiry hairs; upon its head it has large tentacles, with which it seizes its human prey. Measuring forty to a hundred feet in length, its body is as thick and round as a bullock's. By night it is said to make a loud, terrifying, booming cry; by day, as it well might, it makes a rumbling noise like the digestion noises of a herd of grazing elephants.

From Lakes Bangweolo, Nweru, and Tanganyika every hunter of experience has heard inexplicable reports of a huge pachyderm similar to a hippopotamus, but with a large horn rising from its head; this may be the same or a different mystery monster – the brontosaurus or some other.

The level-headed man at home will be tempted to exclaim, 'But this is rubbish, this talk of undiscovered monsters.'

So at first thought it may seem; but it must be borne in mind that such an obvious animal as the okapi, a beast that looks as though it had escaped from a jigsaw zoo, remained undiscovered up till the beginning of the present century, when Sir Harry Johnston startled the scientific world by sending home the skin and skeleton of one. Scientists gasped: this cannot be, they said. They said the same about the man who first reported the giraffe; in fact, they tortured him for a downright romancer of the worst description. But there were children feeding giraffes in the London Zoo this week!

The famous chimiset or Nandi bear is perhaps the most notorious of all Africa's mystery monsters.

Speaking of it, Captain A. Blayney Percival, the famous authority on big game, who has lived his life amongst Africa's wild animals and who for twenty-three years was Game Ranger in Kenya, makes a remarkable assertion. 'I do but assert my belief,' he says, 'that some strange animal lurks in the Nandi forests, awaiting discovery and a name.'

Were there no other tittle of evidence to support the real existence of the mysterious chimiset, the word of this famous hunter would be difficult to get round; but nearly every hunter who has safaried through the vast Masai and Nandi Reserves in Kenya and Tanganyika has been implored at the manyattas or villages to track down and shoot the chimiset. Often the weird tracks of this mysterious animal have been found – queer five or three-toed tracks – the tracks of no known animal.

Fear and superstition have embroidered the native accounts of this uncanny beast; but, while allowances must be made for the exaggeration to which savages are prone, it must also be borne in mind that both the Masai and the Nandi are courageous and warlike tribes, not easily dismayed by dangerous animals. It is the proud and truthful boast of many of their warriors that they have walked boldly up to a savage lion on the veld and pulled it backwards by the tail!* Such is the test of their manhood, and it will be plain in the face of such foolhardy bravery that there must be some good reason to make the Masai and the Nandi stand in abject terror of the chimiset, which they look upon as a monster infinitely more savage and terrible than a lion at bay.

Kitapmetit Kipet, the headman of a Nandi village to which I was sent to investigate raids on stock and children by a chimiset, described the monster to me in these words, which I quote from my report. 'The chimiset is a devil which prowls the nganasa

* 'Pulled it backwards by the tail' . . . ? A full-grown lion can attain a weight of up to 550 pounds. – A.C.J.

(hut settlement) on the darkest nights, seeking people, especially children, to devour; it is half like a man and half like a huge ape-faced bird, and you may know it at once from its fearful howling roar, and because in the dark of night its mouth glows red like the embers of a log-fire.'

During my stay in his village Kipet showed me a hut, in the mud-and-lattice wall of which a large hole had been battered; through that hole the chimiset had dragged a six-year-old girl who had been sleeping in the koimaut or living-room of the hut. On the earth outside the hole were claw furrows. Calves had also been stolen from Kipet's cattle boma. Besides the palisade of poles which surrounds all Nandi cattle kraals, Kipet's men had piled up thorn-bush to a height of six feet in a solid wall eight feet thick. Burrowed through this wall was a tunnel big enough for me, not a small man, to crawl through, and on the bottom of this tunnel were more claw marks. But they were the claw marks of no known animal, unless maybe the aardvaark. But then the aardvaark does not eat young girls or burrow big tunnels through thorn zarebas, nor does it prey on calves; it is content to eat white ants.

Kipet informed me that the chimiset seemed to come from a small forest-clad kopje or boulder hill some five miles from his nganasa. I circled that kopje with spearsmen, and, gradually closing in, beat every bush and twig on it till we got to the summit. We put up baboons, rock-rabbits, some mongooses, some dik-dik antelopes, a bush-buck and its does; we put to flight owls, hawks, bats and guinea-fowls. We found the lair of a porcupine family and a hyaena hole; we dug both out. We put up some wart-hogs, and the dogs turned out innumerable rats, mice, and lizards, and not a few scorpions and snakes. But we found no chimiset; nor trace of it. Nor did we find a trace of the spoor of lion or leopard, which might have been the culprits.

I thought of a score of such hunts after the chimiset, all of which had proved futile, and decided to make quite sure. A huge forest, some twenty miles square, stretched away from the kopje. I could not search that forest, but I could make certain if any beast came to the kopje from the forest and then left the kopje by night for the village.

Around the kopje ran several sandy bush-tracks, which led to water-holes. Cutting down the bush between, Kipet's men joined these paths until they made a sandy track completely encircling the kopje. We brushed this track clean and smooth, so that even a beetle walking over it would leave its trail.

Then I went to bed. I had a small khaki-coloured pi-dog named Mbwambi with me, a mongrel, but a ferocious, plucky little beast, and I tied him up to the door of my tent.

It was well after midnight when he gave a sharp, alarmed, whiny growl and woke me. But before I could get out of bed the whole tent rocked; the pole to which Mbwambi was tied flew out and let down the ridge-pole, enveloping me in flapping canvas. At the same moment the most awful howl I have ever heard split the night. The sheer demoniac horror of it froze me still, and not for some seconds did I hear the clatter of poles in Kipet's nganas, which told of his men, having been aroused, unbarring their hut doors.

I heard my pi-dog yelp just once. There was a crashing of branches in the bush, and then thud, thud, thud of some huge beast making off. But that howl! I have heard half a dozen lions roaring in a stampede-chorus not twenty yards away; I have heard a maddened cow-elephant trumpeting; I have heard a trapped leopard make the silent night a rocking agony with screaming, snarling roars. But never have I heard, nor do I wish to hear again, such a howl as that of the chimiset.

A trail of red spots on the sand showed where my pi-dog had gone. Beside that trail were huge footprints, four times as big as a man's, showing the imprint of three huge clawed toes, with trefoil marks like a lion's pad where the sole of the foot pressed down. But no lion, not even the giant nine feet four and a half inches long which fell to Getekonot, my hunter, at Ussure, ever boasted such a paw as that of the monster which had made that terrifying spoor.

At the first streak of dawn we followed those tracks; they led to the kopje. Over our sandy path they showed as plain as the print on this page; on the farther side of the kopje were more footprints leading to the forest, where, searching with our hearts in our mouths every day for a week and more, we found and lost and found them. But we found no chimiset. Such is the mysterious beast, hunted by many a hunter who has trekked the big-game trail in Africa; a beast which the Game Ranger who lived amongst beasts for twenty-three years believes to be 'awaiting discovery and a name'!

Another mysterious animal – seen, shot at, spoored, but never killed or captured – is the nunda, the giant cat of East Africa's coast. Not long ago a reign of terror gripped a small fishing-village on the coast of Tanganyika, where I was stationed as a native magistrate.

It was the custom for native traders to leave their belongings in the village market every night, ready for the morning's trade; and to prevent theft and also to stop stray natives sleeping in the market-place, an askari or native constable took it in turns with two others to guard the market on a four-hour watch.

Going to relieve the midnight watch, an oncoming native constable one night found his comrade missing. After a search he discovered him, terribly mutilated, underneath a stall. The man ran to his European officer, who went with me at once to the market. We found it obvious that the askari had been attacked and killed by some animal – a lion, it seemed.

In the victim's hand was clenched a matted mass of greyish hair, such as would come out of a lion's mane were it grasped and torn in a violent fight. But in many years no lion had been known to come into the town.

We were puzzling the problem at the boma next morning when the old Arab Liwali or native governor of the district hurried into our office with two scared-looking men at his heels. Out late the previous night, they said, they had slunk by the market-place lest the askari should see them and think them evil-doers; and as they crept by they were horrified to see a gigantic brindled cat, the great mysterious nunda which is feared in every village on the coast, leap from the shadows of the market and bear the policeman to the ground.

The Liwali, a venerable and educated man, assured us that within his memory the nunda had visited the village several times. It was an animal, not a lion nor a leopard, but a huge cat as big as a donkey and marked like a tabby. I had heard this tale, and had put it down as silly superstition, but the Liwali's assertion put a different light on things.

That night we kept watch with two armed askaris at the market; nothing happened. On parade next day we read the native constables a lecture on the stupidity of superstitions.

It seemed that we were slightly premature. That same night another constable was torn to pieces, and clutched in his hands and scattered about the buckles of his uniform was more of that grey, matted fur. The terrified villagers meantime had paid a famous medicine man to work 'dawa' or magic to scare the nunda off, and the village, between fear and rage and witchcraft, was in a ferment. I sent the hair to headquarters for expert examination. They replied, asking me what animal it came from, 'as it was a fur and not a hair as you state: probably cat'.

Followed a month of tragedies at small villages up and down the coast: worried headmen trekking in to say that a huge, grey-striped animal like a cat, but as big as a donkey, was seizing men by night. Traps and poisons were set, and armed police scoured the district. Then, as suddenly as they had begun, the raids of the nunda stopped. The mysterious beast was never found. As in the case of the chimiset many a hunt has been made for it; but, though seen and fought with, it has never been killed or caught.

Of other mystery animals, such as the ngoloko, the man-ape of the Isansu hills, a weird creature that prowls the dismal stretches of Yaida lake, I will not tell, for the certainty of being disbelieved. But such are the mystery animals. There are others – the mpisimbi, the leopard-hyaena, which eats sugar-cane, and which I have hunted many a weary night without success; the yiya, a tiny elephant unknown to science; and, a bit farther abroad, the orang pandak, the man-bear-ape of Malaya – seen, hunted, spoored, but never caught; the migu or snowman-monkey of Tibet – half-animal, half-man, who preys on yaks.

Perhaps Colonel Fenn may discover and bring home one or more of these mystery monsters. At Ngoholi, not far from Lindi on the Tanganyikan coast, in a huge valley, dropping sheer two thousand feet from a plateau top to the primeval jungle down below, I have stood in a graveyard of brontosauri and other mighty monsters of the long-dead past; stood and kicked up the turf and seen in the pale green earth below, only a few inches down, their mighty bones; stood and watched a great tree, perched perilously on the cliff edge, totter and sway and slowly fall, tumbling and hurtling root over branches into the abysmal depths below, rocking the silent grandeur of that mighty valley with the splintering of branches, raising the raucous calls of toucans, the hoarse barking of baboons. So has the valley been crumbling to slow decay for aeons past, since the days when the pterodactyl, the megatherium, the hideous dinosaur, and that long-necked nightmare beast, the brontosaurus, hunted and fought, mated and died, on that very spot.

As science counts the years, that was but yesterday.

Who knows but that, in the unpenetrated depths of the vast mysterious continent, there may yet linger some of those grim monsters of an age when men grew hair for covering, and swung, long-armed, from trees?

Quest for Ivory

Frederick Courtenay Selous

Greed has sometimes led to the wanton slaughter of animals. The search for ivory was one of the worst examples – in addition it was often associated with slave-trading. Mary Kingsley, the nineteenth-century traveller, remarked that 'ivory is everywhere an evil thing, before which the quest for gold sinks into a parlour game'.

Early next morning, as soon as it began to grow light, we were up and stirring, and after looking at the priming of the guns, filling the powder bags (when elephant-hunting on foot, we load with the hand from a leather powder bag hung at the side), and putting ten four-ounce bullets into each pouch, I hastily drank a cup of strong coffee, ate a few mouthfuls of grilled meat, and started for the water, leaving my two youngest Kafir boys to look after my blankets and all the traps at the 'skerm', or temporary camp.

Arrived at the nearest pool, the first glance convinced us that our ears had not played us false in the night when we heard the trumpeting of elephants; for there, deeply impressed in the soft mud, lay the giant footprints of several splendid bulls.

A careful survey round about soon showed us that they had come down by the valley to the right, and after drinking and splashing about at all the pools, had gone out into the low hills on the left; so putting Minyama, my best spooring Kafir, on the track, we lost no time in starting in pursuit. The troop, as well as could be judged, consisted of about ten or twelve bulls, amongst them three or four regular old teasers, with footprints nearly two feet in diameter. The spoor led us in a north-easterly direction, across low undulating hills, and they had evidently taken it easy here, feeding about on the succulent 'machabel' trees, which were very numerous; such havoc, indeed, had they committed, that it was easy to follow them without looking for the footprints, just by glancing on ahead at the trees stripped of their bark, and the clusters of fresh leaves and chewed bark left along their track. After following their spoor for about a couple of hours across this sort of country, it led us to some much higher and more rugged hills, and here they had ceased to feed and taken to an old path, stepping it out at a brisk pace in single file. After following the spoor for about another hour along this path, it once more left it, and struck off again in the old direction across the hills, and, just here getting amongst a lot of yesterday's tracks, we had great difficulty in following it; but at length Minyama, with the sagacity and perseverance of a bloodhound, ferreted it out, and away we went again. About eleven o'clock we got into a patch of very thick scrubby bush (what the Kafirs call 'idoro' bush), in a deep kloof or ravine between the hills, and here we went along with great care and caution, expecting every instant to see the elephants, as I made sure they could not pass a place so favour-able for their midday siesta; however, they went clean out of here, and up the steep hill on the other side. Arrived at the top, we looked down upon a large kloof, enclosed on all sides with steep hills, and covered with dense bush, thicker a good deal than that we had just come through, and as I looked I felt sure my friends were standing sleeping not many hundred yards off (it being now about midday, and the sun very hot).

The Kafirs here took off their raw-hide sandals, that they

might walk more quietly, and following the spoor carefully, we descended cautiously into the depths of the kloof, and near the centre of it came to a place from which they had evidently not long moved on, as the dung was still warm. Before we had proceeded a hundred yards farther, Minyama suddenly came to a halt, and crouching down, with his arm pointing forwards and his head turned towards me, whispered, 'Nansia incubu' ('There are the elephants'). Ah, how those two words thrill through the hunter's breast, making his heart leap again with concentrated excitement!

Stooping down, I now saw them not more than thirty yards off, for the bush was very dense. They were standing huddled together in a mass under the shade of a large tree, gently flapping their huge ears in a sleepy, contented sort of way, all unconscious of the deadly enemy that lurked so near. Judging that when they were started they would make for the steep banks of the kloof, either on the one side or the other, and as what little wind there was was blowing from them towards where we were standing, I sent two of my boys up each side to drive them towards me if they came in their direction (it is usually an easy matter to turn elephants by shouting in front of them, though of course it sometimes happens that, instead of turning, they charge in the direction of the noise). Having made these arrangements, and after taking a gulp of water from the calabash and giving a hitch to my belt, I beckoned to my two gun-carriers, and then taking my first gun, crept quietly to within about twenty yards of the still unconscious elephants, to look for the finest pair of ivories. Owing to the way in which they were crowded together, I could not get a very good view of most of them; one, however, standing to the left of the rest, and turned half away from me, showed a fine long tusk on the right-hand side, offering at the same time a good shot behind the shoulder; and so, not seeing a better chance, I fired. I had hoped to get another shot with the second gun, but the bush was so thick, and the elephants broke away in their panic with such despatch, that I could not get a chance; so calling to my second gun-carrier to keep close, I ran as hard as I could after them. At their first set-off, running all close together, they had cleared a path like a waggon road; but on reaching the steep side of the hill they had to slacken their speed (elephants can only go very steadily up-hill, but down, no matter how rough be the ground, they 'run' at a tremendous pace).

At about 150 yards from the starting-place, the one I had fired at as they stood fell dead, having been shot through the heart, and I dashed past him after the others. Luckily, they ran straight on towards the two Kafir boys that I had sent up the hill on the right-hand side of the kloof before firing, and on their shouting lustily, immediately turned and came rushing down again, carry- ing trees, bushes, stones, and everything before them, right past me. As they went by I gave one a shot somewhere about the shoulder; but the bush being so thick, it was little more than a snap shot, and, although my first gun was loaded again, I had no time for another. However, a four-ounce round bullet, hardened with zinc and quicksilver, is no trifle, even to such a mighty beast as an African bull elephant, and immediately on getting it he slackened his pace, and, not being able to keep up with the rest, turned out and took along the side of the hill. I did my best to keep up with him; but, although he now only went at a sort of long half-walk, half-trot, I had to put my best foot foremost to maintain my position in the thick bush, as an elephant, though so large an animal, is a thing easily lost sight of. I was careful to keep under the wind, as a wounded elephant is apt to make himself disagreeable,* and trusts more to his scent than his eyesight in charging. Three several times did I range alongside, and take the gun from my Kafir's hands to fire; but the bush was so thick that, though at very close quarters, I could not get a chance, and had to run on again, hoping the ground would get a little more open presently. At last, having crossed the bottom of the kloof, he either heard something or got a whiff of tainted air, and turning suddenly round, with his huge ears extended, his trunk stretched straight out, and his wicked, vicious-looking eyes gazing in our direction, stood ready to charge, no doubt, if he could but ascertain our exact whereabouts. But small time was allowed him for consideration, for to get the gun to my shoulder and plant a bullet in his exposed chest was the work of but few seconds. On receiving the ball he fell on his knees, but recovering, picked himself slowly up, turned, and resumed his retreat, but now only at a slow walk.

At this instant, glancing to the right, I perceived four more elephants coming down the side of the hill a little on ahead (my boy Minyama afterwards claimed to have headed these and turned them back towards the bottom of the valley); so, believing that the one to which I had been paying attention was all but done for, and wishing to secure another if possible, I sent my second gun-carrier and two more boys after him, telling them to finish him, or at any rate keep him in sight, and then ran to intercept

* In other words, 'this animal is dangerous – it defends itself when attacked!' – A.C.J.

the other four. I was just in time, and as they passed in front of me, at not more than forty yards' distance, in single file, I gave the last one (he having the finest ivory) a shot in the middle of the shoulder, but a few inches too high; however, it slackened his speed considerably, and he left the others. Quickly reloading, I followed, and getting to where the bush was a little more open, shouted behind him, 'Hi there! Woho, old man!' and fatal curiosity or perhaps a wish for vengeance inducing him to turn, I planted another four-ounce ball in his chest. He wheeled round immediately, but, his strength failing him, only walked a few yards, and stood under a tree and, after receiving another bullet square in the shoulder, gave a fierce shake of his head, making his huge ears flap again, and, sinking slowly down with his hind legs doubled out, surrendered up his tough old spirit – looking for all the world, though dead, like a tame elephant when kneeling for people to ascend to the howdah.

Having heard some shots fired by my gun-carrier at the one first wounded, I now made all haste in the direction where the last shot fell; when suddenly, not far to my left, the silent forest rang again with short piercing trumpetings, repeated so quickly one after another, and continuing for such a time, that I made sure one of my boys was caught – as when an elephant is either very near on to his persecutor, or has actually overtaken him, he emits scream upon scream in quick succession, all the time stamping upon and ventilating his enemy with his tusks, and only ceasing to scream when he has done with him; and persons thus operated upon are seldom known to complain of their treatment after it is over.

Before I could reach the scene of action the trumpeting had

ceased; so, calling to my gun-carrier by name, I listened anxiously, and in another instant was much relieved to see him, still alive, but looking very crestfallen. There he was, without gun or assegais, all scratched and bleeding from violent contact with the bushes, and his eyes almost starting out of his head with fright, which was scarcely to be wondered at considering the trying ordeal he had just gone through. He said that, having given the elephant two shots, it just walked slowly on without appearing to take any notice, and that then, having stopped to reload, he had lost sight of him for a moment, and so running on the spoor with eyes bent on the ground, had got almost under the brute's very tusks before he saw him, as the elephant, having turned and waited behind a bush, let him come quite close, and then rushing out, had kept him literally under his trunk for about a hundred yards, and would no doubt have eventually caught him if he had not been so weakened by his previous wounds. In his flight my gun-carrier had thrown the gun and assegais away, and he must indeed have had a miraculous escape, for his back and the calves of his legs had drops of blood upon them, that could only have come from the trunk of the elephant. The two other Kafirs who were near him, and had bolted on seeing the elephant charge, now coming up, I told them to take the spoor, that we might get the gun and then despatch him, as I was sure he was not far off. After picking up the gun and the assegais (one of which had been trodden on and smashed by the elephant), we took up the spoor, and, as I had predicted, had not gone far before we saw him walking slowly along, the blood dripping from his trunk, looking very sick – though he would very likely have tried another charge if he had got the chance, as sometimes they are game to the very last, and have been known to fall dead whilst in the act of charging. I now ran a little wide of him, in a half-circle, and getting in front waited for him, and as he passed gave him a ball, at about twenty yards' distance, through the heart. Directly the bullet struck him he broke into a run, and, after going for about a hundred yards, fell with a crash stone dead, bringing a small tree down in his fall.

On examination this proved to be the finest of the three, his teeth weighing 55 lb. and 57 lb. respectively. Those of the one that fell on his knees, though long, were thinner, and weighed 42 lb. each; whilst, on examination, the one I shot first proved to have but one tusk (not a very uncommon thing in South Africa, though more often met with amongst the cows than the bulls), which I did not know when I fired at him. This single tusk weighed 53 lb.

As there was not time to chop out the teeth of all three elephants and get back to the skerm before nightfall, I resolved to chop out those of the largest, and send my boys back the next day for those of the remaining two. After about an hour and a half's hard work the tusks were laid on the grass, and after cutting out the heart (the tit-bit in my opinion, though some people prefer the foot or trunk), all the inside fat – which, when rendered down, is nearly as good as butter – and some meat from the thick part of the trunk, we proceeded to make tracks homewards, reaching the skerm just about sundown; and I soon had a piece of elephant's heart, nicely salted and peppered, roasting on a forked stick over the coals; and if I had but had a white companion with whom to talk over the day's sport and fight the battle o'er again, my happiness would have been complete.

In the course of four months I killed to my own gun forty-two elephants, eleven of which were big bulls, whose tusks averaged forty-four pounds apiece; I also shot several very fine cow-elephants, whose tusks weighed from fifteen to sixteen pounds. The tusks of the largest bull I killed, when thoroughly dried out, weighed seventy-four pounds each. During the same time, George Wood (my hunting-partner) shot about fifty elephants, whose tusks, however, did not weigh quite as much as mine, and our Kafir hunters also shot nearly forty more, so that altogether we made a very profitable hunt. Until the latter end of November (1871) we continued hunting with varying success and at the onset of the rainy season trekked back to Gubulawayo, carrying with us nearly five thousand pounds of very fine ivory.

The Story of the Milu

Willy Ley

A landmark in man's changing attitude towards wildlife was the discovery by Père David, nineteenth-century missionary and naturalist, of the deer which was named after him. His efforts led to its rescue from near-extinction and his name will always be linked with Woburn Park, where one of the Dukes of Bedford successfully reared a herd of these all-but vanished animals.

'My preparations for the journey were completed several days ago,' the missionary wrote, 'and I could have gone ahead by about the end of February.'

These lines were written in March 1866, possibly in Peking, or else en route between Peking and a place their writer called Suen-Hoa-Fou (Suan-Hwa), the first stopover on a long journey of exploration. The writer was a French missionary of Basque ancestry, Jean Pierre Armand David by name. When he wrote those lines he was Père David; later, after his final return from China, he became the Abbé David. But the fact that he was the Abbé David in the latter years of his long life is important only to clerics and to historians. Naturalists cannot help thinking of him as Père David, because it was under this designation that he made the journeys and the discoveries for which he is famous among naturalists. Before discussing the numerous and varied contributions of the naturalist-missionary to the natural history of the Far East, let's go on with his diary, because the delay in departure implied in the lines already quoted had a good reason.

'Because of this intention' – that of leaving Peking by the end of February – 'I hurried to have my last shipment for the Museum packed up; it consists of the skins of mammals and birds and a few live plants which I have entrusted to the intelligent care of Monsieur Alphonse Pichon, attaché of the French Legation, who is going to return to Paris.'

The importance of that particular shipment was well known to Father David. He probably did not expect that it would make him famous for many years to come, but he did call it *la pièce principale*, writing:

'The principal item in this shipment is the *sse-pu-hsiang*, a kind of large reindeer of which the female is antlerless. For a long time I have tried to obtain a specimen of this interesting variety of *Cervidae*, still unknown to naturalists, which I know to exist in large numbers and for centuries in the Imperial Park Hae-Dze, a few Chinese *li* to the south of the capital.'

The name for the park used by Father David is not the one used by Sinologists, but there is no doubt about the locality to which he referred. Several miles south of Peking was the Imperial Hunting Park called Nan Hai-tzu, which at the time of Father David's visit was considerably larger in extent than the city itself. The area which later became a park seems to have been a hunting and pleasure ground for the emperors of China for many centuries, but for most of the time it was more or less open ground. It was probably around the year 1400 that it was walled in; in any event the wall surrounding the park was centuries old when Father David saw it. Needless to say, nobody was permitted to enter it – especially no foreigner.

Having heard that animals were kept inside the park under the guard of soldiers (mostly Tartars), Father David decided that he would at least look at them, even though there was no way of wangling a permission to enter. Early in 1865 he climbed the wall and saw several game animals which he knew well, but also a large herd – he estimated it at 120 head – of large staglike animals which he had never seen before. He was also certain that no other naturalist had seen them, and it at once became his ambition to place this large unknown animal in the catalogues of science. His diary contains some information which must have been supplied by native friends. He was told that there was a death sentence waiting for anybody who dared to kill one of these animals. But it was also said that the Tartar guards violated that law themselves on occasion when their rations grew too short or too monotonous. However, their fear of the law was strong enough to prevent them from selling anything that might be evidence; they would part neither with a skin nor with the bones nor even with the antlers. As regards the antlers, there seem to have been some exceptions to the rule: Father David reported that the insides of those antlers resembled ivory so closely that pieces of antler were sold as ivory (presumably after the outside had been ground off) and transformed into various utensils by Chinese craftsmen. Many collections of Chinese ivory probably contain pieces which are not ivory at all but parts of illicitly acquired antlers of 'Père David's deer'.

Naturally Father David inquired for the native name of the animal. His friends could tell him. It was *sse-pu-hsiang*, the name he put into his diary. He also knew what the name meant. It is literally 'not like four'. Somewhat more elegantly, it might be translated as 'four dissimilarities'. It is supposed to express the idea that the animal in question does *not* look like a stag, does *not* look like a goat, does *not* look like an ass, and does *not* look like a cow. But there also seems to be an implication that the animal does suggest each of the four in some aspect or feature.

Later a more handy name became known, *mi-lou* or milu. It is mentioned in the first scientific description of the animal but apparently was unknown to Father David. In any event he did what he could to obtain more tangible evidence of the existence of this animal, evidence which could be nailed into a box to be sent to the Museum in Paris. He probably postponed his planned trip into the interior repeatedly just for this reason. But for a long time his quest remained, to use his own term, 'unfruitful'. At long last, in January 1866, he got two complete skins in passable condition, probably by devious and slightly fantastic dealings which he unfortunately did not record in detail. Shortly thereafter the French Legation obtained three live *sse-pu-hsiang* through the good offices of the Imperial Minister Hen-Tchi. Unfortunately they did not survive the trip, but Alphonse Milne-Edward in Paris had the material needed for the first scientific description.

It appeared in the *Comptes rendus des Séances de l'Académie des Sciences*. As is customary, the first describer also has to propose a scientific name, and Milne-Edward chose *Elaphurus davidianus*. In English-speaking countries, 'Père David's deer' has become the usual appellation, which is nice in that it honours the discoverer who may have had to pay dearly for his scientific curiosity, but is not quite as short and simple as milu, which is the commonly used name in continental Europe.

After that description had been published, the directors of zoological gardens all over the world had a brand-new dream –

the future exhibition of a pair of milus. The various legations in Peking suddenly began receiving surprising mail, which dealt, not with trade and tariffs, military matters of hush-hush nature, or trips of dignitaries, but with animals in the Imperial Hunting Park. The diplomats, presumably after shaking their heads in complete and assured privacy, went to work, and they were usually successful on a small scale. After all, the Imperial Hunting Park was not actually used for Imperial hunts, and Father David himself had pointed out that according to his best information no hunt had ever taken place there, not only for as long as anybody could remember, but as long as the records accessible to historians went back.

In 1869 two live specimens were presented to the Royal Zoological Society of London by Sir Rutherford Alcock. Some years later, in 1883, the same Society bought two more in China. One specimen arrived in the Berlin Zoological Garden where it lived, lonely and unhappy, for many years and indoctrinated many Berliners with the belief that 'stags in China look like that'.

Even at first glance Père David's deer appears as peculiar a creature as further study proved it to be. It is rather large: a full grown stag will stand four feet at the withers, about the same as a red deer. But its general carriage is quite different from that of the red deer, a fact that was not always known to taxidermists who mounted specimens. Instead of carrying its head high like a deer, the milu usually carries its head low, more like a cow. Its whole attitude has been termed 'slouching' by Lydekker. The tail is unusually long for a deer and equipped with a hairy tassel like the tail of a donkey. The animal has both neck and throat manes. It has rather large wide-spreading hooves which fall together with a loud clicking noise when it walks slowly. The antlers are especially strange; they are large and at first sight look as if they had been put on wrong. The main fork curves forward, dividing at least once, while the rear prong is undivided, very long, and directed backward in a way which is unlike any other antler known.

Usually only one young is born, in May. The fawns are heavily spotted with white but as the animal grows up the spots vanish, though the females seem to retain them a little better than the males. In summer the adults have a greyish red coat shading to whitish tints on the under side. In winter the coat is a greyish buff. The call of the adults is more like a bray than like the typical call of deer.

While naturalists were recording these facts in zoological gardens, the Duke of Bedford, father of the present Duke, decided to add the milu to the collection of rare mammals which he kept on his estates at Woburn Abbey in England. Of course nobody could possibly have guessed it then, but this decision kept Père David's deer alive. After the Duke of Bedford had decided that there should be milus at Woburn Abbey, they had to be obtained. In all probability he hoped to get some directly from China, but in the meantime he bought as many milus from zoological gardens in Europe as the directors would sell. At Woburn Abbey, during the years 1893-1896, the surprising discovery was made that the milu sheds its antlers twice a year, instead of yearly like other deer.

Other zoological institutions, interested though they were in the reports coming out of Woburn Abbey, preferred to get first-hand knowledge. They wanted more milus themselves, and they kept writing letters which were routed by train and by steamship to wind up in the post office of Peking, unless they travelled in diplomatic pouches. But while many of these letters were still travelling in a ship's hold, the milus of Nan Hai-tzu Park suffered a catastrophe. In 1895 a disastrous flood on the Hun Ho river sentenced thousands of peasants to death from starvation. The same flood also undermined the ancient brick wall of the Nan Hai-tzu Park, and many of the animals penned up there, including the rare milus, escaped and were killed and eaten by the starving populace.

Still, that cannot have been the end of the whole herd. Some must have survived, because it is reported that 'the Imperial Hunting Park was thrown open in 1900 and all the deer in it were killed by the international troops'. In 1901 only one milu, a female, still existed in Peking, and she stayed alive until 1920.

This was the last Chinese milu, for the major mystery surrounding this animal is that it has never been found elsewhere. When Père David's discovery was reported in Europe, most naturalists began to wonder about the milu's normal habitat. Since none was known from the reasonably familiar areas of China near the coast, its habitat was probably to be sought in the interior. The idea that it was otherwise extinct and existed in the Park only was sufficiently 'wild' not to occur to anybody. The natural assumption that there had had to be wild milus somewhere was strengthened by travellers' reports that native guides, especially from the northern parts of China, had told them about occasional small herds of *sse-pu-hsiang*. But all these reports were mistaken. The Chinese really meant reindeer, as was dramatically demonstrated in 1904 when a hunt undertaken by Chinese netted eleven '*sse-pu-hsiang*' to be shipped to Woburn Abbey. Ten of the eleven died during the journey to the coast and the eleventh proved to be a reindeer. Some entries in Père David's later diaries must be founded on the same mistake; it is important to note that Père David never saw any of the animals he was told about.

Possibly native Chinese, living a considerable distance from Peking and knowing nothing about the real milu, took that term 'four not alike' and fitted it to an animal they knew, and the reindeer qualifies reasonably well.

Slowly even the most careful naturalists, as well as the most hardened sceptics among them, had to admit that there were no wild milus. Even then they qualified the admission by the addition of a date of some sort. Obviously there were no wild milus in 1905 or 1906 when that fact had finally to be admitted. Most likely there had been no wild milus when Père David obtained his first information about the animal. And it was probable that there had been no wild milus even in 1800, 1700, or 1600. But at one time, somewhere in East Asia, there must have been wild milus. The question was when and where.

Where there are no facts, hypothesis is called upon to fill the gap. One of the more fanciful ideas was that the milu was not really Chinese at all but had been brought to China by the Manchu. This sounds rather romantic, but has nothing else to recommend it. In fact this particular hypothesis was mainly based upon those faint rumours of *sse-pu-hsiang* in North China and in Manchuria, rumours which were mistaken in themselves. The more likely theory is that the original home of the milu was the large plains of Chihli province which in former centuries were immense reed-covered swamps. As agriculture spread, the reeds were cut or burned and the swamps were drained; the milus gradually became homeless, dwindled in numbers, and finally survived only in the area which became the Imperial Hunting Park.

The idea that the milu preferred such areas as the former swamps of Chihli province is bolstered by observations of the Woburn Abbey specimens. Said Richard Lydekker in *Deer of Many Lands*, 'In England during summer they are very partial to water, often wading out as far as they can go, and sometimes swimming; at this season they feed largely upon water plants, especially rushes. The long and widely expanding hooves, which form one of the characteristic features of this species, are evidently adapted for walking on marshy ground.'

After the destruction of all Chinese milus except that one female, the picture looked quite bleak. A number of zoological parks still had a specimen or two. But even if they did have two and if these two were of different sex, no offspring were forthcoming. I read somewhere a long time ago that 'the milu does not breed when removed from his native soil'. Well, it wasn't quite as noble as that; the specimens were mostly simply too old for breeding. If all the specimens in existence had been pooled at that time, at least a few fawns would have been born.

Some were born at Woburn Abbey, the only place where milus can be said to live. And the Woburn Abbey herd slowly increased in size. Eighteen Père David's deer were originally imported, but of these at least three never bred, so that the present herd is descended from not more than fifteen animals. By the end of 1913, 137 had been born, 48 had died and 35 had been killed owing to old age or disease. During the First World War, quite half of the herd perished of starvation, as the authorities insisted on sheep and cattle being turned into the Park and did not allow enough hay to be provided for winter feeding.

However, Père David's deer was a hardy creature. By 1949, the Woburn herd had increased to 242: 45 stags, 119 hinds and 78 calves from the previous year. Indeed, the herd flourished sufficiently to restock zoological gardens. Seven milus were given to the London Zoological Society. New York received four, while others were sent to Australia's Taronga Park and to Munich Zoo.

In the course of time more and more people in various corners of the world will be able to see live examples of the deer discovered more than a century ago by that devoted naturalist-missionary whose work saved it from extinction.

Island of Dragons

Paul Potous

In addition to being the only way millions of people have any chance of becoming acquainted with wild animals, zoos are both necessary and justifiable for scientific study and research. The (London) Regent's Park Zoo, founded in 1826, still has the largest and most varied collection in the world and this story describes a 'capture' for the Reptile House.

The full moon had not yet set and the sun was still below the horizon as we climbed into the dinghy and were rowed out by an African deck-hand to the smart Government launch anchored a short distance offshore. The launch had been lent by the local District Commissioner, and was to take us to the Island of Boradzulu, tribal burial-ground and home of the Dragon – the giant monitor lizard, or Nile monitor (*Varanus niloticus*). The London Zoo had asked for two four-foot dragons, and we were to catch them alive.

Boradzulu Island lies some twenty-five miles north of Fort Johnston, and approximately eight miles off the western shore of Lake Nyasa. It is uninhabited – in fact no native will set foot on the island. To them it is steeped in superstition and the spirits of their forefathers, for at one time the natives from the mainland would take their dead in canoes and leave the bodies to rest un-buried amongst the rocks and caves of the Island. Even today there are numerous skulls to be found, together with cooking pots, containing beads and other ceremonial regalia.

The island consists of a mass of rock rising straight out of the deep waters of the lake and is splashed white by the guano of the countless cormorants nesting in the stunted trees overhanging the crystal clear water.

Before we were half-way over the sun was rising, while at the same time the orange orb of the full moon sank in the west. The surface of the water, slightly ruffled by the faintest breeze, gradually changed from silver to gold and then to sparkling and shimmering diamonds.

We made for the western shore of the island which would be in shadow, for in the chill of the early morning the dragons are lethargic and will allow one to approach to within a few feet. Even then, if they imagine they have not been seen, they will lie perfectly motionless, trusting to their remarkable camouflage for protection. Immediately they realize they have been seen and are in danger, they attempt to gain the safety of the water, taking the shortest possible route, quite oblivious to any inanimate obstacle in their path.

Dropping anchor less than fifty yards from the shore, we rowed over in the dinghy and scrambled on to the rocks of the island.

The plan of action was for four of the party to make their way slowly along the crest of the island, keeping a sharp look-out for dragons below them. At the same time Bill – the Government entomologist – and I would move parallel to them, but some fifty feet below. Immediately a dragon was spotted by those on the crest, they would remain perfectly still and attempt to point to Bill and me where it lay. The two of us would then get into the best position to intercept its path to the water. When we were ready, those above would throw stones at the dragon, and as it came scrambling down the hillside, Bill and I would attempt to catch it before it reached the water.

We took up our position and slowly moved south, climbing and scrambling over the rocks and through the cactus and patches of sansevieria grass, stunted bushes and coarse grasses. The sansevieria grass is a type of cactus and is related to the cultivated sisal. It is most painful to clamber through it, due to the sharp points at the end of each spear-shaped leaf.

It was not long before we flushed a dragon which we had not seen lying in its hiding-place. It came scuttling down the rocks and without the slightest hesitation took a flying leap on to the rocks twenty feet below. With no apparent injury it waddled to the edge of the rock, falling another ten feet into the water in a clumsy dive. We watched it swim rapidly a few yards then it was lost to sight under an overhanging boulder.

We were astounded by the height from which it leapt into space on to the rocks below, to land with a sickening thud, quite unharmed, and to continue its helter-skelter dash into the water.

Suddenly one of the upper party signalled he had sighted a dragon lying doggo in a clump of cactus. Bill and I scrambled cautiously up the rocks to positions we considered best for intercepting its course to liberty. Bill stationed himself some ten feet below me, slightly to the left, where he would be able to make a second attempt if I missed the dragon.

When we were ready, a stone was thrown from above at the dormant dragon. It landed only a few feet away but the reptile made no move. More stones were thrown and suddenly it leapt into motion, and came scrambling down the slope towards us. Through sheer luck, I was able to grab it by both hands a foot or so above the end of its tail and lift it from the ground. It was not cold and clammy as is the feel of a crocodile, but rough and dry to the touch. It was amazingly strong and I had the greatest difficulty in preventing it from escaping, for it was very heavy and it writhed back and forth, hissing and attempting to bite. All I could do was to hold it in the air, where it was unable to obtain a purchase for its legs and claws. I was balancing somewhat precariously on the steep uneven slope and shouting to Bill for help, when one particularly ferocious effort on the part of the dragon unbalanced me, and I fell over forwards, letting go my grip. At that precise moment, Bill arrived on the scene and flung himself full length on to the dragon. Before it could escape, he had collared it around the back of its neck. Instantly it brought its hind claws into action, and with its left rear leg clawed Bill badly on the inside of his forearm. Still on my knees, I was able to get another grip on its tail and between us it was a simple matter to push the dragon head first into one of the stout sacks we were carrying. Once inside the sack, the dragon made no attempt to escape or struggle further.

After a short rest and a cigarette, we continued.

Our progress was slow, owing to the extreme roughness of the ground. Many times we had to make detours, going around or climbing down gullies and up the other side. We tried not to disturb the dragons, but they were very difficult to see, and more than a dozen came slithering and hurtling down the rocks into the water. It was most amusing to watch their efforts to gain speed. Having landed with a crash on to a rock, all four feet would work overtime in an attempt at quick acceleration. Some of them were so fat, and their legs so short, their claws would slip and gain no hold on the smooth rock surface. They would lie there for a second or so, wriggling, and then suddenly launch themselves off into space.

Eventually we captured a second dragon, a female this time, four feet six inches long. We now had a perfect pair for the Zoo.

It was still early, just after nine o'clock, and we made our way back to the dinghy for breakfast.

During the hunt, two of the boys on the launch had been fishing, and there was delicious freshly caught and fried Lake fish fillets for breakfast.

After breakfast we walked over to the eastern side of the island, hoping to get some movie film of dragons and crocodiles. We were not very successful, for the warmth of the sun had livened up the dragons, and they were scuttling about giving us little opportunity of photographing them.

When we returned to the mainland, each dragon was put into a specially prepared box. These boxes were transported by car to Blantyre, where the following morning they were put on to the aeroplane for England. Within seventy-two hours of having been captured in Nyasaland, they arrived in London, and are now housed in the Reptile House at the Zoological Gardens, Regent's Park.

Pioneer Methods

Richard Kearton

The use of the camera for wildlife photography opened up an entirely new branch of nature study. Pioneers of this were Richard and Cherry Kearton who, nearly eighty years ago, achieved some astonishing results with their cumbersome equipment. They showed men how much more satisfaction and skill there is in 'shooting' animals with a camera rather than with a gun.

As we are often asked how we obtain our pictures, and do not believe in withholding any information likely to be useful to those who desire to share in the fascinating pastime of making studies from the great Book of Nature, I here propose to tell something of how we do our field work.

The great points about successful natural history photography are: the possession of suitable apparatus to work with, an aptitude for taking care in stalking timid creatures, and plenty of patience and determination to wait for and get what is wanted in spite of obstacles.

We take all our photographs with a half-plate camera. This was specially built for us by Dallmeyer, and contains a pneumatically worked silent shutter between the lens and the sensitized plate, in addition to a focal plane one, also worked by compressed air at the back. On top of the half-plate camera is an adjustable miniature camera of the same focus, which is extremely useful in making pictures of flying birds or restless animals. When it is in use, the large camera is charged with a plate ready for exposure, and the photographer manipulates the focusing screw, which moves both in exact ratio at the same time with one hand, whilst he holds the air-ball attached to the pneumatic tube in the other and presses directly a suitable opportunity presents itself. Our india-rubber tubing measures about one hundred feet in length, and is joined in five or six places by hollow pieces of metal, so that almost any length can be used, according to circumstances.

Our climbing ropes are two hundred feet each in length, and an inch and a half and two inches, respectively, in circumference. They were specially manufactured for us from the best Manilla hemp, by Messrs Galloway, Matthews & Co., of Appold Street, E.C. The thicker, or descending rope, has three loops at its end formed by plaiting the strands of which it is made, and then lashing them firmly to the rope above. These the climber puts round his hips and practically sits in them as he descends a cliff.

We carry a revolver for the prosaic and harmless purpose of making a loud report at the top of any cliff in the face of which there is reason for believing some bird's nest, which we desire to photograph, is situated, so that by frightening its owner off we may locate the exact spot at which to make a descent. Our equipment includes climbing-irons which are very useful in ascending tall trees to examine the nests of such birds as build in elevated situations; but my brother, who is a good gymnast and can climb almost any sort of growing timber without assistance, has no great partiality for them. A good pair of field-glasses are indispensible, and more than double the pleasure and profit of a ramble along the countryside. I have a pair of Dolland's, which make me envied by every sea captain who has the good fortune to look through them. One clear day last summer Grace Darling's nephew said to me, as we stood at the foot of St Cuthbert's Tower, on the Farne, 'I can see the halliard rope swing from the Longstone Lighthouse flagstaff with your glasses, sir.' I was incredulous, but this frame of mind soon turned to one of astonishment when I looked for myself and saw it bellying in the wind – the lighthouse was two miles away! We use a powerful bull's-eye lantern for discovering and focusing birds on their natural roosts during dark winter nights, and a small looking-glass with an adjustable handle for attaching to the end of a rod, or long stick, and examining the interiors of such nests as are situated on branches too slender to bear the weight of the climber.

Cliff photography, although really not very dangerous, is at first rather trying to the nerves, as I can testify from experience, having literally walked backwards – of course, with the ropes on – over the edge of a perpendicular precipice seventy feet deep, in order to be in a position to understand and appreciate the sensations of this branch of my brother's work.

Upon reaching a cliff which we desire to descend, and having located the exact position of the nest to be photographed, we drive a moderate-sized crowbar from twelve to eighteen inches into the ground at distances varying from four or five to ten or twelve feet away from its edge, according to circumstances, and sloping slightly out of the vertical in a backward direction. One end of the guide rope is tied securely round it close to the ground, and the rest flung over the cliff. The descending rope is now passed once round the crowbar, as near the bottom as possible, in order to reduce the leverage, and whilst the man who is going to manage the lowering takes charge of it, the photographer, with his camera lashed to his back, slips the loops round his hips, and seizing the guide rope in both hands to steady himself by, prepares to make a descent.

A few of the important points to be remembered in connection with this branch of natural history work are: 1. To use good and reliable ropes, and have a thoroughly trustworthy, level-headed man to work them, as the chief source of danger lies in having a nervous or careless fellow at the crowbar. 2. To see that the last-named tool is driven well into solid ground. 3. To clear away all loose stones and pieces of rubble between the foot of the crowbar and the brink of the precipice about to be negotiated, for, should this precaution be neglected, the descending rope is sure to dislodge them when it is being hauled up; and even a small stone, with the velocity gained by a fall of thirty or forty feet upon it, can do a great deal of damage to the photographer or his camera, if it happens to strike either of them in its downward plunge. 4. Not to allow the descending rope to run in any cleft or crevice, as it may either stick fast altogether when being pulled up again or sustain considerable damage by chafing. In order to prevent either of these awkward eventualities, it is a good plan to run it through a piece of leather tubing over the edge of a cliff. When making a descent, I get into some position from which I can watch my brother's movements, and convey his requirements to the man at the rope, either by word of mouth or by a simple pre-arranged code of signals when the distance is too great to make ourselves heard.

Two of the nastiest sensations connected with the work are stepping backwards over the brink of a very high cliff into space and spinning slowly round like a piece of meat on a roasting-jack, and watching the sea chase the land and the land chase the sea upon becoming insulated through the crags at the top overhanging. Most people in descending a cliff on ropes for the first time prefer, instead of keeping their feet against the rock-face and walking down, to scramble hands and knees against it; but the sharp projections play such havoc with skin and clothing that, if they have nerve enough to persevere in the recreation, they soon try a better way.

On arriving at a ledge with a nest upon it, my brother allows his body to assume a horizontal position almost at right angles to the line of the cliff, and placing the end of one leg of the tripod in a convenient crevice, and the other two through a belt or piece of rope round his waist, he focuses, and generally after a deal of trouble succeeds in making a picture. His pictures of young Peregrine Falcons, for example, were obtained in this way.

Although not particularly dangerous, if carried out with care and proper tools, cliff work of any kind requires a man with a cool head and a strong athletic frame. Most of the danger, as I have already mentioned, comes from the attendant at the crowbar. On one occasion my brother had a very narrow escape from death owing to the fellow who was lowering him neglecting his work to chat with some companions who stood near. The crowbar had not been driven far into the ground, on account of its rocky nature, and just as his head was about to disappear below the edge of the cliff, he happened to look up at it, and was horrified to see the rope running round its top instead of its bottom, and the whole thing so bent over by the leverage of his weight, that, instead of inclining away from him, it was pointing almost straight over his head. A frantic yell brought the careless rascal to his senses, or in another instant the crowbar would have been pulled out of the ground and the rope jerked from his hands. Some attendants have a reprehensible knack of trying to look over the cliff at the descending photographer whilst they manipulate the rope, which is by no means reassuring to the man below.

Nests built near the tops of high isolated trees are often very difficult to photograph, on account of the fact that they are situated amongst slender branches. That of the Carrion Crow comes under this category, as the bird loves a site which commands a good view of her surroundings in order that she may have early intimation of the approach of danger, and make good her escape. Another feature of this bird's nest is that it is extremely deep, thus preventing her eggs from rolling out when the structure is roughly swayed to and fro by a gale of wind, and at the same time necessitating the photographer getting well above it to make his study.

On one occasion in 1896, we were anxious to take a photograph of crows' eggs in the nest, but it was impossible to do so without fixing something up to enable us to get above it. So we borrowed a twenty-foot ladder from a friendly farmer. We hauled the ladder to the top of the tree and lashed it in as nearly perpendicular a position as possible, for otherwise, if it had been at an angle the branches to which it was lashed would have snapped like matches through the leverage produced by our combined weight.

When the legs of the tripod had been lashed to the ladder, and the camera focused, my brother's next difficulty was to get his dark slide in and the plate exposed without interfering with the precise adjustment of the apparatus. In order to accomplish these feats, he was obliged to hold on to one of the rungs of the ladder with his teeth and thus leave his hands free to work with.

But not all situations are as difficult as that. Many birds' nests situated in tall hedges and bushes certainly give the photographer a great deal of trouble, on account of their elevation making it difficult to procure a good view of the eggs or young. But we get over inconveniences of this kind by mounting the tripod on improvised stilts cut from any suitable sticks growing handy – after which my brother clambers on to my shoulders and, in this piggyback fashion, focuses from there.

Such wild animals as Rabbits, Hedgehogs, and Voles require very patient waiting for, with the camera well hidden. We cover ours with a green focusing cloth, which has each of its four corners weighted with gunshot to prevent it from flapping about in a breeze, and then hide the front with bushes, taking care, however, that no drooping leaf stands a chance of interposing itself between the lens and the object to be photographed. My brother then lies up at a convenient distance with the binoculars, and waits until the object he desires to photograph comes within the field of focus, and exposes his plate by a squeeze of the air-ball at the end of the pneumatic tube controlling his silent shutter.

The Way of an Eagle

Guy Mountfort

Pioneer wildlife photographers would have been glad of the tubular scaffolding used by Eric Hosking, the world's greatest bird-photographer, as described in this story. The Coto Doñana, scene of the expeditions led by Guy Mountfort, is a rich natural wilderness, a paradise for naturalists, for apart from other creatures half the bird species of Europe have been seen there. It was purchased by the World Wildlife Fund to ensure its protection as a reserve.

The Spanish imperial eagle had never yet been photographed and this task was given top priority among the objectives for our final expedition. Having carefully studied the eyries on the previous visit, we concluded that in order to do the job thoroughly we should be obliged to build a solid pylon of anything up to forty feet in height, on which to erect the hide. We therefore shipped to Gibraltar, in advance of our arrival, half a ton of Eric Hosking's now famous tubular metal scaffolding, which he had used so successfully for tree-top work in England. As things eventually turned out, the nest we photographed was at an exceptionally low altitude, in the exposed crown of a Stone Pine, only twenty-four feet above ground; but the extra rigidity provided by the scaffolding paid handsome dividends. The site was a very pleasant one, among scattered, flat-topped pines growing in sand, in the region known as the Corral Quemado.

The young eagle was about twenty days old when we arrived. Knowing the penalty for disturbing its parents, we erected the pylon by very easy stages, giving the birds ample time to get used to the strange edifice growing up beside their tree. Each morning we worked for about an hour, at top speed, hoisting the metal tubes into position and securing them by strong clamps. On the sixth day the hide was lashed to the platform and all was ready. Eric Hosking, cautious as ever, wanted to give the birds forty-eight hours' respite, so I asked that nobody should approach within half a mile of the area. Finally, on 12th May, Eric was installed for his first spell of nine and a half hours, in a temperature which by early afternoon soared to 96 F. in the hide.

It was five hours before the eagle returned to the nest, bearing a rabbit, which she quickly plucked and dismembered for the young bird. Twelve minutes later she departed and was seen no more that day. Eric had succeeded nevertheless in obtaining a fine series of pictures, which amply repaid the hardships of his long wait. During the following two and a half weeks he had six more days in the hide, in order to secure photographs of the development of the young eagle. The parent had by then become confident of the harmless nature of the hide and behaved excellently, remaining at the nest on one occasion for three and a half hours.

George Shannon had the honour of making the first cinematograph film in colour ever taken of the Spanish imperial eagle and its young. These were obtained in the course of an eight-hour session on the day following Eric Hosking's first visit. Lord Alanbrooke was the next to use the hide. Although I know of no septuagenarian who looks so deceptively young, or who is more active, I was by no means happy that he should endure the long grilling in the merciless heat of the tree-top hide, much less that he should climb the thirty-foot pylon, with its difficult three-foot 'steps'. But he had already filmed the golden eagle in Scotland, in circumstances little less arduous, and was indignant at the least suggestion that he should be deprived of this opportunity to make an even more exciting film. I accompanied him to the site and watched him climb with complete confidence up the pylon. When he rode back to the *Palacio* that night he appeared less fatigued than any of us and he was in tremendous form later at dinner. The amazing stamina which sustained him under the frightful burden he shouldered throughout the last war, which was the envy and despair of all who served under him, had very obviously not deserted him.

Having satisfied myself that the basic pictorial documentation had now been secured, I had two enchanting days at the eagle's nest, on 15th and 19th May. On both occasions I was able to obtain some good pictures, but most of my time was occupied in studying the behaviour of the young bird and its parent. The copious notes I made, with those compiled by other members, who passed a combined total of eighty-three hours in the hide, provide a valuable consecutive record of the progressive changes in the domestic routine at the nest and the development of the chick. Like most young creatures, the young eagle passed much of its early days in sleep. The nest was completely without shade until evening and I marvelled that the tiny bundle of life, protected from the fierce sun only by a coat of white down, could survive day after day of pitiless heat. In the hide the temperature stood for hours at over ninety degrees. Stripped to the waist, I found it almost unbearable, but refreshed myself periodically by pouring a little water over my head and shoulders. Like Eric

Hosking, I made my midday meal on oranges, lest the crackle of the paper in which the inevitable fish *tortillas* were packed should reach the acute ears of the eagle.

As the days passed, the young eagle developed with great rapidity. At the time of my first full day in the hide it was about twenty-eight days old and the first traces of the brown tips of the scapular feathers formed symmetrical patches on its white down. Four days later the scapulars were completely feathered and brown speckles had appeared on the back, breast and flanks, while the tips of the emergent feathers on the wings and tail were already an inch long. Two weeks later the nestling was almost as big as its parent. Its body was by then well covered with *café-au-lait* feathers, leaving only its head and thighs in white down. On the primary feathers of its wings were two large white patches. Unlike the nestling short-toed eagle, the young Spanish imperial looked every inch a baby eagle, from the fiercely curved black tip of its large yellow bill to the powerful claws on its big feet.

The eagle chick was just learning to stand on its grotesquely long legs during my first visit. It did this experimentally several times, flapping its embryo wings and then collapsing quickly on to its behind. On my second visit it was still unsteady on its legs, but was scrambling all over the nest, often standing on the very edge to look over the side, teetering backwards and forwards so alarmingly that I expected any moment to see it fall to the ground. It had now learned to void its excrement clear of the nest, which it did very neatly by climbing to the rim and elevating its rear. The ground beneath the tree thereafter soon became ringed with 'white-wash'. Whereas the nestling had slept for sixty per cent of the eight hours of my first visit, less than thirty-five per cent of the time was now passed in sleep.

The young eagle was a great favourite with all of us because of its consistently comical behaviour. Even while sleeping it continued to maintain this reputation, by sprawling on its side, with one wing and one long leg fully extended and its head as often as not hanging sideways over the edge of the nest. Before it mastered the use of its legs it often used to sit balanced on its thighs, with its big yellow feet held vertically on either side of its head. It looked laughably uncomfortable. On one such occasion it caught sight of its feet, drew back its head in apparent surprise, looked carefully from one to the other and then tried to swallow one of its toes. A few days previously our field party had come across a semi-wild goat giving birth to twin kids, one of which died. The following day a kid, probably this one, was carried by the eagle to its eyrie. One of the leg bones became the favourite toy of the nestling, which played with it for hours, nearly choking itself in repeated efforts to swallow it. Sometimes it actually swallowed one end and sat with the remaining two-thirds protruding grotesquely from its bill, going through agonizing contortions in attempts to engulf the remainder. Neither did it hesitate to try swallowing the bone crosswise. A large pine cone, was another unfailing attraction and the chick struggled manfully to detach it.

The arrival of the parent was usually heralded by the alarm cries of a pair of magpies, which had a nest a few hundred yards distant. The young eagle soon learned to associate the anxious chatter of these birds with the arrival of food and would instantly raise its head, peering intently to the left of the hide, from which

direction the adult would approach. When later the young magpies left the nest and wandered past the eyrie, the young eagle
did not connect their conversational notes with the alarm, but
merely craned its neck to watch them in the surrounding trees.
As soon as the flying eagle was spotted, the nestling scrambled to
its feet and began crying in an urgent falsetto, a repeated, thin,
wheezy '*see-uk*'. On my second visit it introduced an infant
version of the adult's deep, barking '*owk . . . owk*'. It did this
quite by chance during a spell of play and rehearsed it several
times with evident satisfaction, looking round jauntily to see
whether the performance had attracted attention.

The arrival of the parent with food created an immediate
change in the entire appearance and behaviour of the young eagle.
In place of the self-confident, aggressive little creature I had
been watching, it became a whining, grovelling, incessantly
crying baby. This transformation, which can be seen in most
nestlings, never fails to interest me. It is not without its parallel
in human young, which revert to infantile behaviour in order to
obtain the undivided attention of the mother.

Gradually, as the nestling grew up, it began to lose its baby
ways and became more adept at feeding itself. Lord Alanbrooke
recorded on his film a remarkable demonstration of the process
by which the young eagle was taught to feed itself. While the
parent was away the nestling picked up a young rabbit which
had been left on the nest. Holding it in its bill it tried first to jerk
off some meat. This failing, it then picked up and dropped the
carcase repeatedly, with the obvious desire to tear away a portion. It had not however yet learned the necessity of holding the
prey in its talons while pulling on it, though producing the correct

backward motion of the head in lifting it. At this junction the adult returned, carrying a recently fledged magpie. She stood looking at the nestling for a moment. From what follows in the film one might almost believe she then gave a deliberate demonstration of how to pluck and dismember prey. Placing one huge foot on the magpie, she rapidly and very expertly plucked it, tossing beakfuls of feathers into the air. The nestling watched intently, as though storing up the demonstration for future use. It was then fed. Later in the film the young eagle is seen putting its foot, perhaps accidentally, on its food and thus actually succeeding in tearing off a morsel for itself.

It was a thrilling experience to observe the adult eagle at a distance of only fifteen feet. It appeared completely oblivious of the hide, preening itself and even yawning as an indication of its relaxed attitude. The preening was executed with great care and at the conclusion the eagle shook itself like a large dog, with a loud rustling sound, all its feathers standing on end and looking for a moment as though its skin was much too loose for its body. Each time she left the nest the eagle flew just to the left below the hide, within six feet of me, her great wings making a powerful '*whoosh, whoosh*' as she passed. While examining her closely through my binoculars I noticed an interesting detail, to which Eric Hosking had already drawn my attention. On the iris of each piercing yellow eye was a concentric pattern of short, dark-brown lines, almost like the abbreviated spokes of a wheel.

We never saw the male at the eyrie, though it was frequently observed with its mate in the neighbouring skies. Once the egg hatched, the male contented itself with bringing food to a favourite tree, where it was received by the female and taken to the nest.

The 'food tree' was about 250 yards from the eyrie; when we examined it, a recently killed hare was found waiting on one of the branches. Beneath the tree were about fifty regurgitated pellets, about $3 \times 1\frac{1}{2}$ inches, composed of bones, fur and feathers, which indicated that it was also used as a dormitory. A selection of the pellets was dissected by Tono Valverde, who had been studying food remains at other eyries. These and his other investigations showed that, while rabbits formed the main bulk of the food, turtle doves, wood pigeons, azure-winged magpie, magpie, jackdaw, black-winged stilt, avocet, wigeon, gadwall, mallard, red-legged partridge, cattle egret, coot, unidentified sandpipers and terns, and a variety of mammals, were also taken. We collected pellets at roost-trees used by other pairs of Spanish imperial eagles. One of these was on the Puntal trail, which we frequently used, and as we rode by in the evenings we sometimes saw the silhouettes of the pair sitting side by side on their favourite branch.

These eagles all too frequently fall victims to local 'sportsmen', though not on the well-protected Coto Donana, because of their habit of preying on wounded birds. Seventy years ago Abel Chapman complained that they used to follow him about and snatch birds almost at the muzzle of his gun. He shot a number of them, not only in flight, but also at the nest. In his diary of 1883 he protested: 'I never saw such strong birds. They carry off a skinful of heavy shot and unless a wing is broken seem impossible to kill outright.'

Taping the Swan

Ludwig Koch

*Like the camera, the tape-recorder has immensely increased our oppor-
tunities for enjoying and studying wildlife. Ludwig Koch was one of the
great pioneers of recording bird-song and an interest in nature was stimulated in hundreds of thousands of people who heard his famous radio
broadcasts. Nowadays, with tape-recorders easily available, legions of
amateurs derive pleasure from making their own recordings.*

It was in 1938, during one of my daily walks with Queen Eliza-
beth of the Belgians, that we went one day in May to the far end
of the Royal Park at Laeken, a part that is really still wild, with
swampy reed beds, and with seldom a gardener or other human
being in sight. We saw in the distance a pair of mute swans which
I soon discovered were wild and which, as I later learnt, had
come from the Danube delta. As we carefully drew near, the pen
or female remained sitting, while the cob – although it did not
attack – assumed a very aggressive attitude. With wings raised
and stiffened neck it threw back its head and uttered a loud
trumpeting call. To this day I have never again heard this sound,
but ever since that incident in Laeken I have been haunted by the
idea of studying and recording the call-notes of the bird known
as the 'mute' swan. Like all naturalists and bird-lovers, I knew of
Abbotsbury, the oldest swannery in the world. Its origin goes far
back into history, and it is the only one of its kind in the British
Isles. It was in existence in the days of King Canute. Now it is
part of the estate of the Earl of Ilchester who, with his family, is
greatly interested in the preservation of swans. The swannery is

situated within a kind of natural preserve and harbours over a hundred different varieties of bird. The sea is only a few miles away but cannot be seen, as the view is obscured by Chesil Beach, one of the greatest breeding places of tern in the world. But why did these wild swans ever settle in this one particular spot?

As with human beings, it is the question of food that is decisive. You may approach one of the lovely swans on one of our ordinary ponds and if you do not harm him he will accept titbits from you, for he is domesticated: but the wild swan would not accept bread from you or even suffer you to approach him – in a word, he would not understand. These wild swans feed mainly on a marine grass called *Zostera marina*. It grows under water and the swans seem to love it. There may be a shortage of this grass at Abbotsbury in times of drought or during a severe winter, but in general it is plentiful, and there have sometimes been more than fifteen hundred wild swans settled there. Abbotsbury is situated at the western end of a lagoon called the Fleet. This lies between the Dorset mainland and the eighteen-mile-long shingle beach which I have already mentioned. It is almost landlocked, having just one narrow strait into Portland Bay connecting it with the open sea. The brackish water of the Fleet is subject to quite astonishing and even alarming changes of level. In 1824, for example, the water rose twenty-three feet above the swannery. Normally, however, the Fleet is fully protected by Chesil Beach, and that is why the swans settled there. They always come early in May, and for centuries there has been a family of swanherds who prepare for their arrival and look after their well-being. When I visited Abbotsbury the swanherds were 'Uncle Joe' and his nephew Freddy Lexster – that was in 1946.

My first visit was in March, and Freddy Lexster showed me the work that was going on in preparation for the breeding season in May and June, and this short visit was of great help in arranging my later recordings. On a stormy May morning I was back in Abbotsbury with Eric Hough, a B.B.C. engineer. We transported our gear through the beautiful tropical garden and selected a rather muddy site for the studio about three yards from a swans' nest. The swans looked at us defiantly, but since we took no notice they did not interfere with us as we built our hide-out. Eric Hough switched on the loudspeaker. Later he told me that never before had he seen me look so flabbergasted. The inferno of gale, distorted sea noise, seagulls, and terns came as a great shock, for I still remembered the sweet silence of that summer day in March.

I set out first of all to explore the territory. I went between the bulky nests of breeding swans, and was greeted by an agnry hissing note from the cob, which spread its wings to attack, threatening and challenging any intruder, whether man or one of its own species. Both paths from the actual breeding site led to large swampy places, favoured haunts of the reed-warbler and sedge-warbler. There were no disturbing noises from these places. The brackish water of the Fleet Estuary, the actual feeding and meeting ground of the swans, was at high-tide, and the sand-banks, the feeding place of resident and visiting waders, were flooded.

On the far side of the Fleet I could see Chesil Beach. The wind was coming from the sea, and the distance to my microphone, as the crow flies, was two to three miles. This, with the strong gale, explained the din in the loudspeaker. Through my binoculars I could see, like a black cloud, hundreds of thousands of birds over Chesil Beach, flying to and fro, obviously scared by some beast, an otter perhaps, or a great black-backed gull – or, nastiest of all, a poacher. Chesil Beach is one of the few remaining terneries. The common tern, the little tern, the sandwich tern and even the roseate tern breed there more or less regularly. The sooty tern was a visitor there in 1935. The Arctic tern is also a visitor to this Dorset beach. On this particular day, however, I should have been happier had they all been four thousand miles away, and my first and most important task was to beat the noise of the weather and of the combined team of terns and gulls.

I had also to get closely acquainted with the habits of the swans. Throughout the centuries many naturalists have observed wild, semi-domesticated, and domesticated mute swans. I learned a lot from my old friend and master, the late Dr Oscar Heinroth, co-author of my first sound-book, on the songs of wild birds. Henry E. Dresser and many more have made valuable observations. The wild swan is too shy and cautious to give you a chance to approach it. Though they have not many enemies, apart from man, wild swans choose resorts where they can command a view of the neighbourhood, and at the least sign of danger they fly away. On the Lower Danube I have watched wild swans taking no notice of sea eagles overhead and, contrary to earlier reports, I never saw an eagle even make an attempt to attack swans. The wolf in Russia, however, is known to attack them.

Swans are vegetarians, and protect lakes and ponds against an overgrowth of aquatic plants. They are also dictators. They need *Lebensraum* and, although so graceful, they are aggressive birds, specially during the breeding season, when the male bird will furiously attack not only any intruder of his own species but also man. One once stood between me and my recording gear. I did not want to use force, nor did I wait for one of the terrific blows from the cob's wings. I preferred a tactical retreat through swampy ground, a detour of half a mile.

I have often noticed that rain and storm will suddenly stop for a short period before dawn. I also noticed that this was a favourite bathing hour for the swans of Abbotsbury, who assembled for a family meeting regularly on a certain spot in the Fleet. The terns and gulls were not yet audible or visible. This was perhaps a chance to listen to the conversation of the so-called mute swan. My recording gear was about two hundred yards away and the swans could neither see nor hear us.

When I played back the results of a series of such night recordings, I came to the conclusion that the vocal performances and movements of the swans during the breeding season, before the arrival of the cygnets, are not so limited as a casual observer might believe. There are sounds easy to identify: the clumsy but very rhythmical stepping in and out of the water: wing-flapping: landing in water: taking off: and the unique flight with its strong and powerful vibratory rhythm which so impressed Wagner that, as his wife Cosima told me, it may very likely have inspired him in writing the *Ride of the Valkyries*.

A good many of the various greeting notes, ranging from low and threatening grunts to soft groaning, could be recorded, but they may have a different meaning according to their differing pitches. Most strange was an alarm note, loud, which I was lucky enough to capture. There was danger in the vicinity, and the swanherd believed that it might have been an otter. Freddy

Lexster says that this call is like 'Herbert, Herbert'. I frequently heard a variant of the trumpeting sound, not to be compared with that clear ringing sound but fairly loud and more snorting. Very occasionally I heard the complete call, ending with a tremulous vibration and at a low frequency. I am at a loss to understand the meaning of this call, which I have heard both at night and during the daytime in totally different circumstances. There was nothing that could irritate the bird at night. In the daytime, however, when I saw visitors coming close to the nest, the cob took up its attacking position and, sometimes after people had gone away, he would make the trumpeting, with wings raised and stiffened, ready to strike. It could be a victory call, similar to the 'V' call of a stag in the rutting season.

Family life seems to be impossible without quarrels, even for the swans. I frequently heard hissing notes, furious explosive grunts, and swans chasing each other. Most of these noises have been recorded. I have not heard the cob or pen making any noise when his or her place in the nest was occupied by an intruder. It might happen that two females were sitting together, or another cob was the temporary intruder. Then the legal husband determinedly, but usually quite gently, turns the visitor out.

I left Abbotsbury towards the end of May with an unforgettable memory of two swans dancing round and round in the Fleet estuary. Their grace is unique among creatures, and I can understand the immortal Pavlova's fondness for watching swans at Abbotsbury. In June, when I returned, I was walking through the reeds before 4 a.m. and saw a cygnet far away from the swannery in a pitiful state. I was just about to rescue the little creature when a huge black-backed gull flew into my face.

Everything happened so suddenly that I can only remember walking to our swampy 'recording studio' with the cygnet in my pocket. The young engineer who accompanied me this time found my face fiercely bleeding and a scratch dangerously near one eye. But no great harm was done and after some hours the cygnet was adopted by a cob.

I noticed that the swans were still more aggressive now that they were rearing large families. Once again I chose the same watching post. Cobs, pens, and cygnets were united at the bathing rendezvous. The most remarkable note that I was able to record was the pen calling the cygnets. It is a fairly loud barking noise, probably an expression of alarm used to keep the flock together. It is the most characteristic language of the mother-swan.

Again I heard all the bathing noises, all sorts of grunting, the hasty attacking sounds of the cob, and once even a typical laughing sound, though I do not know whether it was the cob or the pen that was so cheerful on this dull morning. There were more short flights in the water: and I got a very fine sound picture when a redshank intervened in a swan's flight with his lovely song. I was also extremely lucky in recording a pair of swans in full flight round the swannery; they passed very close to my microphone on the way back. I enjoyed, too, the continuous musical peeping of the cygnets, convoyed by their parents, when the whole family took to the water. Late one evening I watched a pen with nine cygnets, comfortably covered with the finest down, and the cob keeping a watchful guard.

There is no such thing as a 'swan-song'. But musicians may be interested to know that the black swan from Australia, domesticated in Britain on lakes and ornamental waters, and not related to our European swans, attaches to his steamboat-like alarm call a very short and soft song. When I heard Grieg's *Lied*, 'Der Schwan', I was almost certain that this Norwegian composer had heard the black swan's song, and enquiries which I made long ago confirmed my assumption.

Footnote – just to illustrate the dangers of taping the swan: spring 1951 was not very favourable for recording. At the end of March I accepted another invitation to spend Easter at Laeken. The Queen Mother was still very anxious to finish the sound-book, the recordings for which we had made in 1938. I took my gear with me in case there should be something of interest to record, but the weather was still cold and rainy. But whenever the rain stopped my wife and I tried to take a walk. Thus it happened one day in April that we were strolling through the silent park. The weather was still wintry, and I wore thick clothes. I remembered my adventure with the swan thirteen years earlier, and automatically we turned our steps towards the spot where I had seen the pair. As we drew near the small pond I noticed, to my astonishment, a pair of obvious wild swans building a nest.

Now, a swan can break a man's leg with the beat of its wings, and so it was half reluctantly that I approached. The pen was busy and took no notice of us, but the cob at once took up his attack position. We retired slowly, hoping that the cob would not follow, but about sixty yards from the pond the cob attacked me, giving me heavy blows with its wings. Although these blows hurt, I was more afraid of the long neck and the beak swaying before my face. Very soon the swan knocked me down. This was perhaps fortunate, since the blows had less force once the swan was sitting on me, but the situation was still serious. I tried in vain to get hold of the swan's neck. With a quick movement I threw the bird off and managed to get to my feet. But again the cob attacked and brought me down. Then my chance came, and I got a grip on its neck and beak. This meant that for the time being they were out of action. Then, thanks to my careful observation at Abbotsbury, I got hold of a certain spot, and the upper part of the swan was completely quiet. This, I knew, would not harm the swan, which was able to breathe freely. It still attacked me with its wings, causing me great pain, and I was beginning to feel exhausted, for the struggle had already lasted five minutes.

My wife had meanwhile succeeded in finding a stick, but at the first blow it broke. After another minute's struggle I managed to get hold of the swan's wings, and as I still had the neck under control I was able to carry the bird back to the pond and throw it in. It was unharmed and so, fortunately, was I, although quite out of breath. I waited a second to see if the cob would attack again. It at first made as if to swim towards me, but then changed its mind, and I was able to retire and sit down on the ground while my wife attended to me. Thus my acquaintance with a swan-keeper at Abbotsbury, whose family had been looking after swans for more than five hundred years, bore fruit. For, having watched not only the swans but also the behaviour of the keeper, Fred Lexster, I had learnt enough to bring my fight with a swan to a happy ending.

Catching a Mermaid

David Attenborough

Television has given millions of people a glimpse into the world of nature and has done a vast deal of good in arousing their concern about wildlife conservation. One of the best-known TV naturalists is the present author, who describes an incident during an expedition to British Guiana (as it was then called). The manatee, one of the so-called 'sea-cows', is a herbivorous, aquatic, slow-moving, harmless mammal and, together with its cousin the Dugong, perhaps gave rise to ancient legends about mermaids.

We spent three more days cruising on the Canje River with our African-Guianese friend Mr King and his crew, searching for manatee. We set nets at night, we set them during the day; we set them in the rain and in sunshine, when the tide ebbed and when the tide flowed, but never did we see any sign whatsoever of our quarry in spite of assurances that each of these conditions in turn was essential for our purpose. Finally we had no more provisions to stay out longer, so dolefully we sailed back to New Amsterdam.

'Well, man,' said Mr King philosophically, as we paid him off, 'I reckon we get bad luck.'

As we walked away along the jetty, an East Indian fisherman ran up to us.

'You de men dat want water-mamma,' he said, ''cause I get one t'ree days ago.'

'What did you do with her?' we asked excitedly.

'Put she in a small lake just outside de town. I easily catch, if you want.'

'Fine,' said Jack Lester, 'we most certainly do. Let's go and catch her now.'

The East Indian ran back along the jetty, loaded his net on to a hand-truck and collected three friends to assist him.

As our little procession wended its way through the crowded streets, I heard the word 'water-mamma' (the local name for manatee) being passed excitedly from person to person and by the time we reached the outskirts of the town and approached the meadow in which the lake lay, we had a loud large crowd trailing behind us.

The lake was wide and muddy, but fortunately it was not deep. Everyone squatted on the banks and silently stared at the water, searching for a sign of the mermaid's position. Suddenly someone pointed to a mysteriously moving lotus leaf. It crumpled and vanished beneath the surface, and a few seconds later a brown muzzle appeared above the water, emitted a blast of air from two large circular nostrils and disappeared.

''E dere! 'E dere!' everyone shouted.

Narian, the fisherman, marshalled his forces. With his three assistants, he jumped into the water. Holding the long net stretched between them, he arranged them in a long line across the small bay where the manatee had been seen. Slowly, chest deep in the water, they advanced towards the bank. As they approached, the manatee betrayed her position by once more coming up for air. Narian yelled to the men on the two ends of the net to wade quickly to the bank and climb out so that the net formed not a straight line but an arc. Now thoroughly disturbed, the manatee rose closer to the surface and rolled over, giving us a view of her great dun-brown flank.

A gasp of astonishment and pleasure rose from the crowd. 'She big t'ing! Maan, she *monstrous*!'

Excitement gripped Narian's assistants on the bank and, enthusiastically aided by some of the onlookers, they began feverishly to haul in the net hand over hand. Narian, still wading in the lake, shouted furiously above the hubbub.

'Stop pullin',' he yelled. 'Not so fast.'

No one took the slightest notice.

'Hundred dollar de net,' Narian screamed. ''E go bust if you no stop pulling.'

But the crowd, having seen the manatee's flank once again, were obsessed by the desire to land her as quickly as possible, and they continued to haul in the net until the manatee lay enmeshed in the water just below the bank. She was obviously a very big one, but there was no time to see more for she suddenly arched her body and thrashed with her enormous tail, soaking everyone in muddy water. The net broke and she disappeared. Narian's fury exceeded all bounds, and he scrambled on to the bank and wrathfully demanded payment from everyone standing near by for repairs to his net. In the ensuing clamour, it did not seem appropriate to suggest that since our mermaid appeared to be a particularly passionate one, we should go and find Mr King so that he could stroke the ropes in his special way and pacify her next time she was netted. The argument proceeded and everyone seemed to forget the manatee except Jack, who wandered off along the bank, tracing her course by swirls in the water.

At last the noise subsided. Jack called to Narian and pointed to where he had last seen the manatee. Narian walked over, grumbling loudly, with a long rope in his hand.

'Dose mad men,' he said contemptuously. 'Dey bus' my net an he wu'th hundred dollar. *Dis* time I goin' in de water an' tie rope roun' her tail so she *cain't* escape.'

He jumped into the lake again and waded to and fro, feeling for the manatee with his feet. At last he found her lying sluggishly on the bottom, and with the rope in his hands he bent down until his chin was just above the surface. He remained in this position for a few minutes as he groped in the water. Then he straightened and began to say something when the rope whipped tight in his hands, and pulled him flat on his face. He struggled to his feet, spat out the muddy water and happily brandished the end of the rope.

'I still got she,' he called.

The manatee, having passively allowed the rope to be tied round her tail, now realized that she was in danger of being caught, and she reared to the surface, splashed and tried to bolt. This time Narian was ready for her and skilfully he managed to lead her towards the bank. His chastened assistants once more encircled the manatee with the net and Narian scrambled up on to the bank with the rope still in his hand. The men on the net pulled, Narian heaved, and slowly, tail first, the mermaid was hauled ashore.

On land she was not a pretty sight. Her head was little more than a blunt stump, garnished with an extensive but sparse moustache on her huge blubbery upper-lip. Her minute eyes were buried deep in the flesh of her cheek and would have been almost undetectable if they had not been suppurating slightly. Apart from her prominent nostrils, therefore, she possessed no feature which could give her any facial expression whatsoever.

From her nose to the end of her great spatulate tail she was just over seven feet long. She had two paddle-shaped front flippers, but no rear limbs, and where she kept her bones was a mystery, for, robbed of the support of the water, her great body slumped like a sack of wet sand.

She seemed entirely indifferent to our exploratory prods, and allowed herself to be turned over without so much as a wriggle of protest. As she lay motionless on her back, her flippers fallen outwards, I became worried that she had been injured during her capture, and I asked Narian if she was all right. He laughed. 'Dis t'ing *cain't* die,' he said, and splashed some water on her, whereupon she arched her body, slapped her tail on the ground, and then returned to immobility.

The problem of getting her back to Georgetown was solved for us by the Town Council of New Amsterdam, who lent us the municipal water-lorry. We tied rope slings round her tail and beneath her flippers. Narian and his three assistants hoisted her from the ground and staggered across the meadow to where the lorry was parked.

Sagging between the slings, her flippers hanging down limply, and dribbling slightly from beneath her vast moustache, she hardly looked alluring. 'If any sailor ever mistook *her* for a mermaid,' said Charles Lagus, our cameraman, 'I reckon he must have been at sea for a very long time.'

'I Mean No Harm'

George B. Schaller

Probably no animal has fired the imagination – or given rise to so many tall stories – as has the gorilla. But nothing could be more expressive of man's changing attitude to animals than the contrast between du Chaillu's description of the gorilla as a bloodthirsty, ferocious creature and this author's remarkable study of the species. He spent many months in the Albert National Park in the Congo, living in close contact with family parties of gorillas, and the present episode is taken from his book Year of the Gorilla.

I found no gorillas on the first day at Kabara nor on the following one, although fairly fresh nests were common. On the third day I took with me N'sekanabo, the guard. He was a huge fellow with a ready grin and muscular arms that would do justice to a gorilla. Our paths led through dense stands of lobelias, each naked stem six feet tall and with a cluster of large leaves at the apex. When injured in some way the plants exude a sticky white fluid that tastes extremely bitter and, when inadvertently rubbed into the eyes, burns with blinding fury. Slightly ahead and to one side of us, we suddenly heard a quarrelsome, high-pitched scream, such as I have heard a captive infant gorilla give when deprived of a favourite toy. Motioning N'sekanabo to wait, I crept ahead and from the cover of a tree trunk looked out over a shallow valley. A female gorilla emerged from the vegetation and slowly ascended a stump, a stalk of wild celery casually hanging from the corner of her mouth like a cigar. She sat down and holding the stem in both hands bit off the tough outer bark, leaving only the juicy centre which she ate. Another female ambled up with a small infant clinging to her back. She grabbed a stalk of wild celery near the base and pulled it up with a jerk. She then pushed a swathe of vegetation down with one hand, squatted and ate, scattering the strips of celery bark all over her lap. Wild celery closely resembles the domestic variety, but, as I later found out, it tastes bitter. This plant turned out to be the second most important food item around Kabara. To obtain a better view of some of the other members of the group, I became incautious and let myself be seen by one female. She emitted one short scream and ran off into the undergrowth. A large youngster, weighing about eighty pounds, climbed up the sloping trunk of a tree, looked in my direction intently, and descended rapidly. Suddenly seven animals, with a large silver-backed male bringing up the rear, filed by only a hundred feet from me. He paused briefly, peering at me from the cover of a screen of herbs, only the top of his head showing. After a harsh staccato of grunts, which apparently functioned as a warning to me as well as to the group, he hurried away, closely followed by three females and four youngsters, two of which rode piggy-back, clutching the females.

Kay and I saw the gorillas only from a distance on the following day, but on the third day I managed to creep to the edge of the group. Crouched in the low crotch of a *Hagenia* tree and partially hidden by some branches, I obtained wonderful glimpses of the apes as they fed and rested among some tall shrubs, completely unaware of my nearness. The silver-backed male moved leisurely up to a *Vernonia*, a tree-like shrub, grasped the stem about six feet above ground, and with a sudden jerk uprooted the whole tree. With the same slow motion he took a branch, splintered and tore it apart with his teeth, and gnawed the tender white pith with his incisors as if eating corn-on-the-cob. A female reclined on her back on a sloping tree-trunk. She had pulled the crown of a near-by *Vernonia* close to her face and was eating the purple blossoms, plucking each one between thumb and index finger before popping it into her mouth. A large youngster climbed into the crown of a shrub and squatted there, swaying gently back and forth. Then it swung its legs free and hung there by one hand, rotating slowly.

A fearful scream shattered the tranquil forest. All feeding ceased as the animals raced to a thicket from which the sound came. Then others screamed with high piercing notes and milled excitedly about. Finally the silver-backed male emitted a series of deep guttural grunts, slow and emphatic. The screaming ceased. Later, after the gorillas had moved over a ridge and out of sight into another valley, I examined the area and discovered the reason for the commotion. A gorilla had apparently fallen some five feet into a cave. Footprints left when it scrambled to get out were clearly visible in the soft earth. A few days later I entered this lava cave with a flashlight and found that equally curious visitors had preceded me. At least three gorillas had entered the cave through a large opening obscured by hanging vines and had explored some hundred feet into the dark and clammy interior. A side chamber in this grotto contained a small lake, terribly still except for a constant drip, drip that seemed to come out of nowhere.

This was not the only group of gorillas I saw around Bishitsi at that time. On 22nd August I heard a male beat his chest about one hundred yards from the animals I was watching, and the following morning inspection of the forest revealed that no less than three groups had nested close to each other. One of these groups was large, comprising nineteen animals as a later count showed, but the third group contained only five gorillas – a male, two females, and two youngsters. These three groups remained in the same part of the forest for five days. Once groups II and III joined briefly, nesting together for a night, and twice groups I and II slept only fifty yards apart. But I was not yet experienced enough to track all the groups through the maze of crisscrossing trails, and the details of their interactions remained obscure to me.

Slowly, as I watched these groups during the latter part of August, I developed techniques for studying the gorilla. Every species of animal presents its own special problems, and not until these have been solved is an intimate study possible. Most of my visits to a group began at the site where I had last seen it the previous day. Cautiously I followed the trails of the gorillas through the trampled vegetation, never certain if the animals had gone a hundred yards, a mile, or doubled back so that now they were somewhere behind me. The trails always had an interesting story to tell, and in many ways I enjoyed my saunterings as much as the sight of the apes themselves. Almost unconsciously I fell into the same unhurried pattern of movement as that of the gorillas, especially when the morning sun shimmered on the leaves and the mountains reached serenely into the sky. When the gorillas were feeding, they fanned out, leaving many trails littered with discarded celery bark and other food remnants. When the gorillas were travelling, they moved in single or double file, only to rest after a while close together on an open slope. Sometimes a musty odour, like that of a barnyard, permeated the air, and I knew that it was the site where the animals had slept the night before. The nests and the area around them were littered with dung, and hundreds of small brown flies darted around laying tiny white eggs on the moist surfaces of the faeces. It often took me over half an hour to find all the nests, since a gorilla occasionally slept sixty feet or more from its nearest neighbour. I mapped each site and paced off the distance between nests. By measuring the diameter of dung in the nests, I could determine the resting place of large silver-backed males and of juveniles. Frequently both medium and small-sized sections of dung lay side by side in the same nest, indicating that a female and her offspring had slept in it.

Somewhere not very far ahead in the undergrowth were the gorillas, often without a sound to reveal their presence. To track them over this last piece of trail, never certain when a shaggy head would rear above the vegetation, never certain that an attack by the male would not follow careless approach, was the most tense and exciting part of the day. Cautiously, I took one, two, three, steps, before stopping, all senses alert, listening intently for the snapping of a branch or the rumbling of a stomach. I climbed up fallen logs or into the low branches of trees to scan the forest ahead for a glimpse of a black body among the weeds. For minutes I stood motionless, nerves so keyed to receive the slightest stimulus that even the distant whirr of a sunbird's wing was enough to startle me.

Frequently my first intimation that the gorillas were near was the sudden swaying of a lobelia or a branch, jarred by a passing animal. Then there were two courses open to me: I could hide myself and watch the gorillas without their being aware of my presence, or I could remain in the open with the hope that, over the days and weeks, the animals would become accustomed to seeing me near them. The former method had a great advantage, since the behaviour of the apes was not influenced in any way by my intrusion. But I soon found out that I often lost useful observations when I hid myself too well, for if I tried for a better view, the animals saw me and grew excited. I usually walked slowly and in full view towards the gorillas and climbed up on a stump or tree branch where I settled myself as comfortably as possible without paying obvious attention to the animals. By choosing a prominent observation post, I was not only able to see the gorillas in the undergrowth, but they could inspect me clearly and keep an eye on me.

Animals are better observers and far more accurate interpreters of gestures than man. I felt certain that if I moved around calmly and alone near the gorillas, obviously without dangerous intent towards them, they would soon realize that I was harmless. It is really not easy for a man to shed all his arrogance and aggressiveness before an animal, to approach it in utter humility with the knowledge of being in many ways inferior. Casual actions are often sufficient to alert the gorillas and to make them uneasy. For example, I believe that even the possession of a fire-arm is sufficient to imbue one's behaviour with a certain unconscious aggressiveness, a feeling of being superior, which an animal can detect. When meeting a gorilla face to face, I reasoned, an attack would be more likely if I carried a gun than if I simply showed my apprehension and uncertainty. Among some creatures – the dog, rhesus monkey, gorilla and man – a direct unwavering stare is a form of threat. Even while watching gorillas from a distance I had to be careful not to look at them too long without averting my head, for they became uneasy under my steady scrutiny. Similarly they considered the unblinking stare of binoculars and cameras as a threat, and I had to use these instruments sparingly. As could be expected, gorillas were more annoyed and excited on seeing two persons than one. My wife, Kay, had to remain at home much of the time, and the park guard, who sometimes accompanied me, had to hide himself while I watched the apes. I decided not to follow the animals once they had moved from my sight, for pursuit could easily frighten them and increase the chance of attacks. In general, I put myself into the place of a gorilla and tried to imagine to what actions I would object if suddenly a strange and potentially dangerous creature approached me. In all the months I spent with the gorillas, none attacked me.

Establishing rapport with the gorillas was fairly easy, because their senses are comparable to those of man – not man of the city who is unable to react to the subtle stimuli of his surroundings amidst the incessant noise of the machine, but man attuned to the wilderness. As with man, sight is the most important sense in gorillas. The apes are very quick at spotting slight movements, and often they watched my approach before I was even aware of their presence. Hearing, too, is well developed in gorillas, but they respond only to strange sounds, like the human voice, or sounds out of context. When a group fed noisily, my approach could be rather casual, but when they were resting all were alert to a stray branch snapping underfoot. The sense of smell seems to be relatively poor in gorillas: they rarely responded to my presence even when I was downwind and within fifty feet of them. Twice, however, gorillas seemed to smell me when I sweated profusely – but, as Kay commented, it does not take an acute sense of smell to do that.

On several occasions resting animals became uneasy while I was watching them from a distance. I was upwind, completely silent, and they obviously had not seen me. Yet they seemed to sense that something was not quite right. Perhaps they responded to subliminal stimuli, too vague to be assimilated consciously; or perhaps some other sense warned them of possible danger. I had had similar experiences when wandering through the forest. Suddenly I had the feeling, in fact, I knew, that gorillas were close by, yet I had neither seen, heard, nor smelt them. More often than not, I was correct. Most naturalists, I feel sure, have had similar encounters with animals.

On the last day of August, as N'sekanabo and I clambered up the boulder-strewn depths of Kanyamagufa Canyon, a tremendous roar filled the chasm and bounding from wall to wall descended the mountains like the rumbling of an avalanche. We started and ducked and then peered up at the silver-backed male who, surrounded by his group, stood motionless at the canyon rim looking down at us. Quietly and as unobtrusively as possible we retraced our steps under the watchful eye of the male, feeling chastised like children for having so crassly intruded into his domain. We climbed up the opposite wall of the canyon, and later, when I was able to see the gorillas well, I found to my delight that they were old acquaintances. Six months previously, in March, Doc and I had watched this group for several hours. Almost daily throughout the month of September I visited these animals, group IV, watching them, enjoying their antics, and worrying over their problems. All members in the group became definite individuals whom I recognized and named. No other group taught me as much or took a greater hold on my affection.

They moved up the precipitous slopes of Mt Mikeno after our first meeting, going higher and higher until the *Hypericum* trees grew stunted and the timber line was not far above. I ascended the mountain daily to be with the animals, my senses vibrant and alive as I clambered up. The silent forests were another world from the villages and fields that lay far below us. On the horizon, past Goma and Lake Kivu, dense ranks of clouds gathered, as they usually did by mid-morning, drawing closer and closer until their advance was halted by the ramparts of the mountains. But drawn inexorably onward they stormed soundlessly up the slopes, fingering the canyons, dodging from tree to tree, until finally they had gathered everything into their clammy embrace.

On 4th September I came upon the gorillas feeding slowly on a steep slope about a hundred yards above me. I sat down at the base of a tree, and, with binoculars resting on my drawn-up knees, I scanned the slope, trying to pinpoint the whereabouts of the four silver-backed males in the group. The large male gorillas are the most alert, unpredictable, and excitable members of the group and hence the most dangerous. Squatting with his back towards me was Big Daddy, easily recognizable by the two bright silver spots on his grey back. As he turned to rest on his belly, he saw me, gave me an intent look, and emitted two sharp grunts. Several females and youngsters glanced from the vegetation in his direction and then ambled to his side, warned that possible danger was near. Big Daddy was the undisputed leader of the group, a benign dictator who by his actions determined the behaviour of the other animals. He stood now looking down at me with slightly parted lips, his mighty arms propped on a knoll, completely certain of his status and his power, a picture of sublime dignity.

D.J. was the striving executive type who had not yet reached the top. He was second in command, a rather frustrating position from a human point of view, for in such matters as determining the direction of travel and the time and duration of rest periods the females and youngsters ignored him completely. He lay by himself on his back, one arm slung casually across his face, oblivious to the world.

The Outsider roamed slowly around the periphery of the group, intent on his own doings. He was a gigantic male in the prime of life, visibly larger than Big Daddy, and by far the heaviest male around Kabara. His nostrils were set like two black coals in his face, and his expression conveyed an independence of spirit and a glowering temper. His gait was somewhat rolling like that of a seaman, and with each step his paunch swayed back and forth. To estimate accurately the weight of gorillas in the wild is difficult, but I believe that the Outsider must have weighed between four hundred and fifty and four hundred and eighty pounds. Gorilla males are often said to weigh six hundred pounds or more, but these are the weights of obese zoo animals. Two mountain gorillas in the San Diego Zoo, for example, weighed that much, and they gained still more before they died. In contrast, of ten adult male mountain gorillas killed and weighed in the wild by hunters and collectors, the heaviest animal reached four hundred and eighty-two pounds, and the average was about three hundred and seventy-five pounds.

The fourth silver-backed male in the group was Splitnose, so named for the ragged cut that divided the upper part of his left nostril. He was young, his back barely turned silver, and he lacked the quiet reserve, the sureness of action, which characterized the other three adult males. As if to compensate for his uncertainty of mind, he was highly vociferous whenever he saw me, roaring again and again, sounding his warning over the mountains. But none of the other animals responded visibly.

Apparently D.J. had hatched a plan, for suddenly he left his resting place and circled uphill. Then stealthily, very stealthily, he angled towards me, keeping behind a screen of shrubs. But gorillas are not very good at this sort of thing. Branches broke underfoot and to orient himself he stood up to glance over the vegetation. As soon as I looked directly at him, he ducked and sat quietly before continuing his stalk. He advanced to within thirty feet of me before emitting a terrific roar and beating his chest. Immediately afterward, before the echo of the sound had died away, he peered out from between the bushes as if to see how I had responded to his commotion. Never, even when I fully expected it, was I able to get used to the roar of a silver-backed male. The suddenness of the sound, the shattering volume, invariably made me want to run. But I derived immense satisfaction from noting that the other gorillas in the group startled to a roar just as visibly as I did.

With the male only thirty feet from me, I became uneasy and thought it prudent to retreat to a safer place. Cautiously, I ascended a tree to a height of ten feet. One of the ten females in the group left Big Daddy and ambled to within seventy feet of me to sit on a stump, her chin propped on her folded arms. Slowly, as if daring each other to come closer, the whole group advanced towards my tree. I felt a brief spasm of panic, for the gorillas had never behaved in this manner before. They congregated behind some bushes, and three females carrying infants and two juveniles ascended a tree and tried to obtain a better view of me through the interlacing vines that festooned the branches. In the ensuing minutes we played a game of peekaboo: whenever I craned my neck in order to see the gorillas more clearly, they ducked their heads, only to pop forth again as soon as I looked away. One juvenile, perhaps four years old, climbed into a small tree adjacent to mine, and there we sat, fifteen feet apart, each somewhat nervously glancing at the other, both of us curious, but refraining from staring directly to eliminate all intimation of threat.

Junior, the only black-backed male in the group, stepped out from behind the shrubbery and advanced to within ten feet of the base of my tree, biting off and eating a tender leaf of a blackberry bush on the way. He stood on all fours and looked up at me, mouth slightly open. In all my hours with group IV, I was never able to fathom Junior completely. He was less than eight years old, still the size of a female, but his body had already taken on the angular and muscular build of a male. There was recklessness in his face and a natural mischievousness, which even his inherent reserve could not hide. At the same time his look conveyed a critical aloofness as if he were taking my measure and was not quite sure if I could be fully trusted. He was the only gorilla who seemed to derive any sort of satisfaction from being near me.

Later in the month, rarely a day went by when he did not leave the group to sit by me, either quietly watching my every action or sleeping with his back towards me. Today he was still somewhat uncertain of himself as his indrawn and compressed lips showed. Man too bites his lips when nervous. Occasionally he slapped the ground with a wild overhand swipe, using the palm of his hand, then slyly looked up at me, apparently with the hope that his wanton gesture had been startling. The other members of the group rested quietly. Every fifteen or twenty minutes one of the males jerked out of his slumber to roar once or twice before re-clining again to continue his nap.

All apprehension of the gorillas had long since left me. Not once had their actions portrayed ferocity or even outright anger. The silver-backed males were excited, but all this was offset by their curiosity concerning me and their rapid acceptance of me. As long as I remained quiet, they felt so safe that they continued their daily routine even to the extent of taking their naps beside the tree in which I was sitting. Early in the study I had noted that the gorillas tend to have an extremely placid nature which is not easily aroused to excitement. They give the impression of being stoic and reserved, of being introverted. Their expression is usually one of repose, even in situations which to me would have been disturbing. All their emotions are in their eyes, which are a soft, dark brown. The eyes have a language of their own, being subtle and silent mirrors of the mind, revealing constantly changing patterns of emotion that in no other visible way affect the expression of the animal. I could see hesitation and uneasin-ess, curiosity and boldness and annoyance. Sometimes, when I met a gorilla face to face, the expression in its eyes more than anything else told me of his feelings and helped me decide my course of action.

The brief morning spell of sunshine had given way to dank clouds that descended to the level of the trees. For five hours I perched on a branch, chilled through and through, my fingers so stiff I was barely able to take notes. It began to rain heavily, and soon the rain turned to hail. The gorillas sat in a hunched position, letting the marble-sized stones bound off their backs. They looked thoroughly miserable with the water dripping off their brow ridges, and the long hairs on their arms were a sodden mass. I sat huddled next to the trunk of the tree, hoping for some protection from the canopy. My face was close to the bark, and I smelt the fungus-like odour of lichen and mouldy moss. I could not leave the gorillas without disturbing them, and I had to wait until they moved away.

During ensuing days the group travelled through several deep ravines parallel to the slope of Mt Mikeno in the direction of Kabara. The gorillas had become used to my presence: the females hardly responded at all, and Big Daddy did little more than grunt briefly in annoyance each time he first saw me. Even Splitnose, though still his old vociferous self, was somewhat subdued. Junior seemed to await my arrival. A juvenile, perhaps four years old, frequently followed him closely, aping his every action. J.J., the juvenile, seemed to be male, although the sex of young gorillas in the wild is impossible to determine with certainty. He was a cute little fellow with a stomach taut as a drum, long unkempt hair on the crown of his head, and with an expression of sauciness that always seemed to herald some prank.

The guard N'sekanabo accompanied me one morning in search

of the group. When I caught sight of the animals about fifty yards ahead, I motioned him to duck behind a tree while I swung up into a low branch. As usual, Junior sauntered over and twenty feet from me climbed the trunk of a fallen tree. He then moved along the log on all fours with curious abrupt and jerky steps. His body was stiff and erect, and his arms were curved outward at the elbows, giving them a bent appearance. Junior was strutting, seemingly trying to show off by making himself appear big and powerful. I was amused by his doings and had forgotten all about the guard. When I looked down, I saw N'sekanabo standing below clutching his machete with both hands, beads of sweat covering his forehead. His lips were grey with fear, but I admired his fortitude in remaining with me in the presence of the beast. Junior retreated casually, looking over his shoulder before hurrying after his retreating group.

On several occasions Junior, or sometimes another gorilla, approached within sixty feet or less and shook his head from side to side. It was an odd gesture, one that seemed to signify 'I mean no harm'. To see what gorillas would do if I shook my head at them, I waited until Junior was thirty feet away and paying close attention to me as I rewound the film in my camera. When I began to shake my head, he immediately averted his face, perhaps thinking that I had mistaken his steady gaze for threat. Then, when I in turn stared at him, he shook his head. We continued this for ten minutes. Once he relaxed the muscles of his lower jaw so that the shaking produced a rattling sound. Later, when I inadvertently met gorillas at close range, I employed head shaking as a means of reassuring them and they seemed to understand my good intentions.

'A Falcon, Towering in her Pride'

Phillip Glasier

The sport of falconry originated perhaps four thousand years ago in the Middle East and is one of the most skilled examples of man's partnership with wild creatures. The Crusaders brought back much knowledge of the 'art', and in mediaeval Europe a strict protocol was maintained whereby only royalty was allowed to use gyrfalcons – princes, dukes and earls might keep peregrines – and a mere priest was allowed only a sparrowhawk! Here a modern falconer describes the initial, vital training of two eyas peregrines.

Try to use an adze, a tool rarely used nowadays except by wheel- and ship-wrights. Of all implements, I think this is the one that holds the most surprises for the uninitiated. It doesn't look anything out of the ordinary, and a skilled man has no trouble in taking the thinnest of wood shavings off the bow of a boat. Wield it yourself. It at once becomes the most awkward-shaped thing you ever handled, and you find yourself so cackhanded that it appears to harbour a malevolent demon, who takes charge in as fiendish a way as possible the instant a novice picks it up.

Much the same applies to falconry. It looks so easy. Any fool, you think, could feed a falcon on the fist. She just sits there eating, and when she's finished you pop the hood on. Nothing could be more simple – until you try it.

Many years ago, when we were flying falcons on Salisbury Plain, an old, retired professional falconer came over to see them.

At the end of the day we asked him to feed one up. The old falconer made himself comfortable on an upturned barrel, placing himself so that the light fell on the meat and no one could pass behind him to disturb the falcon while she was feeding. Not until he was quite ready did he unhood her and let her feed. The whole time she was feeding there wasn't a flap of her wings, or a foot shifted, to show she was unbalanced or worried in any way. There is a Suffolk word, 'suent', that is used to describe anything that runs easily and sweetly, like a well-greased cart-wheel, or applied to things done without fuss or bother. Gently and suently, he gave help when she needed it. Otherwise he left her to herself.

When she had finished he wiped her beak, and let her pick up the small morsels of meat left clinging to her toes, and on the glove. Then, when she had shaken herself, he hooded her. To the layman he was just a white-haired, weather-beaten old man feeding a falcon. To those of us who could, from past experience, appreciate his skill, it was obvious that he had fed falcons, many, many times before. He had anticipated all the possible trouble, so beautifully handling the falcon that she never had a moment of anxiety. One felt like applauding him.

I was most fortunate in having my uncle to teach me falconry. Most beginners have to learn from books, a pretty impossible task, for as yet there has been no book written that is fully detailed enough to cover all the problems likely to face the learner. To be able to see a falcon handled and flown, even if only for a day, is a great help, but to have a willing expert permanently on the spot was of inestimable value.

He was not a particularly patient instructor, and once he had shown me how to do something he expected me to be able to do it perfectly, having forgotten that there was a time when he himself did not have the know-how.

Teaching me to tie a falconer's knot, I can remember him saying, somewhat testily, 'For heaven's sake, boy, it's quite simple: over, under, round and through. Anyone can do it, I should have thought. Must be something wrong with you.'

Bit by bit I learnt, and in due course became reasonably useful to him, and eventually he considered me proficient enough to handle a completely untrained falcon.

As wild as a hawk: it is a common enough phrase, but few of those who use it can really understand what it means. Even now after training so many, their initial wildness still surprises me, as does the swiftness with which their whole attitude suddenly changes towards humans once they learn no harm is meant.

A beginner usually starts with a kestrel or a merlin. Being so small, they are easier to manage, and their disposition is more friendly from the start. However, I had already gained a certain amount of experience from helping him with trained birds, and this particular year we didn't have anything except two large peregrines. At least they seemed very large to me.

They were both falcons, females that is, and they came in a hamper from a keeper in Ireland. On their arrival they were turned loose in an empty shed, specially prepared for them. We had spread peat over the floor and the windows were barred with bamboo rods, placed vertically so that they could not cling to them and break any feathers. They had perches to sit on, a bath, and as much food as they could eat. They ate an enormous amount too, for they were growing fast and, although hardly four weeks old, were already nearly as big as an adult bird.

They still had a lot of the white down with which they are covered when first hatched poking out from their new feathers. The little wispy bits clinging to the top of their heads made them look very babyish. Their tails were only about two-thirds grown, and the long primaries had blue-coloured sheaths showing still. Until these flight feathers were full length and the quills hardened off they were to remain in the mews. Their feet were not yet the bright yellow colour of an older bird and still seemed too big for them. Their long toes – once called petty singles – stuck out in front of them and looked very odd.

At this stage of their life they were left alone to eat, sleep, preen, or do whatever they wished. Unk allowed no one except himself to go into the shed, and only when it was dark did he take in their food, remove any stale pieces left uneaten, and replenish the bath. For they might, if they once associated him with food, start screaming at the sight of him, as they do when their parents bring food to the eyrie. This can easily develop into a habit that is impossible to break, and a real screamer is something to be avoided at all costs. It will scream all day long with a monotonous, rasping screech that you think would give it a sore throat in no time and certainly gives you a headache with its incessant, nerve-jangling clamour. Unk had arranged a peep-hole in the door so that we could see how they were getting on without their seeing us, but he discouraged its frequent use.

The eyas falcons grew fast, and soon Unk decided they were ready to start their training. He routed out some suitable leather for making jesses and laid out everything all ready. The jesses are put on to the falcon's legs by means of a cunning arrangement of slots cut in the leather, and I was made to practise putting them on a pencil, so that I should know how to do it when the time came. At least, that was the idea. We waited till dark before picking them up, as then they would not crash around in the shed. We slipped in quietly and flashed a torch momentarily to see on which perch they were sitting. Unk picked up one of them in the dark and brought her indoors. I slipped a hood on her while he held her with her feet on an old cushion to give her something to grip.

She gripped all right, but the trouble was that she didn't stay gripping the same place, and I was faced with a hissing, snatching falcon who shifted her feet just when I had got one of her jesses half on. The jess would then slip off and I would have to start all over again, getting more and more dithery in my anxiety to do the job properly before Unk's comments became too caustic and at the same time trying to avoid the clutching, grasping, great feet, whose talons I could see were making large holes in the cushion and would undoubtedly be just as happy making some in me. Finally I got the jesses on and, attaching the leash and swivel, I stood back while Unk released her.

She stood up and tried hard to scratch her hood off, but after a short while gave this up and quietened down. He took her on his glove and made her step back on to the arm of the sofa, where we left her while we jessed up her sister. Hooded falcons will always step back on to something if the backs of their legs are gently pressed against it, so one picks up a hooded falcon by pressing the glove against its legs. Because it can see what it is doing, an unhooded bird steps forward.

As I had been so slow, Unk reversed our jobs. Unk flashed the torch on and off, and I felt my way gently towards the perch.

My job was to take hold of her firmly from in front and slightly above her, so that my thumbs met in the centre of her back and my fingers held her wings close to her body.

I anticipated no more trouble than Unk had had with the first falcon. I felt in the dark for the perch but, misjudging it, I touched her by mistake, to be greeted by an ominous hiss more suited to a twenty-foot python crossed in love.

From the darkness Unk exhorted me not to spend all night over such a simple job. So, taking more care, I felt again and, putting my hands over her, grasped her firmly and tried to pick her up. She had no intention whatsoever of coming, but held tightly on to the perch and refused to let go. Unk switched on the torch to see what was happening, and she promptly put her head down and bit my finger. Even at that age a falcon knows how to bite, for she has been tearing her own food up for the last few weeks, learning to rip through shin of beef, old crows and other such tough items. My finger must have been like a piece of fillet steak to her, and I, somewhat reasonably I thought, let go. She flew on to the floor and scuttled away into a dark corner in a huff. Unk informed the heavenly inhabitants above that never had he such an incompetent, fumble-fingered, bungling assistant and asked why was I complaining about a slight nip from an innocent little bird.

In the end he picked her up and I put the jesses on. Either the falcon was satisfied with the lump out of my finger or gave up the struggle when she saw who was in command; for she was no more trouble. They were both left hooded for the night, sitting on blocks under a lean-to shelter, awaiting the start of their training next day.

To most people one peregrine is much like another, but to a falconer they vary in looks, shape, colour, size and, above all, in temperament. As with people, it is very often the most beautiful that does not turn out so well, while the less glamorous surprises everyone by her performance and pleasanter nature. Of the two falcons one was a big dark-headed bird with a smoky front, a real dusky beauty. Her sister was considerably smaller, rather pale in front and with a tawny-coloured head: good-looking but not so gorgeous.

Although both belonged to him, Unk let me choose which bird I would like to handle. I was very attracted by the big one because of her size and looks but, possibly because of my own lack of stature then, I had a sneaking regard for the smaller one and finally chose her – rather to my uncle's surprise, I think, for he mumbled something about my having possibly picked the better one, in spite of appearances.

The following morning we took them up from their blocks and carried them about, stroking them every so often with a feather. This gets them accustomed to movement, but if you use your hand to stroke them the natural grease in your skin removes the water-proofing on the feathers. Then they get far wetter than they should do if they are left sitting out in a shower of rain. A falcon can stand quite heavy rain and has only to shake herself when it is fine again to send the raindrops flying, leaving her bone-dry.

After an hour or so of carrying they were put back on their blocks, still hooded, and left while we got on with other things. It is a curious fact that, while falcons get tamer even when hooded, hawks do not, and are just as wild as before, the moment the hood is removed.

In the evening we carried them again. When it was getting dusk we brought them indoors and unhooded them, the half-light helping to prevent their getting restive, for falcons dislike flying once it begins to get dark. Both immediately tried to fly off, or bated, as it is called. Now, a two-pound falcon flying madly off the fist and not having any notion of sitting still is quite a handful. Like any other wild thing, they try to get away, but, finding themselves tethered, they naturally tend to attack. Unk's dark glamour-puss hung upside-down by her jesses, screaming in anger and biting his hand every time he tried to lift her back on to his glove.

I was very glad that I had chosen the smaller one, for she, after her first bate, most obligingly flew back on to my fist and remained sitting there, looking very surprised and startled.

Her feathers were all puffed out like a rolled-up hedgepig's prickles, her beak was half open, and at any movement she hissed. Her attitude was by no means one of fear alone, indeed hostility glared out of her large dark eyes. An Army N.C.O. would have placed her on a 'fizzer' at once for dumb insolence.

By this time Unk had persuaded his hitherto bat-like bird to sit the right way up. Her attitude was the same as her sister's, but her greater size and darker plumage made her even more impressive. It seemed quite impossible to me that either of them would even deign to consider surrender on any terms, let alone ever be pleased to see us. The idea of flying them free and expecting them to return was quite ridiculous.

I watched my uncle as he slowly, so slowly, stroked his falcon's breast feathers with the hood. Very gradually he worked his way up towards her head, her hissing grew less and her beak closed, but her eyes watched every move he made. Still working quite slowly, he deftly put the hood over her head and, with a neat movement of his fingers, pulled the braces tight to prevent her shaking it off.

It was like a conjuror's sleight of hand, so smooth and unhurried till the last slick movement that the falcon hadn't realized she was being hooded till it was too late to do anything about it. Like the showman's patter when he does the three-card trick, 'the quickness of the 'and deceives the h-eye'.

I tried to do the same with my falcon. I'd hooded trained falcons before, so I had a good idea of what to do. She hissed hard as I raised my hand. Her hot breath puffed out over my face with a curious scent quite unlike any I had smelt before. It was unexpectedly pleasant, like the intriguing smell of burnt horse-hoof in a smithy, or leather in a saddler's shop. It should obviously be bottled in little model falcons of Lalique glass and sold in only the most exclusive shops to very special order.

I copied Unk's movements with the hood and, to my surprise, got it on with no trouble whatsoever. For the next hour we sat quietly unhooding and hooding them every few minutes. While a falcon is still apprehensive of the falconer is the time to accustom her to the hood. Once she loses her fear of him she is far more difficult to break to the hood, for her whole attention is then riveted on avoiding it.

Hooding is an art that is either acquired fairly quickly or not at all. Some people never master the knack and so bungle things that the falcon becomes hood-shy and bates away, screaming in annoyance at the sight of a hood. If it is done properly at the very beginning, they soon learn to think no more of being hooded than we do of wearing a hat. Hoods are said to have been brought into this country from Syria by the returning crusaders. Richard Coeur de Lion took falcons with him to the Crusades, war being carried on in a far more civilized manner then.

I have had falcons that would put their heads forward into the hood; and a red-tailed buzzard from America used to go to sleep on my fist almost as soon as the hood was put on. She would tuck her head into the top of her back, and it looked most odd as I walked along with an apparently headless bird.

Next they had to be persuaded to feed on the fist. It is very easy to get them to feed with a hood on, but they get no tamer, make the hood dirty, are obviously miserable because they cannot see what they are eating, and pick up the bad habit of pulling at one's glove when they are keen, in the hopes of finding food there. So ours were to feed bareheaded on the fist and, to impress on them that we were the providers of all their food, they were to be allowed to feed nowhere else for the time being.

At first they won't start to eat until their fear of man, and of their strange surroundings, has been overcome. Unk gave me a rough idea of how to manage and then took his bird off to another room so that we should not disturb each other.

I settled myself comfortably in an arm-chair and, holding a nice tempting piece of raw beef in my gloved left-hand, close to the falcon's feet, I unhooded her. She bated off as I had expected her to, but half flew, half scrambled on her own. She caught sight of the meat and looked down at it for an instant, then looked up at me and just sat and stared. I remained quite still, hoping she would start to feed. She stayed motionless, still glaring. Her big eyes never blinked nor altered their penetrating gaze. Her expression was that of immutable stubbornness. More than that, for she obviously dared me to outstay her.

Just then a slight breeze from the open window lifted the curtain and made her bate. I hooded her, got up and shut the window, sat myself down and tried once more.

After about ten minutes one of my feet began to go to sleep. I shifted as gently as I could to relieve it but disturbed her, and again she bated.

I tried drawing her attention to the meat by rubbing her foot; she looked down, half inclined to eat, changed her mind and stared straight in front of her. She had obviously decided that there was a catch in it somewhere and that she was not going to be had. I rubbed her foot again, and once more she looked down but in a flash was looking back at me.

I cut off a small piece of meat very carefully, juggling the penknife open with my free hand, and offered it to her. She opened her beak as my hand came near, but closed it just as I was about to put the meat in. I tried again, moving more quickly, and this time I succeeded. I took my hand away, and she sat there with the meat in her beak for a brief while. Then, with a quick movement of her head, she flicked it away across the room as though it were distasteful to her, resuming her inscrutable, sphinx-like gaze.

I moved my glove under her feet; she involuntarily gripped as though to stop the meat escaping and so nearly took a bite that I drew in my breath rather sharply, and the noise stopped her.

After several more minutes of her fixed gaze, my throat began to tickle, and I felt a desperate desire to cough. Suddenly she put her head down, took a good mouthful, and swallowed it. I could stifle the cough no longer, and she naturally bated at the explosion. I was furious with myself.

Then, to my utter amazement, she shook herself, looked round the room as though to make sure it was unaltered, and began to feed steadily. The food slipped once, but she only paused when my hand caught and replaced it. In five minutes or so she had finished the lot and was sitting there contented, with a fair-sized crop. She cleaned her beak, stropping it on my glove like a razor, first to one side then the other – feaking as it is properly called. I gently hooded her without any fuss and got to my feet, appreciating my regained freedom and delighted with my success.

Just as I was stretching my cramped limbs the telephone rang with the suddenness and persistence of an alarm clock. 'Been trying to get you for the last ten minutes,' the voice said. I thought to myself that, had it rung ten minutes sooner, it might well have been at least another half-hour before I persuaded the falcon I meant no harm and that my offering was genuine.

A few minutes later Unk came in. His falcon had taken a small crop after, so he told me, a lot of encouragement on his part. So I felt very pleased. I looked at the clock. We had been over an hour just feeding them – an hour that seemed very short now it was successfully over, but that had been endless when only half-way through with nothing to show for the discomfort but frustration. A very concentrated but rewarding hour.

That evening we discussed names for the falcons. Unk was rather fussy and a little superstitious about this. He preferred not to give any falcon a name that he considered she might well fail to live up to. 'If you call her Diana you can be quite sure that all the hunting she will ever do will be for fleas.'

I must say this seemed to work out, for the previous year we had had three merlins, called Mayfly, Maynotfly and Won'tfly. Won'tfly had been by far the best.

A book on falconry that had been sent to him for reviewing made him roar when he looked at the first chapter. 'Just listen to this,' he said. 'This chap has the audacity to put a photograph of himself in the front of this book and entitle it "The author with his trained kestrel Thunderer". Ha, blooming ha! That shows you at once what an able and knowledgeable bloke he must be on the subject! Thunderer! What a name! I bet it just sits on his fist and goes "squeak, squeak, squeak" at him.'

So I was pretty wary about the names I suggested. Finally we chose Bonus for his and, because of her tawny colouring, Cheetah for mine.

For the first three days they were unhooded only when on the fist. We carried them as much as possible – two or three hours each day – and continued to get them used to their hoods and to feeding on the fist.

The second time they were fed was far easier. Though still shy and suspicious of us, they both remembered the previous feed and, after a short delay, soon settled down. They were easily put off by any sudden movement or unusual sound but would shortly be on the feed again.

In the evenings, the day's chores done, we would take them round to friends, or drop in at the local pub, and get them accustomed to noise and chatter. The regulars in the King's Head knew all about it and took quite an interest in their education, but strangers often looked a bit astonished, and would sometimes ask if the falcons talked. If Unk was feeling expansive he would give them a free lecture on falconry, but if he had already been badgered with a lot of questions he would pull their legs.

'What sort of bird is it, mister?'

'Well it's a very interesting bird that comes from the West Indies,' he would reply. 'Feeds entirely on bananas; won't eat anything else.' Quite often they would swallow it and turn to tell their friends about it with the air of superior knowledge only just learnt.

Years later, in a train, I was tempted to do the same thing myself. As we drew into the station and I got up to leave with my falcon, an old lady handed me two bananas in a paper bag. 'For your birdie's lunch, my dear.'

By the end of three days the two were showing great progress and rarely bated now except for good reasons. A violent sneeze, or a strange dog rushing up were the sort of things they disliked.

Unk said that they could now be left unhooded on their blocks for an hour or so at a time. So we put them where we could watch from the sitting-room window, and, unhooding them, we walked quietly away.

After a few minutes Bonus bated off and, coming up against the restraint of her leash, stood looking bewildered. Cheetah followed in like manner. Their wings were half spread and their feathers all puffed out, and they looked as they do when about to take a bath. Cheetah walked forward but was brought up short by her jesses and promptly bent down to peck at them. She soon gave this up as a jackdaw, flying over the garden, distracted her attention. She watched it go overhead, shook herself and turned to jump back on to her block.

The block has evolved as the best possible sort of outside

perch. It is very like the rock the falcon would naturally sit on, serving also as a means of securing her, while being portable too, and designed to prevent entanglement and damage to feathers. To accustom them to this perch we had put some blocks on the floor in their mews, so they already knew what they were for.

Cheetah sat there, fanning her wings hard but holding on to the block with her feet to avoid becoming airborne. Once or twice she let go, and her wings lifted her into the air a few inches, but she slowed up the beat and dropped on to her block again. It was a form of physical jerks: upwards jumping with wings flapping sideways.

After a few minutes of this exercise she stopped, bobbed her head at Bonus, shook herself thoroughly and, puffing out her feathers in front, drew up one foot underneath them, letting the feathers fall back into place, concealing her foot entirely. It was rather like a schoolgirl who, lacking pockets, discreetly tucks her handkerchief into her bloomers.

She sat there as composed as a falcon who has already spent many hours on the block.

Bonus acted in much the same way, and they copied each other, for if one bated the other followed suit a moment later – a sort of sympathetic detonation. But they quickly returned to their blocks and settled down. Everything that moved in the garden caught their attention, particularly any birds that flew past. These they watched most intently, though showing no signs of wishing to chase them. In fact they looked amiably at a hen blackbird, worm-hunting on the lawn, which hopped well within their reach at times.

Keeping falcons in no way lessens the number of other birds

in the garden. Blackbirds will often eat the meat fat that a falcon has discarded while she watches them unconcernedly. In fact, birds use the feathers lying around the falcons' blocks to line their nests. One bottle-tit's nest we found was upholstered in regal style with Ramshaw's* moulted feathers.

About tea-time we went out and hooded them up again. We took a piece of meat with us, but as Unk had warned me, they both bated away and refused to jump to the fist. They appeared to have forgotten entirely and hissed at us. To me, our three days' work on them seemed wasted, but after a few minutes on the fist they relaxed, behaving in a more friendly fashion.

Now that they were both feeding without hesitation on the fist, we encouraged them first to step, then jump, and finally fly from the arm of a chair, or from the top of a gate if we were out of doors, to the food held in our gloved hands. Bonus did this at once, but Cheetah was very reluctant to trust herself in the air even this short distance, and sidled along the perch in an endeavour to reach the food without having to fly. Finally she made it, after screwing up her courage. Once she had made the initial effort, I had a job to get my hand back into position before she was on it again.

Each day they progressed more rapidly and gained more confidence. They spent longer unhooded on the lawn, bathing with great enjoyment, splashing about and dipping their heads under the water, letting it run down their backs and rolling from side to side, before jumping back on the block, to sit wings spread in the sun to dry.

Once dry, they would preen, an operation that they were as

* A golden eagle trained by Unk.

fussy over as a girl at her dressing-table before a dance. They were very thorough about it, and would go back time after time to run their beaks down the full length of one particular primary that was being recalcitrant. As their beaks neared the end of the shaft, it would bend more and more, curving outwards, till, as the tip was reached, it flicked back into position, all breaks in the webbing invisibly mended.

Every so often they would get a fresh supply of oil from the gland hidden under the tail coverts, and so re-waterproofing was accomplished at the same time. To do their throat feathers they would draw their heads backwards and nibble at the feathers, looking rather like someone trying to hide a double-chin. They would take maybe an hour or more over their toilet, and would invariably end it by shaking themselves, or rousing. Very slowly all their small feathers would stand up, like the bristling hackles on a watchdog, then they would pause, as if a sudden, very important thought had crossed their minds, and the feathers would slowly subside, only to rebristle anew as the thought was dismissed. Their feet would grip the block instead of just standing relaxed, and they would gather themselves up, the shake beginning at the head and travelling down their bodies, gaining momentum as it went. Loose pieces of down would float away, and finally they would indulge in a spell of energetic wing-fanning before relaxing and tucking up a foot to sit contentedly, yet always on the alert for anything of interest.

By the afternoon of the sixth day they both jumped eagerly from their blocks to our outstretched gloves when we went to pick them up.

To get them used to travelling around we would take them into

Sevenoaks when we went shopping. I would take one on my fist, while the other sat on the perch in the dicky of the old Austin. On the return journey we exchanged positions, so that each got the same amount of handling. In this way they kept fairly level with each other in their training. One day Bonus might be slightly ahead, but by the next Cheetah would have caught up.

A week after being taken from the mews we introduced them to the lure. This consisted of an old pair of well-dried rook's wings, tied together and adorned with a piece of meat or a chicken's head. This tempting affair was attached to a line about four yards long. On the far end was the lure-stick, a short length of broom-handle, on which the line was wound when not in use. This also served to slow a falcon up if she tried to carry the lure away after catching it in mid-air.

Unk was very particular about the way the lure-line was wound. It had to be done in figure-of-eight fashion, the same way that a gardener's line is wound. Nothing infuriated him more than if someone just did it round and round, for then it might jam when he wanted it in a hurry, and if the culprit were in earshot, woe betide him, for he soon knew he was not in favour.

It wasn't that Unk was fussy about the way he liked things done; in fact he was most untidy as a rule and once returned from one of his American trips to discover a chicken's head still in the pocket of a coat. It was a bit fruity and his pocket was full of maggots by then. Like most untidy people, he preferred to have his things left alone, for apart from his spectacles, which, like everyone else's, were always lost, he knew where he had put things even if it was in a different place each time. But when it came to falconry he insisted on having things done his way, because he had tried others and learnt from bitter experience which was the most efficient.

I use the term bitter experience only too feelingly, for falconry is a very exacting sport that tends to make you pay rather heavily at times for a mistake. An apparently trivial error may result in a lost hawk, and may well mean hours or even days of searching before she is found, possibly even permanent loss.

The lure having been made up under Unk's supervision, and checked by him to ensure that all the knots were tight (for if the lure came loose the falcon might carry it away with her), we hooded them up and took them across the road into the park.

Here there was an area of short grass, close-cropped by sheep and suitable for our purpose. A falcon on a line, or creance as it is called, gets caught up easily if the grass is long, or there are tussocks or thistles round which she can get tangled.

We stuck an old fence-post into the ground and put Bonus, unhooded, on this perch. Unk unwound the creance as he walked back a short way, then, whistling to Bonus to attract her attention, he threw the lure out on to the grass a few yards in front of her. She bobbed her head up and down in the curious way that all the falcon tribe have when they are particularly interested in a thing. Not sure what the lure meant, she looked away. Unk gave it a short jerk, which drew it a few inches towards him, and the movement of it attracted her again. This time she saw the meat and, after bobbing her head again and opening and closing her wings a few times, she flew down on to the lure in a clumsy, cumbersome way. She leant down looking at it closely and then struck at it with one foot and remained there looking rather foolish, not knowing quite what it was all about.

Unk stood there watching her, making no attempt to move to pick her up in case he frightened her, as she might then try to carry the lure away to eat it uninterrupted. Once a falcon starts to carry, it soon becomes a habit, and the owner looks very silly if she takes it into an unclimbable tree and sits there eating it, ignoring both blandishments and unprintable remarks. This sort of thing generally happens when you are trying to show an important guest just how good your falcon is and how well you have trained her. So bad habits must be avoided, for once started they are almost impossible to eradicate. A falcon can only be coerced; she cannot be corrected by chastisement or admonishment, as a dog can.

So we stood and waited till Bonus got hold of the lure with both feet and began to eat. Then Unk slowly moved in towards her. Every time she stopped feeding he stood still till she started again. She was not unduly suspicious of him, and when he was within a few feet of her he knelt down on one knee and offered her a piece of meat in his gloved hand. She tried to eat from this, but, as he let her pull it towards her every time she pecked at it, she finally had to put one foot on it to hold it down. He raised his glove slightly then, so that she let go of the lure in order to put her other foot up and get herself comfortable. He now lifted her right up, at the same time deftly popping the lure into his bag with his free hand. The whole action was so neatly done that Bonus never realized she had lost the lure.

He gave her some of the meat from his glove as her reward and put her back on the post. Then he waited till she had finished picking the odd bits of meat from her toes and was in the right frame of mind to pay attention to him. Again he whistled and threw out the lure, but this time the distance she had to fly was increased by a few yards. She came almost immediately, so quickly had she learnt her lesson. The slow procedure of making in was again gone through, but this time she was offered small pieces of meat from his hand and was left on the lure to continue her meal for a time, while Unk untied the creance from her swivel and replaced the leash.

Every so often he offered her extra pieces from his hand, and soon she looked eager whenever his hand came near. When she had eaten half her daily ration he persuaded her on to his fist again, where he gave her the remainder of her meal. In this way she learnt that the lure meant food, but did not forget the fist. He hooded her, and it was now time for me to try Cheetah, who had been hooded all this time so that she would not be jealous of Bonus.

Cheetah took longer to grasp the meaning of the lure, but the second time she was called off the post she came while I was still swinging the lure in the air and I had to throw it out to her quickly.

We walked back across the park, both very pleased. Even though my falcon had only flown a short way to the lure, the knowledge that she did so solely because I had taught her, gave me a feeling of immense satisfaction and pride.

Rescue Operation

Desmond Varaday

All too often it has been man who has caused tragedy and destruction in the world of Nature. But Nature has her own tragedies, and sometimes man comes to the rescue, as in this instance.

There is a wonderland of wild bush country in the triangle of the Shashi and Limpopo Rivers – a broad wedge which forms the east border of the Bechuanaland Protectorate where I was warden of a private reserve. This fifty square miles of territory is a wild-life paradise, with roaming herds of elephant, led by venerable old bulls with almost 200 pounds of ivory in their huge tusks; eland, kudu, and impala mix with troops of zebra and wildebeest, while the great hunting-cats live here in luxury on Nature's fully stocked larder.

Dangers await the unwary, and often the four-footed hunters become the hunted too – as on that late afternoon at the Limpopo when I was taking water-level readings on marked poles near the shore.

An almost imperceptible furrow on the water's surface gave the signal. The movement was directly ahead near a pole in deeper water, and could only have been caused by the tail of a crocodile. This was no unusual occurrence, for nearly all of Africa's waters house crocodiles, but in this case I hastily withdrew to the bank, for by the way the murky water churned under that furrow, it was clear that a huge reptile lurked there, a menace to any living creature that might venture to the water's edge.

While I made the requisite notes on the readings, some thirty yards upwind a magnificent cheetah stepped out of cover, testing the wind with highheld shiny nose. Satisfied, it walked obliquely down to where I had been only a few minutes earlier.

Then as the cheetah slowly lapped up water, it found itself looking into the glassy yellow-green eyes of the huge crocodile, which had been approaching the shore since it had first seen me. The cheetah uttered a sharp bird-like cry of surprise.

For one instant the flat nose and the eyes of the reptile looked like any of the numerous small rocks pitting the water's surface; in the next, there was a terrible commotion as the crocodile sped through the narrow space of shallows separating it from its intended victim. The great wide mouth opened in a loathsome caricature of a smile, and then the jagged teeth clamped together over the cheetah's head. The victim never had a chance.

The water boiled during the momentary tug of war. The hapless hunting-cat fought desperately to free itself. But the attacker was dragging it into the water, where it could hold its prize until it drowned.

I lifted my ·375 Magnum H. & H. sporting rifle and fired a snap shot at the reptile's head. The crocodile was submerged only a few inches below the surface. Water splashed at the impact and I clearly heard the 'flup' of the bullet striking and then the whine of a ricochet.

The monster reared up, dropping the cheetah, and fell backwards into the water with a resounding crack. But it seemed to be dazed only temporarily, for it made its way off rapidly. By the chain fastened to its right armpit, I recognized Mulembe, the sacred crocodile of the Ba-Kwena tribe, who, several decades before, used to come out of the water in response to the call of his worshippers to be fed and honoured. Long since, however, the tribe had become civilized, leaving Mulembe to provide his own fare.

After the shot, I reloaded at once and ran across the sand to see if I could help the cheetah. It was lying in the shallows – dead. Its head had been terribly mauled by those powerful jaws. I noticed with regret that the cheetah was a nursing mother; her teats were swollen with milk. She had hoped, it seemed, to drink a sundowner before returning to feed her family. Her death was just one of many unrecorded tragedies daily enacted in the wild bushlands of Africa.

Since cheetahs are clannish animals, living and hunting in pairs or families, it was likely that the male would automatically take on the task of feeding the cubs if the mother failed to return to the nursery. The only question was whether the cubs were old enough to feed on what the father could provide. I was curious to find out.

The report of my shot brought Freddie, my Tswana tracker, to the spot. He carried the cheetah's carcase to our Land Rover. I was not happy to have it on hand, for cheetahs are Royal Game – protected by law – and to have its pelt around my quarters could have led to unfair conclusions. But then I realized that its head injuries would be visible, and so I had the pelt pegged out to dry in the camp. That was the action which led to our finding the cubs.

On the second night after the tragedy, I awoke to the sound of a plaintive miaow, a cheetah call. Rex, my fox terrier bitch who had recently had a litter, lifted her head and gave a low growl.

The cheetah's cry had come from close by. I suspected it was the male calling its dead mate, for these large hunting-cats are very shy and normally avoid a camp.

I must have dropped off to sleep again, because I was awakened now by the eerie moaning wails of hyenas: 'Aar-u-ee, aar-u-eee' they complained. The hideous cries came nearer and nearer the camp. After several minutes of quiet a sudden burst of savage snarling, growls, and cat-like spitting rent the night air. In half a minute it was over. All was silent. But not for long. There came a fresh outburst – this time wilder.

Taking my flashlight and my rifle I went out, Rex following. There was a wild rush of shadowy forms; eyes shone green in the flashlight beam; then came the crazy laughter-like howl of disturbed hyenas: 'Ti-tatata, tita-tatata.'

A yellowish body dashed through the grass and out of sight. It was a large cheetah: there was no mistaking its long-legged bound and long thick tail. Rex rushed into the scrub to scare away the hyenas who appeared intent on stealing the dead cheetah's pelt which the male had apparently been defending.

At sunrise we read the spoors – the newsprint of the bush – and saw that the cheetah had come upon the scent of his missing mate, approached the camp while calling to her, and at lack of response had come into the camp and found her pegged-out pelt. In the meantime hyenas had also come on the scent.

Two or three hungry hyenas together often become daring, as these had. Many a time they had passed through camp at night snatching away biltong, fleshy oddments and supper left-overs, bones and even old skins. This time there was a fierce guardian to keep them from the drying pelt.

In the scuffle the cheetah had obviously received a bite, for on his spoor we found drops of blood. Freddie (an expert in bush-craft), Rex and I followed the spoor on foot. We must have gone nearly five miles into gradually thinning bush, losing the spoor, then finding it again, before we came upon a wide depression in the ground. It was densely covered with tall green grass. In the middle of the depression stood a solitary marula tree. Freddie indicated the tree with his eye. We stood and listened – to the unmistakable squeals of hungry cubs. This was the cheetah's lair.

A 'koto-koto' – yellow-billed hornbill – was sitting on one of the high branches. When we moved forward, it gave the alarm. I saw the father cheetah slink away from the lair to draw us off the track of the cubs. At the same instant the koto-koto winged off, protesting loudly at our intrusion.

The long grass, fallen leaves, and dead branches under the marula tree did not afford a hiding place for a pair of grown cheetahs, but the cubs were so well hidden by a branch that, but for Rex, we would probably not have found them. They must have heard the fall of our steps, for they lay still and silent – a litter of three.

A few feet away on a clear patch there were small mounds of chewed meat, evidently regorged by the father. None of the mounds appeared to have been touched. For lack of teats and mother's milk, the parent instinctively did what he thought the next best thing. But such food was for cubs many weeks older than these.

I realized that although the father was trying, he would be unable to save the cubs, and so I decided to take them. By their size and unspotted tawny grey-coloured fur, we judged them to be no more than a couple of weeks old. They had not received nourishment now for over two days, and as I picked up two of them it was obvious that they were famished, for they were as light as bundles of feathers.

I made Rex lie down beside the cubs, and I put the three starved orphans to her teats. As soon as the cubs began to swarm on her, nuzzling her underside hungrily, Rex lifted her lips in a warning snarl. I stroked her and cajoled, and at length my words and possibly her motherly instinct got the better of her repulsion for the strange litter. She let the cubs suckle. For a while noisy feeding was heard.

One of the three, the only female cub, appeared to be the liveliest and fiercest of them all. She had emptied a teat and high-handedly fought one and then the other of her brothers for possession of the remaining milk faucets. She succeeded in getting them, too. I had to laugh at her antics, and, despite her sex, there and then named her Cheeky Charlie. Freddie shook his head in disapproval of the name.

While we carried the cubs back to camp, I wondered whether Rex was sufficiently equipped to cope with three additional boarders. Her two healthy pups were always ravenous and there was possibly not enough milk for the newcomers.

Once home, Rex refused absolutely to accept the duties of foster mother. So I had to adopt them and care for the orphans. I groomed them by brushing out their matted fur and wiping them over with a warm, damp cloth. We fed the brood every two hours on powdered milk mixed with water and administered with an eyedropper. It was a long and tedious performance, because we had only one dropper. By the time I had completed the round, the first one was almost due for another feed. It was a full-time job.

To remedy the unavoidable running stomachs, I mixed finely powdered charcoal with the milk and added a pinch of bismuth. Diarrhoea, however, got the upper hand. I then resorted to chlorodine, the taste of which did not quite make feeding an unqualified success.

Cheeky Charlie had the 'I want to live' instinct and the stronger constitution of a female. She took to the artificial nourishment and, in a way, flourished. Her brothers barely existed and began to look dehydrated and scruffy. I had fears for their survival.

In fact, from the very first day I had doubts about the smaller of the two. After a few days, while feeding him I found that the milk was coming back through his nostrils. On examining his mouth I noticed that he had something like a cleft palate which diverted much of every pull of food to his nose. In the second week he died.

Rex still determinedly refused to assist with the feeding. At night she would stealthily remove her pups from the basket, leaving squeaking cheetah cubs to huddle together for communal warmth. When this warmth proved insufficient, the cubs protested loudly, waking me. I gave Rex a dark look but she always pretended a deep sleep, though I knew she was shamming. Eventually there was nothing to do but to take the cubs into bed with me. One at a time I popped them under the blanket and pushed them down to my feet. When they were snug I would try to continue the broken night's rest. They remained quiet and slept, pressed against my feet. The nights were getting colder.

Food was the all-important commodity for my fluffy pair, and they made their demands known as long as they were awake. Freddie shared the duties of feeding because I could no longer cope alone. One day, he took one of the cubs out of the basket and stood holding it in his arm while putting the feeder, a lemonade bottle fitted with a rubber teat, to the cub's mouth. The hungry little thing lunged forward and slipped from Freddie's grasp, falling with a dull thud on the hard floor. Its tender young body was internally injured, and after that it refused all food. In spite of our efforts to nurse it back to health, it faded away. Both Freddie and I were very upset at the loss of the cub.

I have never heard of cheetahs breeding in captivity and it seemed that even those born in the wilds were difficult to rear.

Now the only survivor was the female: still as lively and demanding as on the first day. She accepted the feeding device as naturally as though it were the real thing, wrapping her tongue around the teat and holding the bottle with forepaws, purring and suckling contentedly on it long after it was empty, like an old man sucking a pipe. She allowed only me to feed her, spitting and striking out at all who came near her.

I suppose the name Cheeky Charlie would have remained hers had not a primitive, dishevelled specimen – a detribalized Bushman – arrived at my camp to seek employment as a game scout. I was busy feeding the little cub when Freddie escorted the man to me. As no African is more cunning in the craft of tracking than a Bushman, I engaged him. The way Piet looked at the cub convinced me immediately that he was a keen animal-lover and had a passion for handling wild game. Respectfully he asked permission to stroke the cub: this I granted.

But Piet had hardly reached out to stroke the cub's head when

she spat at him so fiercely and loudly that he instinctively withdrew his hand. He laughed at the savagery of the small unspotted
fur-ball, and also at his own fright. 'Ow!' he exclaimed. 'This is
Gara-Yaka, mother of the monsters and the ghosts that walk by
night!'

And from then on she was called Gara-Yaka. In a short while
her ears became so attuned to the sound of this name that she
answered to no other.

Somehow Rex had become less harsh to the lone cub. She even
permitted the cheetah to share the family basket. I was surprised
to find Gara-Yaka also sharing Rex's milk with the pups, but she
condescended to accept this belated hospitality only during the
daytime. The nights she still spent with me, smuggled under the
bedclothes, occasionally coming up for air.

Soon she was running and gambolling around with the pups,
an absolute picture of health and happiness, scratching at fleas as
vigorously as the dogs did. She had learned how to ask to be
picked up: she would stretch her long arms, place them on me,
and look until I gathered her up.

At three months Gara-Yaka was big. She appropriated the dog
basket, using it as her daytime apartment. She was always quick
to mete out punishment to the dogs if they ventured too near the
comfortable basket.

My pet was by now a cuddlesome, feline beauty, with long
gangling dog legs. She was a strange mixture of dog and cat.
Polka dots were becoming clearly defined on her tawny, golden
side. The fur on her rounded belly was creamy, the texture of
swan's-down.

As on grown cheetahs, Gara-Yaka's head was her most typical

feature. The lyre-shaped black lines were already fully marked on her cheeky face, starting at the inner corner of her eyes and ending at her upper lip, where, like badly applied make-up, the 'tear-stain' became smudged and lost in the growing whiskers. She was still quite fluffy, and her loose coat was well padded with puppy-fat. By the day she grew more affectionate.

At about this time she began serious bouts of hide-and-seek with her stepbrothers. It was mostly she who stalked. Instinct gave her the know-how. The game usually ended with a rush and a charge in which the pups were caught at a hopeless disadvantage. They rolled over with stumbling clumsiness. But there were times when they came on Gara-Yaka unexpectedly, and this scared her. I noticed that she was easily frightened. On these occasions, she would rise to her full height, get up on her toes, arch her back, and stretch her tail out stiff, its hairs bristling like a bottle brush, and then hop sideways, stiff-legged. Then she would get even with the pups by spitting at them and cuffing them repeatedly. At times when they charged her she raced up a tree like a cat, still with that wild look in her eyes.

This appeared to be the age for ratifying established relationships. She spat and growled at all Bantu except Freddie and Piet, whom she accepted as part and parcel of the camp.

To all intents and purposes I was still Mama, and this was confirmed daily when she clambered into my lap while I was relaxing. She would creep up to my chest and lie there, purring in a strange, deep, throaty gurgle and 'making puddings' – kneading me with her semi-retractile claws. Then the real caressing would begin: she would rub her face against my cheeks and gaze into my eyes. In bright sunlight her large eyes shone like polished jasper.

Her attitude towards Rex became very frivolous, and gradually she looked upon the mother dog as an equal. In spite of the dog's cool superiority and occasional chastisement – in what seemed to be a last effort on Rex's part to establish her waning authority – the cheetah accepted no such discipline.

When Gara-Yaka was with the dogs, she considered herself one of them, even trying to behave like them. She learned everything and did everything the dogs could do, except bark. Her voice remained that of a big cat.

Then there were times when Gara-Yaka behaved like a human baby, especially when she lay on my chest. She made no secret of her own belief that I was still Mother, and that she lived only to love me. I had noticed this very deep affection among wild cheetahs, who, at the finish of a meal, with much ado, lick each other's face clean and then lie sleeping with arms and legs entwined like human lovers.

My cheetah did this to her foster brothers, who, although visibly disliking this sort of familiarity, put up with it for the sake of peace, while lifting their lips in a warning grimace. Gara-Yaka would have one or the other pup by the throat and gently but firmly squeeze her jaws together to force the pup to accept whatever she was meting out. The happy family circle would then break up with much squealing and howling on the part of the dogs. At this, Gara-Yaka would be thoroughly fed up with the unsporting attitude of the pups and come and join me. She was obviously self-willed and independent, her wild heritage showing through her every act.

Wherever I went, she came too. I had no choice, for she would follow anyway. The moment she opened her eyes in the morning, she would greet me with an affectionate whistle-like miaow. She shared my tea, lapping out of my saucer, but if I was too slow pouring hers first, she would firmly but politely remind me of my negligence by placing her paw on the tray, almost upsetting it. Even when the saucer was empty, she made quite sure that no dregs were left: she held it firm while she ran her tongue over it looking for the last drop, tea-leaves and all.

Eventually, Gara-Yaka was weaned from her liquid diet to solids. At the first attempt I chopped the meat finely for her. To my consternation she would not even look at it. Taking a leaf from her father's book, I chewed raw liver for her, but achieved similar results. The raw offal tasted horrible, but anything for a good cause!

Patiently I dipped my finger into the chewed bloody mess and smeared it across her lips. Surprisingly she took my finger in her mouth and sucked off the blood. This manoeuvre, repeated three or four times, comprised the meal. Later I purposely dropped minced liver on the floor. She picked up the small lumps, and from then on she took to raw meat almost eagerly. Her survival as a carnivore was thus assured.

Gara-Yaka's happy relationship with the Game Warden continued, and half-tame, half-wild, she grew up in the reserve and eventually mated and became a mother.

The Forest by Night

Gerald Durrell

Capturing wild animals for zoos is an arduous and sometimes hazardous job, but it has its lighter moments – at least seen through the eyes of this well-known zoo-man. Here he is at work on an expedition to the Cameroons in West Africa.

The results of our days spent hunting in the forest, and the prodigious efforts of the villagers for miles around, soon filled my cages to overflowing, and then I found my whole day taken up with looking after the animals. The only time I had for hunting was after the day's work was done, and so it was that we took to hunting at night with the aid of torches. I had brought four great torches out from England with me, and these threw a very strong beam of light. I supplemented our lighting with four more torches purchased on arrival in the Cameroons. Armed with this battery of lights we would scour the forest from midnight to three o'clock in the morning, and by this method we obtained a number of nocturnal beasts which we would otherwise never have seen.

The forest at night was a very different place from the forest by day: everything seemed awake and watchful, and eyes gleamed in the treetops above you. Rustles and squeaks came from the undergrowth, and by the light of the torch you could see a creeper swaying and twitching, indication of some movement one hundred and fifty feet above you in the black treetops. Ripe fruit would patter down on to the forest floor, and dead twigs would fall. The cicadas, who never seemed to sleep, would be screeching away, and occasionally a big bird would start a loud 'Car . . . carr . . . carr' cry, which would echo through the forest. One of the commonest night noises was caused by an animal which I think was a tree hyrax. It would start off its piercing whistle softly, at regular intervals, then gradually it would work faster and faster until the sounds almost merged, and the whistle would get shriller and shriller. Then, just as it reached a top note and its highest speed, the cry would stop, as though cut short with a knife, leaving the air still quivering with the echoes of the cry. Then there were the frogs and toads: as darkness fell they would start, whistling, hooting, rattling, chirruping and croaking. They seemed to be everywhere, from the tops of the highest trees, to the smallest holes under the rocks on the river banks.

The forest seemed twice as big as normal when you were hunting at night: you moved along under the great, rustling canopy of trees, and outside your torch beam everything was a solid wall of blackness. Only in the small pool of light cast by your torch could you see colour, and then, in this false light, the leaves and the grasses seemed to take on an ethereal silvery-green hue. You felt as though you were moving in the darkest depths of the sea, where there had been no light for a million years, and the pathetically feeble glow of your torch showed up the monstrous curling buttress roots of the trees, and faded the coloration of the leaves, and the silver moths fluttered in groups across the beam, and vanished into the gloom like a silvery school of tiny fish. The air was heavy and damp with dew, and by shining your torch beam upwards, until it was lost in the intricate maze of trunks and branches above, you could see the faint wisps of mist coiling sluggishly through the twigs and creepers. Everywhere the heavy black shadows played you false, making tall slender trees seem to crouch on deformed trunks; the tree roots twisted and writhed as you moved, seeming to slide away into the darkness, so that you could swear they were alive. It was mysterious, creepy, and completely fascinating.

The first night I ventured into the forest with Andraia and Elias we started early, for Elias insisted that we hunted along the banks of a largish river which was some distance from the camp. Here, he assured me, we would find water-beef. What this beast was I had only the haziest notion, for the hunters employed this term with great freedom when discussing anything from a hippo to a frog. All I could get out of Elias was that it was 'very fine beef', and that I would be 'glad too much' if we caught one. We had progressed about a mile down the path that led into the forest, and we had just left the last of the palm plantations behind, when Elias suddenly came to a halt, and I walked heavily on to his heels. He was shining his torch into the head foliage of a small tree about forty feet high. He walked about, shining his torch from different angles, grunting to himself.

'Na whatee?' I asked, in a hoarse whisper.

'Na rabbit, sah,' came back the astonishing reply.

'A *rabbit* . . . are you *sure*, Elias?' I asked in surprise.

'Yes sah, na rabbit for true. 'E dere dere for up, sah, you no see 'e dere dere for stick?'

While I flashed my torch about at the tops of the trees I hastily ran over my knowledge of the Cameroon fauna: I was sure no rabbit had been recorded from the Cameroons, and I was certain an arboreal one had not been recorded from *any* part of the world. I presumed that a rabbit sitting in the top branches of a forty-foot tree could be termed arboreal with some justification. Just at that moment two ruby-red spots appeared in my beam: I had located the 'rabbit'. There, sitting peacefully on a branch high above us, nonchalantly cleaning its whiskers in the torch light, sat a fat grey-coloured rat.

'That's a rat, Elias, not a rabbit,' I said, rather pleased to find my zoological knowledge still secure. The appearance of an arboreal rabbit in the zoological world would, I felt, cause rather a stir.

'Na rat, sah? Here we call um rabbit.'

'Well, can we catch him, do you think?'

'Yes, sah. Masa and Andraia go wait here, I go climb de stick.'

We kept our torches aimed at the rat, and Elias disappeared into the darkness. Presently the tree began to shake as an indication that he had started to climb, and the rat peered downwards in alarm. Then it ran to the end of the small branch it was sitting on and peered down again to get a better view. Elias's head came into view among the leaves directly below the branch on which the rat was sitting. 'Which side 'e dere?' he enquired, screwing up his eyes against the light.

'E dere dere for up, on your left side.'

As we shouted our instructions the rat slid down a creeper with great speed and landed on a branch about fifteen feet below Elias.

''E done run, Elias,' screamed Andraia shrilly, ''e dere dere for under you now . . .'

Painfully, following our shouted directions, Elias descended until he was on a level with the rat. The quarry was still sitting on the branch, putting the finishing touches to his toilet. Slowly Elias edged his way out along the branch towards him, one hand cupped ready to grab. The rat watched him in a supercilious manner, waited until Elias lunged forward, and then launched itself into space. Instinctively we followed it with our torches, and watched it crash into a small bush and disappear. From above came a crack, a roar of anguish and fright, and the sound of a heavy body descending slowly and painfully earthwards. Flashing our torches up we found Elias had disappeared, and only a few leaves fluttered slowly down to show that he had once been up there. We found him nursing his leg in the bushes at the base of the tree.

'Eh . . . aehh!' he groaned, 'dat stick no give me chance. It done broke, and I de get wound plenty.'

Careful examination disclosed only a few scratches, and after soothing Elias's hurt feelings we proceeded on our way.

We had been walking some time and carrying on a lively discussion on the difference between rabbits and rats, when I found we were walking on white sand. Looking up, I discovered that we had left the forest, and above us was the night sky, its blackness intensified by the flickering stars. We were actually walking along the banks of the river, but I had not noticed it, for here the brown waters flowed sluggishly between smooth banks, and so there was no babble of water; the river flowed slowly and silently past us like a great snake. Presently we left the sand beach and made our way to the thick fringe of waist-high growth that formed a border between the sand and the beginning of the forest. Here we paused.

'Na for dis kind of place you go catch water-beef, sah,' whispered Elias, while Andraia grunted in agreement. 'We go walk softly softly for dis place, and sometime we go find um.'

So we commenced to walk softly, softly through the lush undergrowth, shining our torches ahead. I had just paused to pluck a small tree frog from a leaf and push him into the bottle in my pocket, when Elias hurled his torch at me and dived full length into the leaves. In my efforts to catch his torch as it whirled towards me I dropped my own, which hit a rock and promptly went out. I bungled the catch, dropped the second torch as well, and that followed the first into oblivion. Now we only had the illumination of Andraia's, which was very anaemic, for the batteries were damp and old. Elias was rolling about in the undergrowth locked in mortal combat with some creature that seemed frightfully strong. I grabbed the light from Andraia, and in the feeble glow I saw Elias rolling about, and held in his arms, kicking and bucking for all it was worth, was a beautiful antelope, its skin patterned with a lovely pattern of white spots and stripes.

'I done hold um, sah,' roared Elias, spitting leaves, 'bring flashlamp, sah, quickly, dis beef get power too much . . .'

I sprang forward eagerly to help him, tripped heavily over a hidden rock and fell on my face. The last torch flickered and went out. I sat up in the gloom and searched frantically for the torch. I could hear Elias desperately imploring someone to help him. Then as my groping fingers found a light, a sudden silence fell. I switched on the torch, after several attempts, and shone it on Elias. He was sitting mournfully on his ample bottom getting leaves out of his mouth. ''E done run, sah,' he said. 'Sorry too much, sah, but dat beef get power pass one man. Look, sah, 'e done give me wound with his foot.' He pointed to his chest, and it was covered with long deep furrows from which the blood was trickling. These had been caused by the sharp, kicking hooves of the little antelope.

'Never mind,' I said, mopping his chest with the iodine, 'we go catch dis beef some other time.'

After a search we found the other two torches, and discovered that both bulbs had been broken by the fall. I had forgotten to bring any spare ones and so our only means of illumination was the third torch, which looked as though it was going to give out at any minute. It was plain that all we could do was to call off the hunt and get back to camp while we still had some means of seeing our way. Very depressed we set off, walking as fast as we could by such a poor light.

As we entered the fields on the outskirts of the village Elias stopped and pointed at a dead branch which hung low over the path. I peered at it hopefully, but it was quite bare, with one dead and withered leaf attached to it.

'Whattee?'

'Dere, for dat dead stick, sah.'

'I no see um . . .'

Disturbed by our whispering the dead leaf took its head out from under its wing, gave us a startled glance, and then flew wildly off into the night.

'Na bird, sah,' explained Elias.

It was, altogether, a most unsuccessful night, but it was interesting, and showed me what to expect. The fact that the birds slept so close to the ground amazed me, when there were so many huge trees about in which they could roost. But a little thought showed me why they did this: perched on the end of a long slender twig they knew that, should anything try and crawl along after them, its weight would shake the branch or even break it. So, as long as the branch was long, thin, and fairly isolated, it mattered not if it was a hundred feet up, or five feet from the ground. I questioned Elias closely about this, and he informed me that one frequently came across birds perched as low as that, especially in the farm lands. So the next night, armed with large soft cloth bags, we set out to scour the fields. I was armed with a butterfly net with which to do the actual capturing.

We had not gone far when we found a bulbul seated on a thin branch about five feet above us, an almost indistinguishable ball of grey fluff against the background of leaves. While the other two kept their torches trained on it, I manoeuvred my net into position and made a wild scoop. I don't suppose the bulbul had ever had such a fright in its life; at any rate it flew off into the darkness tweeting excitedly. It was then I realized that the upward sweeping motion I had employed was the wrong one. So we went a bit further, and presently came across a pygmy kingfisher slumbering peacefully. I scooped the net down on him, he was borne to the ground, and within a couple of seconds was in the depths of a cloth bag. Birds, if placed in a dark bag like this, just lie there limp and relaxed, and do not flutter and hurt themselves during transportation. I was thrilled with this new method of adding to my bird collection, as it seemed far superior to the other methods employed. We spent three hours in the fields that night, and during that time we caught five birds: the kingfisher, two forest robins, a blue-spotted dove, and a bulbul. After this, if I was feeling too tired to wander into the forest at night, we would just walk for an hour or so in the fields a mile or two from the camp, and it was rarely that we returned empty-handed.

Elias felt very deeply the loss of the water-beef, and it was not long afterwards that he suggested we should again hunt by the river, mentioning as additional bait, that he knew of some caves in that area. So we set off at about eight o'clock one night, determined to spend all the hours of darkness in pursuit of beef. The night did not start well, for a few miles into the forest we came to the dead stump of a great tree. It had died and remained standing, as nearly all these giants did, until it was hollowed out by insects and the weather into a fine shell. Then the weight of the mass of dead branches at the top was too much, and it snapped the trunk off about thirty feet from the ground, leaving the base standing on its buttress roots like a section of a factory chimney, only much more interesting and aesthetically satisfying. Half-way up this stump was a large hole, and as we passed our torches caught the gleam of eyes from its dark interior. We stopped and held a hasty consultation: as before, Andraia and I kept our torches trained on the hole, while Elias went round the other side of the trunk to see if he could climb up. He returned quickly to say that he was too short to reach the only available footholds, and so Andraia would have to do the climbing. Andraia disappeared round the trunk and, shortly after, scraping noises and subdued ejaculations of 'Eh . . . aehh!' announced that he was on his way up. Elias and I moved a bit closer, keeping our torches steady on the hole. Andraia was two-thirds of the way up when the occupant of the hole showed itself: a large civet. Its black-masked face blinked down at us, and I caught a glimpse of its grey, black-spotted body. Then it drew back into the hole again.

'Careful, Andraia, na bush-cat,' whispered Elias warningly, for a full-grown civet is the size of a small collie dog.

But Andraia was too busy to answer, for clinging to the bark of the trunk with fingers and prehensile toes was a full-time job. Just as he reached the edge of the hole the civet launched itself out into space like a rocket. It shot through the air, and landed accurately on Elias's chest with all four feet, its weight sending him spinning backwards. As it landed on his chest I saw its mouth open and close, and heard the chop of its jaws. It only missed making its teeth meet in his face because he was already off his balance and starting to fall backwards, and so its jaws missed him by about three inches. It leapt lightly off his prostrate body, paused for one brief moment to stare at me, and then in a couple of swift leaps disappeared into the forest. Elias picked himself up and grinned at me ruefully:

''Eh . . . aehh! Some man done put bad *ju-ju* for dis hunting I tink,' he said. 'First we lose water-beef next dis bush-cat . . .'

'Consider yourself lucky you've still got a face left,' I said, for I had been considerably shaken by this display of ferocity on the part of the civet, an animal I had always thought was shy and retiring. Just at that moment a strangled yelp came from above us, and we shone our torches up to where Andraia was clinging like a lanky black spider.

'Na whatee?' asked Elias and I together.

'Na something else dere dere for inside,' said Andraia shrilly. 'I hear noise for inside hole . . .' He felt in his loin-cloth, and with some difficulty he withdrew his torch and shone it into the hole.

'Eh . . . aehh!' he shouted, 'na picken bush-cat here for inside.'

For a long time Andraia performed the most extraordinary contortions to try and cling on to the tree, while shining the torch
into the hole with one hand and endeavouring to insert the other
into the hole to catch the baby. At length he succeeded, and his
hand came into view holding a spitting, squirming young civet
by the tail. Just as he got it out of the hole and was shouting,
'Look um, look um,' in triumph, the baby bit him in the wrist.

Now Andraia was a complete coward about pain: if he got the
smallest thorn in his foot he would put on an exaggerated limp
as though he had just had all his toes amputated. So the sharp
baby teeth of the civet were like so many hot needles in his wrist.
Uttering an unearthly shriek he dropped the torch, the civet,
and released his precarious hold on the tree. He, the torch, and
the civet crashed earthwards.

How Andraia was not killed by the fall I shall never know: the
torch was smashed, and the baby civet landed on its head on one
of the iron-hard buttress roots of the tree, and was knocked unconscious. It had a severe haemorrhage about ten minutes later
and died without regaining consciousness. Andraia, apart from
being severely shaken, was unhurt.

'Eh . . . aehh! Na true some man done put *ju-ju* for us,' said
Elias again. Whether it was *ju-ju* or not, we were not worried by
ill-luck for the rest of the night: on the contrary, we had very
good luck. Shortly after our little affair with the civet we came to
the banks of a wide stream, about three feet deep in the middle.
The water was opaque, a deep chocolate brown colour, and even
our torch beams could not pierce it. We had to wade up this
stream for about half a mile, until we came to the path on the
opposite bank which we were following. Though the surface of

the stream was unruffled, there was a considerable undercurrent, and we felt it clutch our legs as we waded in. The water was ice-cold. We had reached the centre and were wading along as swiftly as the deep water and the current would let us, when I became aware that we were not the only occupants of the stream. All around us, coiling and shooting through the dark waters, were dozens of brown water snakes. They swam curiously along-side us, with only their heads showing above water, their tiny eyes glittering in the torch light. Andraia became conscious of the snakes' presence at the same moment, but his reactions were not the same as mine.

'Warr!!' he screamed, and dropping the collecting bag he was carrying, he tried to run for the bank. He had forgotten the water. Here it was almost waist high, and any attempt at running was doomed to failure almost before it was started. As I had antici-pated, the strength of the current caught him off his balance, and he fell into the water with a splash that sent every water-snake diving for cover. He surfaced some yards downstream, and struggled to his feet. His lovely sarong, which he had been carefully carrying on his head to protect it, was now a sodden mass.

'Na whatee?' asked Elias, turning round and surveying Andraia, wallowing in the stream like a wounded whale. He, apparently, had not seen the snakes.

'Na snake, Elias,' spluttered Andraia, 'na snake *too much* for dis water. Why we no fit pass for land?'

'Snake?' asked Elias, shining his torch about the calm waters.

'Na true, Elias,' I said, 'na water-snake. Andraia de fear too much.'

'Eh . . . aehh!' exclaimed Elias wrathfully. 'You stupid man, Andraia. You no savvay dis beef no go bite you if Masa be here?'

'Ah!' said Andraia, humbly, 'I done forget dis ting.'

'What's all this?' I asked. 'Why snake no bite Andraia if I'm here?'

Standing in the middle of the stream while Andraia fished about for the collecting bag, Elias explained to me:

'If black man go for water him only, some kind of bad beef, like snake, go smell him, he go come one time and chop him. If black man go for water with white man, de beef smell de white man and he de fear too much, so he no go come.'

'Only when we go for water dis ting happen?' I asked.

'Yes, sah.'

It was a useful piece of knowledge, and I stored it away in my memory for future use. Andraia had by now collected all the things he had dropped, and I suggested that we should turn out the torches and wait to see if the water-snakes returned and, if they did, try to catch some. With a certain lack of enthusiasm my hunters agreed. We stood there in the water, in complete darkness, for about half an hour and then, at a prearranged signal, we all switched on our torches together. All around us were water-snakes, weaving silver patterns in the torchlight. Seizing the net I plunged after the nearest, and after a scramble, managed to get him hissing and wriggling into the net, and from there into the bag. Thus encouraged, Elias and Andraia joined in and within a very short time we had captured twenty of these snakes. But now they were growing wise, and the slightest movement on our part would send them all diving to the murky depths of the river, so we called off the hunt and continued on our way.

I don't know what the attraction of that river was for these snakes, as I never saw them congregated in one spot in such numbers again. Often in the day, and also during our night hunts, we had waded long distances up rivers, but only occasionally had we seen an odd water-snake. In the half-mile we travelled up that stream we saw hundreds of them. It may have been some sort of mating gathering, or maybe a sudden abundance of food in that particular area which had attracted them. We never found out. Some weeks later we crossed the same stream at the same point during the night, and not a snake was to be seen. In places like this you come into contact with many enigmas of this sort, but, unfortunately, you have not the opportunity to investigate as fully as you would like. You can do little more than note them, and wonder about the reason. It is one of the most annoying things about collecting, that you have not the time to investigate these riddles and find an answer, fascinating though that investigation might prove.

We came at last to the place where we had our meeting with the 'water-beef', and though we beat the low growth thoroughly, we did not flush another. So we gave it up as a bad job and walked along the sandy banks towards the cliff where Elias said there were some caves. As we rounded the bleached carcase of a huge tree that had fallen across the bank, I saw something glowing on the sand ahead of us.

'Elias, na whatee dat?' I asked, pointing.

'Na fire, sah,' he replied.

'A fire, out here?'

'Yes, sah, I tink some hunter man sleep here.'

As we walked nearer I saw that the glow was caused by the

embers of a small fire. Next to the fire was a tiny, frail lean-to made out of saplings and creepers.

'Ahey!' called Elias, 'someone 'e dere dere?'

There was a stirring in the depths of the hut and a black face, sleep-crumpled, peered out at us.

'Na who?' asked the stranger, and I could see he was reaching for his muzzle-loader which lay beside him. Hastily we turned our torches on to ourselves so that he could see who we were.

'Eh . . . aehh!' he gasped. 'Na white man dis?'

'Yes,' said Elias, 'na white man dis.'

'What thing white man do for bush for night time?' asked the stranger, and I could see a suspicion dawning on his face that perhaps we were some sort of terrible *ju-ju* in disguise.

'We hunt for beef,' said Elias.

I kicked the dying fire into a small flame, sat down beside it and produced cigarettes. The stranger accepted one, but he still kept a hand on his gun.

We built up the fire and sat round it smoking, while Elias explained to the man who we were, and what we were doing, and from whence we came. The man, it transpired, was a wandering hunter. These men live in the forest, shooting what they can, and drying the meat. When they have as much as they can manage they trek into the nearest township and sell the meat at the market, buy fresh powder with the proceeds and set off to the bush again. This man had had very good luck, for he had shot four full-grown drills, and he showed us the dismembered bodies, dried by wood smoke. The largest male must have been a magnificent brute in life, and his dried arm, strangely like a mummy's, was knotted with great muscles. His hands and his skull with the flesh dried close to the bone looked decidedly human. We, in our turn, explained what we were doing, and showed the hunter the water-snakes, which he was not enthusiastic over. When we rose to go I dashed him four cigarettes and he, in turn, presented me with a drill leg, saying that it was 'very fine chop for white man and black'. I ate this leg in a stew, and the hunter was proved correct: it was very fine chop indeed, with a delicate and succulent flavour of beef with the faintest tang of wood smoke about it.

At last we came to the caves: they were in the face of a cliff heavily overgrown with ferns and moss, intermingled with the long creepers that hung down from the trees that grew on the top of the cliff. The usual tumbled mass of boulders littered the base, intergrown with shrubs and bushes. The largest cave was the size of a small room, and from it ran a number of narrow, low tunnels. These, however, were too small to allow us to crawl up them, so we had to content ourselves with lying on our stomachs and shining the torch up in the hopes of seeing something.

Presently we each took a section of the cliff and started a search on our own. I came to another series of these small tunnels, and as I walked along flashing my torch about, something leapt out of the undergrowth ahead and shot into one of them. I hurried to the spot, but I had not much hope of being able to corner whatever it was now that it had gained the sanctuary of its tunnel. Crouching down I shone the torch inside, and discovered that it was a false tunnel, that is to say it ran about eight feet back into the cliff face and then ceased abruptly. The floor of the tunnel was covered with various sized boulders, and the walls were gnarled and full of dark corners and crevices. I could not see the animal, but I presumed that it was hiding somewhere in there as there was, as far as I could see, no exit. Andraia and Elias were some distance away, and I did not like to shout to them to come and help as the more silently one worked the better one's chances of surprising an animal. So I lowered myself to the ground, hung the collecting bag round my neck, put the torch in my mouth, and proceeded to crawl up the tunnel on my stomach. This method is supposed to be the time-honoured one for stalking game, but I found it quite the most painful means of progression known to man. Erosion had given the boulders, which so liberally littered the floor of the tunnel, a razor-like cutting edge to their corners, and most of them had apparently been carefully designed to fit snugly into the more delicate parts of the human anatomy, and thus cause the maximum amount of pain.

I crawled on grimly until I reached the small circular 'room' at the end of the tunnel leading off into the depths of the earth. I struggled towards it, and as I reached its mouth a curious sound issued from it, a harsh, rustling rattle, a pause, two thumps, and then silence. I started to crawl closer when the rattling recommenced, a pause, the two thumps were repeated, and then silence. I hastily ran over the list of Cameroon fauna in my mind, but the noise did not seem to belong to anything that I knew of, so I continued my advance with increased caution. Reaching the tunnel I shone my torch inside and found to my surprise that it was also a cul-de-sac, only a much shorter one than the one I was in. As I was flashing my torch round in an effort to see what had produced the noise, there was another burst of rattling, something jumped forward, the torch was knocked out of my hand, and a sharp stinging pain assailed my fingers. I grabbed the torch and backed away hurriedly, and then sat down to examine my hand. On the back of it were a number of spots of blood, and a few deep scratches which now commenced to sting. It looked as though I had plunged my hand into a blackberry bush. I thought about this for a few minutes and then suddenly I realized what it was I had to deal with, one of the commonest animals in the Cameroons, and the only one that could make that noise: a brush-tailed porcupine. I was annoyed that I had not thought of it before.

I crawled back, and, with greater care, shone my torch in: there, sure enough, was the porcupine, standing half-turned to me, his spine bristling, and his curious tail rattling like mad. He would give a prolonged rattle on his tail, and then follow it up by stamping his hind feet petulantly, exactly as a rabbit will do when it is scared. He was about the size of a cat, though it was a little difficult to judge accurately, as his erect spines made him look larger. As all his spines pointed backwards he naturally had to stand with his bottom half turned to me, and he peered over his shoulder with his moist black eyes prominent with a mixture of anger and fear. He was mostly black in colour, except for the spines that covered his lower back, which were handsomely patched with black and white. His long tail, which he kept in a U-shape half over his back, was bare of both fur and spines. On its very tip was a curious cluster of spines which had no points: they looked like a head of wheat, pure white, thick and long. It was this appendage on his tail which produced the rattling noises, for now and again he would stiffen his tail and rattle these hollow, harmless spines together with a crisp crackling sound. He was all keyed up and alert for trouble.

I began to wonder what to do. It really needed two people to capture him, but even if I enlisted the aid of Andraia or Elias, there was not room in this narrow tunnel for two people. There was nothing for it but to try and capture him myself. So I carefully wrapped my hand in a canvas bag, laid another bag out on the floor in readiness to put him in, and proceeded to crawl cautiously towards him. He rattled and stamped, and uttered shrill squeaks of warning. I manoeuvred into position and then suddenly grabbed him by the tail, as this seemed the least protected and most easily handled part of his body. I got it, and immediately he backed with full force on to my hand, and his spines ran straight through the canvas that I had wrapped round as protection, as though it was so much paper. It was extremely painful, but I hung on and dragged him towards me, for I felt that if I let go I might not get another chance to grab him now that he knew my plan of attack. Slowly I wriggled backwards dragging the reluctant porcupine with me, until we were in the small room at the end of the first tunnel. Here there was slightly more room to move, and I tried to get the bag over the animal's head, but he struggled madly, and backed into my chest, the spines going through my thin shirt and well into my flesh. The confined space was in his favour, for whichever way he turned he managed to dig a spine into me, while I had not room to evade his attentions. The only thing to do was to keep on crawling until I reached the open air. So I wriggled along backwards dragging the porcupine, and those last few feet seemed like miles. Just as we reached the open air he gave a terrific bound and a wriggle in an attempt to throw off my hand, but I hung on like grim death. I got shakily to my feet and kept the animal aloft so he could do no damage to me or himself. He hung there quite quietly, all the fight seemed to have gone out of him.

'Andraia . . . Elias . . . come quick, I done catch beef,' I called.

They came running, their torches bobbing through the rocks. When they saw what I held they were astonished.

'Na chook-chook beef,' said Elias. 'Which side Masa done fine um?'

'Here for dis hole. But he done chop me too much. Get a bag to put him into, my hand done tire.'

Elias opened a big canvas bag and I neatly dropped my capture into it. This was my first meeting with a porcupine, and to have captured it single-handed was, I felt, something of a feat.

The brush-tailed porcupine, or, as it is known locally, the chook-chook beef, is one of the commonest animals in the Cameroons: it is found everywhere and in almost every type of country. Most of the faint, twisting paths one found in the forest were the result of the nightly perambulations of this rodent. They would, I found later, make their homes anywhere, but they seemed to favour caves, and particularly caves with small openings under a massive rock, or piles of rocks. In nearly every cave one came across signs of their tenancy: footprints on a sandy floor, a few cast quills, or a half-eaten fruit. In one cave I found fresh palm nuts, which showed that this porcupine in question must have travelled very long distances at night, for the nearest native farm at which he could have obtained this commodity was some six miles away. In another cave I found indications that these porcupines play in much the same way as an English otter will. In this cave there was one wall which was a natural slide, a wall of rock some eight feet high sloping to the ground at a gentle angle of forty-five degrees. This slide had been worn smooth by the constant passage of porcupine bodies or bottoms. Judging by the tracks in the sand, they scrambled up to the top of this slope, slid down, walked round, climbed up again, and slid down once more. They must have been indulging in this game for a number of generations, as the rock-face was worn as smooth as glass. The pidgin-English term for this animal is derived from the word 'chook', which means any thorn or spike, and particularly the doctor's hypodermic needle. In pidgin you form the plural of a word by repeating it, so the brush-tailed porcupine became naturally the chook-chook beef. I decided that this was a good name for the animal, as I was sore and smarting all over from contact with it. Within two days this specimen had become very tame, and would come to the door of his cage to take fruit from my hand. He would only put up his spines, rattle his tail, and stamp his feet if I put my hand right inside the cage and tried to touch him. Later on he would even come to the bars and let me tickle his ears or scratch a soothing spot under his chin, but this was only allowed if there were bars between us.

After I had finished my smoke and had described in boastful details to my hunters how I had captured the porcupine, we continued on our way. Presently I made another capture, and this made me feel better still: true, it was not such an important specimen as the porcupine, but it was worth while, nevertheless. Clasped tightly to a branch, some ten feet from the ground, my wandering torch beam picked out a pair of sleeping chameleons. They were lying close together, their big eyes closed, their legs tucked carefully in, and body-colour a pale and deceiving silvery-green. We had broken the branch and shaken them into a bag almost before they had woken up and realized what was happening. I presumed, since they were sleeping together like that, they were either in the process of mating, or had just mated. It turned out that I was right, for some weeks later the female laid five white eggs the size of a sparrow's, in the bottom of her cage.

By the time we had bagged the chameleons I was in such an elated mood that I would have hurled myself unhesitatingly into a single-handed battle with a leopard if one had happened along. Luckily, the great cats in the Cameroons are retiring in the extreme. What did make their appearance in the torch beams, shortly afterwards, was a diminutive pair of galagos or bush-babies. Now there are three species of galago found in the Cameroons, and two of these are rare and have not, to the best of my knowledge, been represented in any zoological collection in England. Accurate identification as to species when an animal is twenty feet above you, and only lit by a torch beam, becomes impossible, so the rule was that any animal remotely resembling a galago was always pursued with determination and vigour. This we proceeded to do with this pair, who were dancing about on some lianas, occasionally looking down at us so that their enormous eyes glowed like outsize rubies. It was definitely a two-man job, so, leaving Andraia to shine the torch on the prey, Elias and I went aloft in different parts of the tree, and started to converge on the animals. They looked not unlike a pair of fluffy grey kittens dancing about from creeper to creeper with a fairy-like grace and lightness, their eyes glowing as they moved. Slowly Elias and I drew nearer, and I manoeuvred the butterfly-net into position for capture. After catching two chameleons and a porcupine, I felt that this was going to be child's play. Just as I leant forward to swipe at them, three things happened with startling suddenness: my hand I placed on something long and thin and cold which wriggled vigorously, making me let go of the net which sailed downwards to the forest floor. The galagos took fright at this and leapt wildly out into space and disappeared. I crouched very still on my branch for I was not certain of the location of the snake I had leant on, nor was I certain of its species.

'Andraia,' I shouted down, 'give me some light here. Na snake for dis stick and he go chop me if I no get light.'

Andraia moved round and shone the battery of torches at the place where I clung, and I saw the snake. It was coiled round a bunch of twigs and leaves about a foot from my hand. I surveyed it cautiously: the hind end of its body was tangled and twisted round the twigs, but the forequarters were hung forward in the shape of a letter S, apparently ready for action. It was very slender, with a brown skin and darker markings, and a short blunt head furnished with an enormous pair of eyes. It was about two feet long. I watched it, and it watched me, with approximately the same amount of suspicion. I had nothing with which to capture it, except a small length of string which a frantic search through my pockets disclosed. I fashioned a slip-knot out of this and then broke off a large twig to tie my improvised trap to. At this the snake decided to depart, and proceeded to glide through the branches with a fluid rapidity. Hanging on with one hand and my knees, I made three attempts to get the noose over its slender neck, and with the fourth attempt I succeeded. I drew it tight, and the snake hissed and bunched itself into a knot at the end of the string. I tied my handkerchief round the twig to act as a marker and dropped it down to Andraia with instructions. By the time I had reached the ground he had got it safely into a bag. I was extremely annoyed at the loss of the galagos, for we never saw any more specimens in spite of numerous night hunts.

My First Stag

Charles St John

Sport and a love of nature are not necessarily incompatible. In Britain there has existed for a long time a tradition of sportsmen-naturalists, foremost among whom was Charles St John (1809-56) and though he was primarily interested in the pursuit of sport, his observations on natural history, exemplified in his Wild Sports and Natural History of the Highlands, *were of great interest and value.*

Where is the man who does not remember and look back with feelings of energy and delight to the day, the hour, and the wild scene, when he killed unaided his first stag? Of course, I refer only to those who have the same love of wild sport, and the same enjoyment in the romantic solitude and scenery of the mountain and glen that I have myself: shooting tame partridges and hares from the back of a well-trained shooting-pony in a stubble-field, does not, in my eyes, constitute a sportsman; though there is a certain interest attached even to this kind of pursuit, arising more from observing the cleverness and instinct of the dogs employed, than in killing the birds. But far different is the enjoyment derived from stalking the red deer in his native mountain, where every energy of the sportsman must be called into active use, before he can command success.

Well do I remember the mountain-side where I shot my first stag, and though many years have since passed by, I could now, were I to pass through that wild and lovely glen, lay my hand on the very rock under which he fell.

Though a good rifle-shot, indeed few were much better, there seemed a charm against my killing a deer. On two occasions, eagerness and fear of missing shook my hand when I ought to have killed a fine stag. The second that I ever shot at came in my way in a very singular manner.

I had been looking during the chief part of the day for deer, and had, according to appointment, met an attendant with my gun and pointers at a particular spring in the hills, meaning to shoot my way home. The spring was situated in the midst of a small green spot, like an oasis in the desert, surrounded on all sides by a long stretch of broken black ground. The well itself was in a little round hollow, surrounded by high banks.

I was resting here, having met my gillie, and was consoling myself for my want of success by smoking a cigar, when, at the same moment, a kind of shadow came across me, and the pointers who were coupled at my feet pricked up their ears and growled, with their eyes fixed on some object behind me. My keeper, who had been out with me all day, was stretched on his back, in a half slumber, and the gillie was kneeling down taking a long draught at the cool well, with the enjoyment of one who had had a long toiling walk on a hot August day. Turning my head lazily to see what had roused the dogs, and had cast its shadow across me, instead of a shepherd, as I expected – could I believe my eyes! – there stood a magnificent stag, with the fine shaped horns peculiar to those of the Sutherland forests. He was standing on the bank immediately behind me, and not above fifty yards off, looking with astonishment at the group before him, who had taken possession of the very spot where he had intended to slake his thirst. The deer seemed too much astonished to move, and for a moment I was in the same dilemma. The rifle was on the ground just behind the slumbering Donald. I was afraid the deer would be off out of sight, if I got up to take it, or if I called loud enough to awake Donald. So I was driven to the necessity of giving him a pretty severe kick, which had the effect of making him turn on his side, and open his eyes with a grunt. 'The rifle, Donald, the rifle,' I whispered, holding out my hand. Scarcely knowing what he was at, he instinctively stretched out his hand to feel for it, and held it out to me. All this takes some time to describe, but did not occupy a quarter of a minute. At the same instant that I got the rifle, the gillie lifted up his head from the water, and half turning, saw the stag, and also saw that I was about to shoot at him. With a presence of mind worthy of being better seconded, he did not raise himself from his knees, but remained motionless with his eyes fixed on the deer. As I said before, I had never killed a deer, and my heart beat. I fired however with, as I thought, a good aim at his shoulder. The deer at the instant turned round. After firing my shot, we all (including Donald, who by this time comprehended what was going on) ran to the top of the bank to see what had happened, as the deer disappeared the instant I fired. I had, I believe, missed him altogether, though he looked as large as an ox, and we saw him going at a steady gallop over the wide flat. Donald had the glass out immediately, and took a steady sight at him, but having watched the noble animal, as he galloped up the opposite slope and stood for two or three minutes on the summit, looking back intently at us, he shut up the tele-scope with a jerk that threatened to break every glass in it, and giving a grunt, vastly expressive of disgust, returned to the well, where he took a long draught. His only remark at the time was,

'There's no the like of that stag in the country; weel do I mind seeing him last year when shooting ptarmigan up yonder, and not a bullet had I. The deil's in the rifle, that she did na kill him; and he'll cross the river before he stops.' It required some time and some whisky also, to restore Donald to his usual equanimity.

This was on Saturday. On the Monday following at a very early hour Donald appeared, and after his morning salute of 'It's a fine day, Sir,' he added, 'There will be some deer about the west shoulder of the hill above Alt-na-car. Whenever the wind is in the airt it now is, they feed about the burn there.' We agreed to walk across to that part of the ground and were soon en route. Bran galloped round us, baying joyously, as if he expected we should have good luck. We had not gone half a mile from the house, when we met one of the prettiest girls in the country, tripping along the narrow path, humming a Gaelic air, and looking bright and fresh as the morning. 'How are you all at home, Nanny, and how is your father getting on? Does he see any deer on the hill?' said I. Her father was a shepherd not far from the house, and she was then going down on some errand to my servants. 'We are all no' that bad, thank you, Sir, except mother, who still has the trouble on her. Father says that he saw some hinds and a fine *stag* yesterday as he crossed the hill to the kirk; they were feeding on the top of Alt-na-car, and did na mind him a bit.'

Donald looked at me, with a look full of importance, at this confirmation of his prophecy. 'Deed, Sir, that's a bonny lass, and as gude as she is bonny. It's just gude luck our meeting her; if we had met that auld witch, her mother, not a beast would we have seen the day.' I have heard of Donald turning home again, if he met an old woman when starting on any deerstalking excursion. The young pretty girl, however, was a good omen in his eyes. We passed through the woods, seeing here and there a roebuck standing gazing at us as we crossed some grassy glade where he was feeding. On the rocks near the top of the woods, Donald took me to look at a trap he had set, and in it we found a beautiful marten cat, which we killed, and hid among the stones – another good omen in Donald's eyes.

On we went, taking a careful survey of the ground here and there. At a loch whose Gaelic name I do not remember, we saw a vast number of wild ducks, and at the further extremity of it a hind and calf feeding. We waited here for some time, and I amused myself with watching the two deer as they fed, unconscious of our neighbourhood, and from time to time drank at the burn which supplied the loch. We then passed over a long dreary tract of brown and broken ground, till we came to the picturesque-looking place where we expected to find the deer – a high conical hill, rising out of rather flat ground, which gave it an appearance of being of a greater height than it really was. We took a most careful survey of the slope on which Donald expected to see the deer. Below was an extensive level piece of heather with a burn running through it in an endless variety of windings, and fringed with green rushes and grass, which formed a strong contrast to the dark-coloured moor through which it made its way, till it emptied itself into a long narrow loch, beyond which rose Ben Cleebrich and some more of the highest mountains in Scotland. In vain did we look, and Donald at last shut up his telescope in despair: 'They are no' here the day,' was his remark. 'But what is that, Donald?' said I, pointing to some bluish-looking object I saw at some distance from us rising out of the heather. The glass was turned towards it, and after having been kept motionless for some time, he pronounced it to be the head and neck of a hind. I took the glass, and while I was looking at it, I saw a fine stag rise suddenly from some small hollow near her, stretch himself, and lie down again. Presently six more hinds, and a two-year-old stag got up, and after walking about for a few minutes, they, one by one, lay down again, but every one seemed to take up a position commanding a view of the whole country. We crept back a few paces, and then getting into the course of the burn, got within three hundred yards of the deer, but by no means whatever could we get nearer. The stag was a splendid fellow, with ten points, and regular fine-shaped horns. Bran winded them, and watched us most earnestly, as if to ask why we did not try to get at them. The sensible dog, however, kept quite quiet, as if aware of the importance of not being seen or heard. Donald asked me what o'clock it was; I told him it was just two. 'Well, well, Sir, we must just wait here till three o'clock, when the deer will get up to feed, and most likely the brutes will travel towards the burn. The Lord save us, but yon's a muckle beast.' Trusting to his experience, I waited patiently, employing myself in attempting to dry my hose by wringing them, and placing them in the sun. Donald took snuff and watched the deer, and Bran laid his head on his paws as if asleep, but his sharp eye, and ear pricked up on the slightest movement, showed that he was ready for action at a moment's warning. As nearly as possible at three o'clock, they did get up to feed: first the hinds rose and cropped a few mouthfuls of the coarse grass near them: looking at and waiting for their lord and master, who, however, seemed lazily inclined and would not move; the young stag fed steadily on towards us.

Frequently the hinds stopped and turned back to their leader, who remained quite motionless, excepting that now and then he scratched a fly off his flank with his horn or turned his head towards the hill side when a grouse crowed or a plover whistled. The young stag was feeding quietly within a hundred and fifty yards of us, and we had to lie flat on the ground now and then to escape his observation. The evening air already began to feel chill, when suddenly the object of our pursuit jumped up, stretched himself, and began feeding. Not liking the pasture close to him, he trotted at once down into the flat ground right away from us. Donald uttered a Gaelic oath, and I fear I added an English one. The stag that had been feeding so near us stood still for a minute to watch the others, who were all now several hundred yards away, gazing steadily at him. I aimed at him, but just as I was about to fire he turned away, leaving nothing but his haunch in view, and went after the rest. Donald applauded me for not shooting at him, but told me that our case was hopeless, and that we had better make our way home and attempt no more, as they were feeding in so open a place that it was impossible to get at them: even Bran yawned and rose, as if he too had given up all hope. 'I will have one try, Donald; so hold the dog.' 'You need na fash yoursel, Sir; they are clean out of all hope and reason.' I determined to make an effort before it became dusk; so leaving Donald, I set off down the burn, looking for some hollow place that might favour my getting up to them, but I could find none: at last it struck me that I might by chance get up within a long shot by keeping a small hillock, which was in the middle of the plain, between me and the deer. The hillock was not two feet high, and all depended on the animals keeping together and not outflanking me.

On I went, not on my hands and knees, but crawling like a snake, and never rising even to my knee. I could see their hind-quarters as they walked away, feeding, however, most eagerly, and when they looked up I lay still flatter on the ground with my face buried in the heather. They appeared, however, not to suspect danger in the open plain, but often looked anxiously to-wards the burn or the rocky side of the mountain. One old long-legged hind kept me in a constant state of alarm, as she fre-quently looked in my direction, turning her ears as if to catch some suspicious sound. As for the stag, he never looked about him once, leaving that to the hinds. I at last got within about a hundred yards of the whole of them: as they fed in a group turned away from me, I could not get a shot at anything but their hindquarters, and I did not wish to shoot unless I could get a fair broadside towards me. While waiting for an opportunity, still flat on the ground, a grouse cock walked out of the heather close to me, and strutted on with head erect and his bright eye fixed on me till he came to a little hillock, where he stopped and began to utter a note of alarm. Instantly every deer left off eating. I saw that no time was to be lost and raised myself on my elbow, and with cocked rifle waited for the hinds to move, that I might get at the stag, who was in the midst of them. The hinds soon saw me and began to trot away, but their leader seemed determined to see what the danger was, and before he started turned round to look towards the spot where the grouse was, giving me a good slanting shot at his shoulder. I immediately touched the trigger, feeling at the same time sure of my aim. The ball went true and down he fell. I began reloading, but before I had half done the stag was up again and making play after the hinds, who were galloping up a gentle slope of the hill. The poor beast was evidently moving with the greatest difficulty and pain; sometimes coming to his knees, and then recovering himself with a strong effort, he still managed to keep not far behind them. I sat down in utter despair: looking round too for Donald and Bran I could see nothing of them. Between anxiety and vexation I did not know what to do. All at once I saw the hinds dash away in different directions, and the next moment my gallant Bran appeared in the midst of them. I shouted with joy. On came the dog, taking no notice of the hinds, but making straight for the stag, who stood still for one instant, and then rushed with apparently full vigour down the hill. Down they came towards the burn, the dog not five yards behind the stag, but unable to reach his shoulder (the place where he always struck his game). In a few moments deer and hound went headlong and seemingly both together into the burn. Donald appeared running like a lunatic: with good judgement he had, when I left him, gone to cut off the deer in case I wounded one and it took up the hill. As good luck would have it, the hinds had led off the stag right up to where Donald and Bran were, notwithstanding his inclination to go the other way. I ran to see what had become of them in the burn, expecting to find the stag at bay. When I got there, however, it was all over. The deer had probably tumbled from weakness, and Bran had got his fangs well into the throat of the poor brute before he could rise again. The gallant dog, when I was up with him, lay down panting with his forepaws on the deer, and wagging his tail seemed to congratulate me on my victory, and to expect to be caressed for his share in it. A fine stag he was, in perfect order, with noble antlers. Donald added to my satisfaction by applauding my manner of getting up to him, adding that he never would have thought it possible to kill a stag on such bare and flat ground. Little did I feel the fatigue of our three hours' walk, two of them in the dark and hard rain. We did not go home, but went to a shepherd's house, whose inhabitants were at evening prayer when we arrived; we did not interrupt them, but afterwards the wife prepared us a capital supper of eggs and fresh trout, which we devoured with vast relish before the bright peat-fire, our wet clothes steaming all the time like a boiler.

Such was the death of my first stag.

In the Service of Man

Alan C. Jenkins

Edward Topsell, the early seventeenth-century author of The History of
Four-Footed Beasts, *wrote: 'There is no creature among all the beasts of
the world which hath so great and ample demonstration of the power and
wisdom of almighty God as the Elephant.' It is extraordinary not only that
such a massive, marvellous creature should have survived, but also that for
several thousand years man should have been able to train it for use in
peace and war. Here is a description of a capture of a young Indian elephant
and its first lesson.*

I met Pyari or Little Darling, as she eventually became known,
several times before she acquired a name. It is only on the evidence of my Indian hosts at an elephant camp in Mysore that I
can say this. For to my inexpert eye most elephants of a similar
age looked the same – just as the Chinese say that all Europeans
look the same to them, and vice versa.

Anyway, Pyari-to-be was about ten or eleven years of age, and
she lived with her mother and relations in deep bamboo jungle,
which provided her and them with most of their food – though
they greatly appreciated the odd pineapple or cabbage whenever
there was a handy property to raid.

At times I was accompanied – it was really the other way round
– by a little Coruba tribesman named Bapundi, an expert ele-
phant-tracker. On sight he could of course identify any individual
animal – while out of view he could tell them by their footprints
which if necessary he would measure with lengths of grass.
Whenever we came across a portentous pile of elephant dung he

would nonchalantly stick a bare toe in it as a sort of improvised thermometer to check how old it was and thus how close the elephants might be.

I saw Little Darling first when she was enjoying her obligatory evening bathe, for elephants are almost as ritualistic about this as the Hindus themselves. Very often when they amble down to a bathing-place they are pink – patched with red at times – with the eternal dust of India with which they have sprayed themselves. When they emerge from the water they gleam blackly as if carved from ebony.

No doubt because she was a female, Little Darling was well aware of the beautifying effects of the mud-pack and on this occasion she spent most of her time solemnly squirting dollops of liquid mud on the crown of her head, frequently squealing in sheer delight. Evidently she felt that her mother was in need of similar treatment and from time to time plastered a trunkful of mud over Mum's massive hindquarters, perhaps to smoothe out the wrinkles.

Meanwhile, however, the other elephants were becoming restive. The herd, including Little Darling and some other young elephants, began to move off, striding up the bank and crashing through the jungle. Little Darling was quite peevish at having her fun cut short and within a few minutes had come trundling back to the lake. She straightway resumed her mud-larking, using her trunk rather like an enormous icing-sugar syringe.

But she wasn't allowed to enjoy this for long. While Bapundi and I continued to watch from our boat some distance away in the shelter of overhanging trees, Mum came storming back, the essence of maternal crossness and anxiety. She made straight for

Little Darling, administered with her trunk a resounding slap that rang out like a rifle-shot and chivvied the truant away at a smart pace. This time there wasn't any arguing.

I saw Little Darling on other occasions, often on the same lake. Once the elephants were swimming across, the tips of their trunks curling up above the surface, nature's own version of the 'schnorkel', while one small elephant was glad to hold on to its mother's tail. Little Darling's penchant for mischief seemed to be highly developed, for on one occasion she caused havoc in a planter's bungalow some miles away – this accusation being supported by Bapundi's testimony that it was she. The young elephant and her mother and an 'auntie' elephant had visited the place one night, in search of any available variation in their staple diet of bamboo. Having thoroughly ravaged the garden, the elephants decided to quizz the bungalow itself. The planter was away on leave and only the kitchen quarters were occupied – by the chowkidar or caretaker and his family. Little Darling managed to barge her way through the French windows into the drawing-room, but once inside she had great difficulty in getting out again.

When she realized her plight she became extremely vocal and in general displayed some pretty unladylike manners. Her panic-stricken squeals drove Mum and Auntie frantic with rage and the night rang with their trumpeting while they besieged the bungalow. The chowkidar and his various relations sought refuge in the loft until Little Darling had bashed her way to freedom. But the end of Little Darling's freedom was near. A day arrived when she was trapped in earnest. In India the elephants are completely protected and only the occasional 'rogue' is shot – though in general life becomes increasingly difficult for them because of pressure of space by swarming humanity. It's been estimated that there are possibly about seven thousand elephants left in India.

A certain number are caught each year to be trained for work in the forests. In the past the 'keddah' was the method employed, especially in southern India: a whole herd of elephants would be ringed in a huge area and gradually driven into a funnel-shaped stockade. But spectacular as the keddah was, it was far too expensive and impractical. It took many days to accomplish, it involved many men and trained elephants – and often the devastation of cultivated land.

Nowadays, in the brief catching-season that takes place between January and March, a simpler, age-old method is usually employed. Herds of elephants have their different feeding grounds, to and from which they travel many miles along veritable roads through the jungle. Near one of the haunts of Little Darling's herd, pits had been dug and then disguised with an astonishingly skilful covering of grass and foliage and branches, quite indistinguishable from the surrounding scrubby ground. I was shown one or two of these elephant traps and would certainly have walked into them if I hadn't been warned.

Unfortunately for Little Darling, she did walk into such a trap and as a result her life of freedom came to an abrupt end.

When a messenger arrived at the camp with the news that a young elephant had been caught, the camp officer at once sent off three mahouts and their trained elephants. Some time later we followed in a Land-Rover, starting along a road that turned into a track – and this in turn became little more than a gap in the jungle. We drove through a dense wilderness of feathery bamboo and wild almond trees and teak and the occasional sandalwood tree which is so precious because of its perfumed wood.

Blackfaced monkeys vaulted through the trees. Every now and then mongooses bounded across our path. Huge fruit bats hung in clusters from the branches, like black umbrellas. The trees were alive with colour – the lovely petals of the flame-of-the-forest, the scarlet cups of tulip-trees: alive with birds, too – golden orioles, blossom-headed parakeets, racket-tailed drongos. Cicadas kept up their endless chizzing like a sizzling electric current. I was assured that there wouldn't be many leeches as it was the dry season – but that if one did happen to drop on me from a tree the easiest way of getting rid of it would be to apply a lighted match to it. As for snakes, not to worry, either – they would get out of my way – the only really pugnacious snake was a king-cobra when it was guarding its eggs . . .

We drove as near as possible to the pit-trap and finished the journey on foot. Bapundi and his fellow Corubas were already at work trying to get Little Darling out of the trap, while the mahouts and their trained elephants stood by nonchalantly, ready to help at the crucial moment. Everyone was delighted at the quality of the catch – just right in age, she would prove very tractable – older elephants were much more difficult to train. Sometimes the catch wasn't as welcome as this one: on one occasion two female elephants and their babies had been caught in a trap, on another an extremely unco-operative wild buffalo.

Yes, everyone was delighted – except Little Darling. She was exceedingly angry at the practical joke that had been played on her – and even a young elephant's rage can be impressive. However, there was nothing she could do about it. What surprised me was the comparative smallness and shallowness of the pit. But the strange thing about the elephant is that despite its size and strength, it can't jump or stride more than six feet – a fact which gives point to the special elephant trenches protecting many dwelling-places in southern India.

So Little Darling was well and truly caught in this cunning pit-trap. Now she had to be got out of it. You might think that extracting an elephant – even a young one – from a pit-trap would present considerable difficulties. But nothing could have been simpler. The trappers cut quantities of branches and brushwood which they chucked into the pit. Little Darling became crosser than ever at this and trampled the stuff underfoot. She didn't realize that this was just what was wanted of her. Gradually the floor of the pit was being raised – and the captive with it!

Meanwhile, a rope noose had been got round a hind-leg and another noose round her neck – a more difficult operation than it sounds as she was lashing out with her trunk all the time. Both these ropes were attached to two of the trained elephants who were ready to take the strain. Eventually Bapundi's patent jungle lift brought Little Darling near enough to the surface and she was able to clamber out. She immediately vented her fury in every direction. But she was in a hopeless situation, for at the end of each rope was a living anchor in the shape of a five-ton camp elephant. If Little Darling tried to stomp off back to her native jungle, she was brought up short by one of the elephants. If she refused to budge, she was gently shoved by the other – and there was still a third blasé camp elephant in reserve.

Little Darling was frog-marched into captivity.

For a week or two Little Darling was confined in a strong teak-wood cage in the elephant-camp. Elephants and human-beings lived very much cheek by jowl – the Corubas in their flimsy shacks and various elephants tethered here and there. At night some of the working-elephants, impeded by lengths of chain so that they could not go too far, were allowed to wander into the jungle to supplement their ration of rice and jaggary-sugar. In the morning, the mahouts would trace them by the sound of their bells – though one cunning animal used occasionally to stuff his bell with mud.

At first Little Darling certainly didn't live up to her newly acquired name. Her trunk was constantly in use to express her feelings. When she wasn't squealing, she would bash her forehead unavailingly against the bars of her cage. Once when I turned up at the camp clad in newly dhobied clothes, she ambushed me through the bars with a shattering blast of red dust. Her triumphant squeal was echoed by the subdued giggling of the mahouts.

Day by day, however, she grew calmer. Before long she was allowed out, tethered to a tree-stump in the middle of the camp so that she became used to the presence of human-beings and the constant comings and goings. The company of other elephants too, helped to make her feel at home. Bapundi petted her and fed her large balls of boiled rice mixed with jaggary and ghee, which she accepted gracefully though eagerly.

At the end of three weeks' probation she was deemed ready for her first outing – and lesson. It was an important day in her career.

Once again she was roped to two camp-elephants, with a third in reserve in case she was fractious. The little tribesmen dodged about quite unconcerned under the legs of the adult elephants. As for Little Darling, she practically disappeared between those enormous elephants. What was so nice was to see how gentle they were. They knew just what to do. If Little Darling was at all difficult, they simply gave her a little squeeze or a nudge – and she realized she had to do what she was told. They exuded an atmosphere of melancholy sympathy, as if they remembered their far-off days in the jungle and knew how bewildered Little Darling must be feeling.

Off we all trooped to the river – a tributary of the Cauvery – and once again I was astonished at the silence with which the elephants moved. The effect was all the greater because they disappeared completely in a thick curtain of dust – there's always dust in India during the dry season. Away the elephants trudged, probably sixteen or seventeen tons of them – and they made no more noise than a deer would – except for the jangle of the bell swinging at the throat of each of them.

Little Darling's first lesson was as simple as it was important. No work-job she was taught to do in the future would be as vital as this first lesson. It consisted of making her sit in the river. While two of the trained elephants stood around squirting water over themselves, the third, who looked a mixture of boredom and fatherly patience, led the pupil into midstream. He stood knee-deep in the water, with his trunk draped over one tusk – rather like an old gentleman carrying an overcoat on his arm. His wrinkled grey hindquarters looked as if he was wearing very baggy trousers that were in danger of falling down. If ever Little Darling showed signs of rebelling, he just leaned mightily on the long rope to make her behave.

Meanwhile, half a dozen tribesmen had surrounded Little Darling and proceeded to beat her with sticks, slap her, splash water over her, while they kept up a constant exhortation in Hindi to sit. Again and again and again – she was told to sit, an order reinforced by sticks and hands. It's hardly necessary to say that this 'beating' on her thick skin was more like a vehement caress.

Sit! Sit! Sit! Sit! Sit!

Little Darling stood there with bowed head, utterly at a loss. For a long time she sulked and resisted, while the Corubas went on smacking her and shrilling out their chorus.

Sit! Sit! Sit! Sit! Sit!

At last the idea sank in. With an air of resignation she sat down obediently in the water. A cry of approbation rang out. But there was no respite. No sooner had Little Darling sat down than she was told to get up. The Hindi chorus rang out again – this time in a command to stand up.

Get up! Get up!

Little Darling, with all the flexibility of youth, was an apt pupil. After some minutes she began to take in this new order. Obediently she floundered to her feet – only to be told immediately to sit down again.

Sit! Sit! Sit! – Get up! Get up! It was all very confusing. You could almost hear her saying 'For heaven's sake, what is the point of all this? Can't you leave me alone? It's so hot!'

But of course there was very much a point in this apparently childish lesson. This young elephant, so recently snatched from her native jungle, had learned for the first time to obey man. It was a critical moment in her new life – indeed, life would never again be the same for her.

In due course school was over for the day. The Corubas were delighted with Little Darling's response. They praised her, calling her sister, affectionately splashed water over her and began to scrub her with huge burrs that resembled scrubbing-brushes as she lay relaxing in the turgid water. She wasn't just an animal. She was one of the family and these merry little jungle tribesmen and their Indian boss were proud that she had been so good – especially in front of a visitor.

This tractability is the most astonishing characteristic of the elephant. Nothing can be wilder, fiercer, stronger than the jungle elephant. On occasions it can become a terrible killer – it can deal out a death-blow with its two-hundredweight trunk – kneel on the object of its dislike and squash it flat – devastate vast areas of jungle as if a storm had passed by.

Yet in the right hands it can become a patient, gentle, skilled worker. And now, even though it would be another ten years before Little Darling started her working-life in earnest, she was the latest recruit in the service of man. Away in the jungle the wild herd went its way, ever more menaced by the rising tide of humanity.

The Arrival

Walter von Sanden

In the past generation a veritable explosion in pet-keeping has occurred, involving creatures as varied as agoutis and alligators. The pet otter in this story may not be in his natural habitat but he knows how to make himself thoroughly at home.

Ingo is not of course a human being, he is an otter; and so from the first day of our being together I have had to apply to him a different standard from that which I apply to people. This has been difficult for me, and I shall probably never master it properly. I believe that Ingo and I understand each other, and we afford each other so much pleasure that I will even now try to describe our life together at the risk of having to correct myself in time to come.

His very arrival and first appearance were unusual. An animal dealer whom I knew sent a telegram: 'Offer tame otter. Superb specimen.' Since for a long time it had been my wife's dearest wish to possess an otter, I answered without hesitation: 'Despatch immediately.'

Ingo, at that time still nameless, had to endure a journey right across Germany, and so two and a half days later I was in a state of anxiety as to the condition in which he would arrive, and as to what was to be inferred from the somewhat elastic term 'tame'.

A telephone call from the railway station ended our waiting. A packing-case had arrived for me, with an unknown animal inside. It was crying incessantly, scratching and biting the wood,

330

and would I please fetch it immediately: the railway authorities could take no responsibility for it. The advice on the despatch-note seemed to read, 'Live *adder*', but the beast certainly wasn't a snake.

This was no time for delay! I jumped into my car and raced to the station. Just before I left I shouted to Lisa, our maid, to get a pail and net some live perch out of my fish-weir in the river, to leave them in my bedroom, and to fill the bath with cold water.

At our little station I could hear, even through the closed door of the shed, an improbably high-pitched voice. It sounded like a short, sharp bird-cry. Quickly I ran into the shed and stopped beside the crate. Ingo had heard my steps and was silent. The air-holes in the lid were so small that I could see nothing. After I had stood quietly waiting for a short while, there came a pitiful whimpering from Ingo's prison. He must have thought that he was alone again and was giving voice to the unhappiness in his heart. I moved and laid the palm of my hand on the largest hole in the lid. Silence. Then I heard and felt the air being breathed in, and out, and in again under my hand. Ingo was making use of his nose to discover what was outside. Those deep, exploratory sniffs founded our friendship.

We had not even seen each other yet. But what need has an otter of visible, outward appearances when his nose can explore a thing? Also his sense of hearing helped. I spoke a few friendly words, and Ingo gave vent to such a tender whiffle that I would have dearly loved to tear open the lid then and there.

Rapidly I carried the crate to the car and drove away. The bumping and shaking was nothing new to Ingo, who had experienced it for several days on end; but the hand on top, from which he expected something nice – the hand was no longer there. There was a horrid smell of petrol. Overcome with grief and loneliness, Ingo began to cry again heartrendingly.

I then steered with one hand and put the other on the lid. Silence. Deep, exploratory sniffs, soft whiffling. Thus we drove home at no great speed, and mentally I made a favourable diagnosis of the expression 'tame'.

When, just before the end of our journey, there was a difficult stretch of road, I had to use both my hands for steering, Ingo remained silent. He had fallen asleep. The presence of a human being had reassured him. Weariness had won; fear, hunger and thirst were vanquished.

At home my wife and Lisa were waiting for us. We carried the crate up to my bedroom and shut all the doors. I sat down on the floor and broke open a part of the lid. Before this I had let my hand rest on the lid for a while.

Ingo saw the daylight shine in; this was pleasant. But he would not come out. The sniffing nose moved in the background. 'I'd like to come out,' it seemed to say, 'but everything is strange and the lid above me is my protection.'

So far as I could see, there was neither food nor water in the crate. I splashed with my hand in the tin of fish beside me. Quick as lightning the flat head appeared at the opening, two black expressive eyes stared at me briefly: 'Have you got some water?' And Ingo had already disappeared again.

Was he perhaps very hungry? I held a fish in the opening of the lid. A swift, strong snatch was followed by loud sounds of crunching. Nothing was to be seen. Ingo lay in the farthest corner of the crate.

Well, he was healthy all right. He was enjoying his food. Now only patience was necessary. I made myself comfortable beside the crate and waited. Ingo's head appeared again: 'Where's some more fish?' But I only splashed in the water and spoke to him.

'Ingo, do come out. We'd so much like to see you.'

Again came the head, the enquiring eyes. 'Can I trust you? There's such a delicious smell of water and fish. But everything's so strange here!'

'There, Ingo – smell my hand, you know it. I'll stretch it out to you – quite slowly. There, you see. It's all right. No need to be afraid. No need at all. Now, put your forepaws on my knee. It doesn't smell so strongly of fish, but it will remind you of my hand.'

'I'm coming,' said Ingo's eyes: 'in fact, I'm already there; but first my nose must be quite sure of everything.'

The outside of the crate, my hand, my knee, the air above – all was thoroughly appraised. An impatient sound came from Ingo's little mouth, and he had vanished again into the darkest corner of the crate. But this time not for long. He appeared once more. A look of enterprise shone in his eyes. Soon one foot rested on my knee, and immediately after, a second. The toes were splayed out so that the brown webs were visible between them.

Now the strange unknown had been conquered. Whiffling softly, he came right out and sat on my lap. The floor was sniffed, my whole person investigated, and then it was the fish pail's turn.

'I'm familiar with things like that,' said Ingo. 'There's something to eat or drink inside.' His head dipped in. The pail began swaying precariously because the perch had no wish to be caught. But soon he had one and lay down beside me. With the fish between his forepaws, his thick tail stretched out behind, he ate it, starting with the head. Ingo's upward directed gaze seemed to say: 'tastes excellent; nothing will be left, not even the tip of the tail.'

When he got near the tail, his forepaws, which were used like human hands, let go of what remained and Ingo swung it right up in the air so as to lose nothing and swallowed it at a gulp. 'There were more like that in the tin,' the thought suddenly occurred to him. He stood up and gave free play to his lust for fishing. Out with the fish! They flopped and writhed on the floor beside him, but he paid no attention to them until he had thoroughly satisfied himself that there was none remaining in the water.

'I'm still exceedingly hungry,' said Ingo. Again he took a fish between his paws. Only a tiny heap of scales was left after he had finished devouring his prey. The next two he consumed just as heartily, and the fourth he only half ate. 'Thirsty,' he said, and plunged his head deep into the pail.

Water dripped from his long whiskers, and his expressive eyes said: 'Now I must find out what else there is to be discovered here.'

Every inch of the floor was investigated, every corner, every space under the furniture. 'And what does it look like higher up?' His head lifted, his eyes roved all around, his nose sniffed the air. When he got to the bath, he sat up on his hind legs, rested his forepaws on the edge, smelt and saw the water. 'I don't dare to jump, but I know very well what a chair is. 'What's standing beside the water certainly looks a bit different, but it's good enough or me,' and then he was up on the stool and from there slid cautiously into the water.

'This is nice, this is delicious, this is really marvellous,' said his movements, which sent the water splashing over the edge of the tub. Backwards and forwards he raced, sometimes above, sometimes under the water, and he could not have enough of it after that long, dry journey.

When the pool round the bath had grown to such an extent that I began to have fears for the ceiling of the room underneath, I let out the water. 'What a remarkable thing!' said Ingo, and stuck his nose as far as it would go into the plug-hole. He could not reconcile himself to this, kept sitting up on his hind legs and looked at me questioningly. I turned on the tap and sprayed him with a hose. He did not at all like this on his body, especially on his back, but he thought the jet of water was a wonderful thing to play with. He bit at it, tried to catch it between his forepaws, flung himself on his back and grabbed at it. This was a wonderful game which was in his blood. His ancestors used to play it at suitable natural places, and his relatives still do today. Wherever a little stream flows out of a rock or a water-drain pours out of a bank into a river, there is their water-toy, and there they will play so long as they feel themselves safe from their worst enemy – man.

Ingo did not hate human beings. That was obvious. He was familiar with them, seemed acquainted with many of their furnishings, and loved their company. Of his earlier life I knew nothing, not even where he came from. From my knowledge of wild otters I judged him to be about two years old. One couldn't help loving him, the way he lay in the bath-tub, oblivious to all around him and determined to catch that jet of water.

Finally I turned off the tap and went into the next room where my bed was. Ingo was playing with my sponge in the bath, but soon followed me, and when he discovered my bed he was on it in a flash and rolling himself dry on my clean pillows.

So he knows what a bed is, too, I thought. I let him be; on his first day he should have only what he enjoyed. He seemed to be just as happy on the bed as in the bath. When he felt himself to be dry enough, he went on with his voyage of discovery. He climbed up on to the little table by the side of the bed and walked round it without upsetting the alarm clock or the carafe of water. Then he sprang back on to the pillows and from there to the floor.

Meanwhile, being tired of standing, I had lain down on the chaise-longue, and from there observed Ingo's activities. Suddenly he missed me because I was lying quite still. Snuffing, he searched round the room, until his nose discovered me: 'There he is!' A bound and he was up beside me; he sniffed me and began playing with my hand, taking each finger in turn, like a dog, and holding it gently between his teeth. At the same time he rolled and wriggled on me and the chaise-longue and whiffled incessantly. There was such an expression of tender happiness about him that I was entirely unworried about my fingers, although he could easily have reduced them to pulp. But he never thought of it, and neither did I.

When he had played enough, the window-seat attracted him. From my sofa he climbed on to it, looked attentively through the panes into the garden, and walked backwards and forwards without upsetting one of the flower-pots. Then he climbed down to me again, took my ear gently between his teeth and nibbled at my hair, whiffling happily the whole time. 'I'm so pleased that you're here, that I can always find you when I've finished with my explorations. But now I'm tired, and there's still something missing to make me really comfortable.'

He walked round investigating. At my head, he caught one corner of the cushion with his teeth and tugged the whole cushion on to the floor. He rolled it about a few times, and then, comfortably half curled up, lay down on his side. At the same time, like a baby with its bottle, he held the corner of the cushion between his forepaws and muzzled at it; the suckling sounds were clearly to be heard. After a while he fell fast alseep.

How very different had been my previous encounters with otters! I knew them only in their wild state, only in those places where man does not hold the centre of the stage and where the otter reveals himself as one of the shyest and most retiring of our wild creatures.

The Chase

Francis Parkman

This piece could aptly be called 'The Beginning of the End'. When the author set out into virtually unknown America along the Oregon Trail in 1846, he thought the vast herds of buffalo were inexhaustible. Yet in little more than a generation the species was all but wiped out. Only by the devoted efforts of a few conservationists, led by the New York Zoological Society, were any survivors rescued.

The country before us was now thronged with buffalo, and a sketch of the manner of hunting them will not be out of place. There are two methods commonly practised, 'running' and 'approaching'. The chase on horseback, which goes by the name of 'running', is the more violent and dashing mode of the two; that is to say, when the buffalo are in one of their wild moods; for otherwise it is tame enough. A practised and skilful hunter, well mounted, will sometimes kill five or six cows in a single chase, loading his gun again and again as his horse rushes through the tumult. In attacking a small band of buffalo, or in separating a single animal from the herd and assailing it apart from the rest, there is less excitement and less danger. In fact, the animals are at times so stupid and lethargic that there is little sport in killing them. With a bold and well-trained horse the hunter may ride so close to the buffalo that as they gallop side by side he may touch him with his hand; nor is there much danger in this as long as the buffalo's strength and breath continue unabated; but when he becomes tired and can no longer run with ease, when his tongue lolls out and the foam flies from his jaws, then the hunter had better keep a more respectful distance; the distressed brute may turn upon him at any instant; and especially at the moment when he fires his gun. The horse then leaps aside, and the hunter has need of a tenacious seat in the saddle, for if he is thrown to the ground there is no hope for him. When he sees his attack defeated the buffalo resumes his flight, but if the shot is well directed he soon stops; for a few moments he stands still, then totters and falls heavily upon the prairie.

The chief difficulty in running buffalo, as it seems to me, is that of loading the gun or pistol at full gallop. Many hunters for convenience' sake carry three or four bullets in the mouth; the powder is poured down the muzzle of the piece, the bullet dropped in after it, the stock struck hard upon the pommel of the saddle, and the work is done. The danger of this is obvious. Should the blow on the pommel fail to send the bullet home, or should the bullet, in the act of aiming, start from its place and roll towards the muzzle, the gun would probably burst in discharging. Many a shattered hand and worse casualties beside have been the result of such an accident. To obviate it, some hunters make use of a ramrod, usually hung by a string from the neck, but this materially increases the difficulty of loading. The bows and arrows which the Indians use in running buffalo have many advantages over fire-arms, and even white men occasionally employ them.

The danger of the chase arises not so much from the onset of the wounded animal as from the nature of the ground which the hunter must ride over. The prairie does not always present a smooth, level, and uniform surface; very often it is broken with hills and hollows, intersected by ravines, and in the remoter parts studded by the stiff wild-sage bushes. The most formidable obstruction, however, are the burrows of wild animals, wolves, badgers, and particularly prairie-dogs, with whose holes the ground for a very great extent is frequently honeycombed. In the blindness of the chase the hunter rushes over it unconscious of danger; his horse, at full career, thrusts his leg deep into one of the burrows; the bone snaps, the rider is hurled forward to the ground and probably killed. Yet accidents in buffalo running happen less frequently than one would suppose; in the recklessness of the chase, the hunter enjoys all the impunity of a drunken man, and may ride in safety over gullies and declivities where, should he attempt to pass in his sober senses, he would infallibly break his neck.

The method of 'approaching', being practised on foot, has many advantages over that of 'running'; in the former, one neither breaks down his horse nor endangers his own life; he must be cool, collected, and watchful; must understand the buffalo, observe the features of the country and the course of the wind, and be well skilled in using the rifle. The buffalo are strange animals; sometimes they are so stupid and infatuated that a man may walk up to them in full sight on the open prairie, and even shoot several of their number before the rest will think it necessary to retreat. At another moment they will be so shy and wary that in order to approach them the utmost skill, experience, and judgement are necessary. Kit Carson, I believe, stands pre-eminent in running buffalo; in approaching, no man living can bear away the palm from Henry Chatillon, our professional hunter.

After Tête Rouge had alarmed the camp, no farther disturbance occurred during the night. The Arapahoes did not attempt mischief, or if they did, the wakefulness of the party deterred them from effecting their purpose. The next day was one of activity and excitement, for about ten o'clock the man in advance shouted the gladdening cry of *buffalo, buffalo!* and in the hollow of the prairie just below us a band of bulls were grazing. The temptation was irresistible, and Shaw and I rode down upon them. We were badly mounted on our travelling horses, but by hard lashing we overtook them, and Shaw running alongside a bull, shot into him both balls of his double-barrelled gun. Looking round as I galloped by, I saw the bull in his mortal fury rushing again and again upon his antagonist, whose horse constantly leaped aside and avoided the onset. My chase was more protracted, but at length I ran close to the bull and killed him with my pistols. Cutting off the tails of our victims by way of trophy, we rejoined the party in about a quarter of an hour after we had left it. Again and again that morning rang out the same welcome cry of *buffalo, buffalo!* Every few moments, in the broad meadows along the river, we saw bands of bulls, who, raising their shaggy heads, would gaze in stupid amazement at the approaching horsemen, and then breaking into a clumsy gallop, file off in a long line across the trail in front, towards the rising prairie on the left. At noon, the plain before us was alive with thousands of buffalo – bulls, cows, and calves – all moving rapidly as we drew near; and far off beyond the river the swelling prairie was darkened with them to the very horizon. The party was in gayer spirits than ever. We stopped for a nooning near a grove of trees by the river.

'Tongues and hump-ribs tomorrow,' said my friend Shaw, looking with contempt at the venison steaks which Deslauriers placed before us. Our meal finished, we lay down to sleep. A shout from Henry Chatillon aroused us, and we saw him standing on the cart-wheel, stretching his tall figure to its full height while he looked towards the prairie beyond the river. Following the direction of his eyes, we could clearly distinguish a large dark object, like the black shadow of a cloud, passing rapidly over swell after swell of the distant plain; behind it followed another of similar appearance though smaller, moving more rapidly, and drawing closer and closer to the first. It was the hunters of the Arapahoe camp chasing a band of buffalo. Shaw and I caught and saddled our best horses, and went plunging through sand and water to the farther bank. We were too late. The hunters had already mingled with the herd, and the work of slaughter was nearly over. When we reached the ground we found it strewn far and near with numberless carcases, while the remnants of the herd, scattered in all directions, were flying away in terror, and the Indians still rushing in pursuit. Many of the hunters, however, remained upon the spot, and among the rest was our yesterday's acquaintance, the chief of the village. He had alighted by the side of a cow, into which he had shot five or six arrows, and his squaw, who had followed him on horseback to the hunt, was giving him a draught of water from a canteen, purchased or plundered from some volunteer soldier. Recrossing the river, we overtook the party, who were already on their way.

We had gone scarcely a mile when we saw an imposing spectacle. From the river bank on the right, away over the swelling prairie on the left, and in front as far as the eye could reach, was one vast host of buffalo; the outskirts of the herd were within a quarter of a mile. In many parts they were crowded so densely together that in the distance their rounded backs presented a surface of uniform blackness; but elsewhere they were more scattered, and from amid the multitude rose little columns of dust where some of them were rolling on the ground. Here and there a battle was going forward among the bulls. We could distinctly see them rushing against each other, and hear the clattering of their horns and their hoarse bellowing. Shaw was riding at some distance in advance, with Henry Chatillon; I saw him stop and draw the leather covering from his gun. With such a sight before us, but one thing could be thought of. That morning I had used pistols in the chase. I had now a mind to try the virtue of a gun. Deslauriers had one, and I rode up to the side of the cart; there he sat under the white covering, biting his pipe between his teeth and grinning with excitement.

'Lend me your gun, Deslauriers.'

'Oui, Monsieur, oui,' said Deslauriers, tugging with might and main to stop the mule, which seemed obstinately bent on going forward. Then everything but his moccasins disappeared as he crawled into the cart and pulled at the gun to extricate it.

'Is it loaded?' I asked.

Oui, bien chargé; you'll kill, mon bourgeois; yes, you'll kill – c'est un bon fusil.'

I handed him my rifle and rode forward to Shaw.

'Are you ready?' he asked.

'Come on,' said I.

'Keep down that hollow,' said Henry, 'and then they won't see you till you get close to them.'

The hollow was a kind of ravine; it ran obliquely towards the buffalo, and we rode at a canter along the bottom until it became too shallow; then we bent close to our horses' necks, and, at last, finding that it could no longer conceal us, came out of it and rode directly towards the herd. It was within gunshot; before its outskirts, numerous grizzly old bulls were scattered, holding guard over their females. They glared at us in anger and astonishment, walked towards us a few yards, and then turning slowly round retreated at a trot which afterwards broke into a clumsy gallop. In an instant the main body caught the alarm. The buffalo began to crowd away from the point towards which we were approaching, and a gap was opened in the side of the herd. We entered it, still restraining our excited horses. Every instant the tumult was thickening. The buffalo, pressing together in large bodies, crowded away from us on every hand. In front and on either side we could see dark columns and masses, half hidden by clouds of dust, rushing along in terror and confusion, and hear the tramp and clattering of ten thousand hoofs. That countless multitude of powerful brutes, ignorant of their own strength, were flying in a panic from the approach of two feeble horsemen. To remain quiet longer was impossible.

'Take that band on the left,' said Shaw; 'I'll take these in front.'

He sprang off, and I saw no more of him. A heavy Indian whip was fastened by a band to my wrist; I swung it into the air and lashed my horse's flanks with all the strength of my arm. Away she darted, stretching close to the ground. I could see nothing but a cloud of dust before me, but I knew that it concealed a band of many hundreds of buffalo. In a moment I was in the midst of

the cloud, half suffocated by the dust and stunned by the tramp-
ling of the flying herd; but I was drunk with the chase and cared
for nothing but the buffalo. Very soon a long dark mass became
visible, looming through the dust; then I could distinguish each
bulky carcase, the hoofs flying out beneath, the short tails held
rigidly erect. In a moment I was so close that I could have touched
them with my gun. Suddenly to my amazement, the hoofs were
jerked upwards, the tails flourished in the air, and amid a cloud
of dust the buffalo seemed to sink into the earth before me. One
vivid impression of that instant remains upon my mind. I
remember looking down upon the backs of several buffalo dimly
visible through the dust. We had run unawares upon a ravine.
At that moment I was not the most accurate judge of depth and
width, but when I passed it on my return, I found it about
twelve feet deep and not quite twice as wide at the bottom. It was
impossible to stop; I would have done so gladly if I could; so,
half sliding, half plunging, down went the little mare. She came
down on her knees in the loose sand at the bottom; I was pitched
forward against her neck and nearly thrown over her head among
the buffalo, who amid dust and confusion came tumbling in all
around. The mare was on her feet in an instant and scrambling
like a cat up the opposite side. I thought for a moment that she
would have fallen back and crushed me, but with a violent effort
she clambered out and gained the hard prairie above. Glancing
back I saw the huge head of a bull clinging as it were by the fore-
feet at the edge of the dusty gulf. At length I was fairly among the
buffalo. They were less densely crowded than before, and I could
see nothing but bulls, who always run at the rear of a herd to
protect their females. As I passed among them they would lower

their heads, and turning as they ran, try to gore my horse; but as they were already at full speed there was no force in their onset, and as my horse Pauline ran faster than they, they were always thrown behind her in the effort. I soon began to distinguish cows amid the throng. One just in front of me seemed to my liking, and I pushed close to her side. Dropping the reins I fired, holding the muzzle of the gun within a foot of her shoulder. Quick as lightning she sprang at Pauline; the little mare dodged the attack, and I lost sight of the wounded animal amid the tumult. Immediately after, I selected another, and urging forward Pauline, shot into her both pistols in succession. For a while I kept her in view, but in attempting to load my gun, lost sight of her also in the confusion. Believing her to be mortally wounded and unable to keep up with the herd, I checked my horse. The crowd rushed onwards. The dust and tumult passed away, and on the prairie, far behind the rest, I saw a solitary buffalo galloping heavily. In a moment I and my victim were running side by side. My firearms were all empty, and I had in my pouch nothing but rifle bullets, too large for the pistols and too small for the gun. I loaded the gun, however, but as often as I levelled it to fire, the bullets would roll out of the muzzle and the gun returned only a report like a squib, as the powder harmlessly exploded. I rode in front of the buffalo and tried to turn her back; but her eyes glared, her mane bristled, and, lowering her head, she rushed at me with the utmost fierceness and activity. Again and again I rode before her, and again and again she repeated her furious charge. But little Pauline was in her element. She dodged her enemy at every rush, until at length the buffalo stood still, exhausted with her own efforts, her tongue lolling from her jaws.

Riding to a little distance, I dismounted, thinking to gather a handful of dry grass to serve the purpose of wadding, and load the gun at my leisure. No sooner were my feet on the ground than the buffalo came bounding in such a rage towards me that I jumped back again into the saddle with all possible despatch. After waiting a few minutes more, I made an attempt to ride up and stab her with my knife; but Pauline was near being gored in the attempt. At length, bethinking me of the fringes at the seams of my buckskin trousers, I jerked off a few of them, and, reloading the gun, forced them down the barrel to keep the bullet in its place; then approaching, I shot the wounded buffalo through the heart. Sinking to her knees, she rolled over lifeless on the prairie. To my astonishment, I found that, instead of a cow, I had been slaughtering a stout yearling bull. No longer wondering at his fierceness, I opened his throat, and cutting out his tongue, tied it at the back of my saddle. My mistake was one which a more experienced eye than mine might easily make in the dust and confusion of such a chase.

Then for the first time I had leisure to look at the scene around me. The prairie in front was darkened with the retreating multitude, and on either hand the buffalo came filing up in endless columns from the low plains upon the river. The Arkansas was three or four miles distant. I turned and moved slowly towards it. A long time passed before, far in the distance, I distinguished the white covering of the cart and the little black specks of horsemen before and behind it. Drawing near, I recognized Shaw's elegant tunic, the red flannel shirt, conspicuous far off. I overtook the party, and asked him what success he had had. He assailed a fat cow, shot her with two bullets, and mortally wounded her.

But neither of us was prepared for the chase that afternoon, and Shaw, like myself, had no spare bullets in his pouch; so he abandoned the disabled animal to Henry Chatillon, who followed, despatched her with his rifle, and loaded his horse with the meat.

We encamped close to the river. The night was dark, and as we lay down we could hear, mingled with the howling of wolves, the hoarse bellowing of the buffalo, like the ocean beating upon a distant coast.

We meant to remain at this place long enough to prepare provisions for our journey to the frontier, which, as we supposed, might occupy about a month. Had the distance been twice as great and the party ten times as large, the rifle of Henry Chatillon would have supplied meat enough for the whole within two days; we were obliged to remain, however, until it should be dry enough for transportation; so we pitched our tent and made other arrangements for a permanent camp. The California men, who had no such shelter, contented themselves with arranging their packs on the grass around their fire. In the meantime we had nothing to do but amuse ourselves. Our tent was within a rod of the river, if the broad sand-beds, with a scanty stream of water coursing here and there along their surface, deserve to be dignified with the name of river. The vast flat plains on either side were almost on a level with the sand-beds, and they were bounded in the distance by low, monotonous hills, parallel to the course of the stream. All was one expanse of grass; there was no wood in view, except some trees and stunted bushes upon two islands which rose from the wet sands of the river. Yet far from being dull and tame, the scene was often a wild and animated one; for twice a day, at sunrise and at noon, the buffalo came issuing from the hills, slowly advancing in their grave processions to drink at the river. All our amusements were to be at their expense. An old buffalo bull is a brute of unparalleled ugliness. At first sight of him every feeling of pity vanishes. The cows are much smaller and of a gentler appearance, as becomes their sex. While in this camp we forbore to attack them, leaving to Henry Chatillon, who could better judge their quality, the task of killing such as we wanted for use; but against the bulls we waged an unrelenting war. Thousands of them might be slaughtered without causing any detriment to the species, for their numbers greatly exceed those of the cows; it is the hides of the latter alone which are used for the purposes of commerce and for making the lodges of the Indians; and the destruction among them is therefore greatly disproportionate.

Our horses were tired, and we now usually hunted on foot. While we were lying on the grass after dinner, smoking, talking, or laughing at Tête Rouge, one of us would look up and observe, far out on the plains beyond the river, certain black objects slowly approaching. He would inhale a parting whiff from the pipe, then rising lazily, take his rifle, which leaned against the cart, throw over his shoulder the strap of his pouch and powder-horn, and with his moccasins in his hand, walk across the sand towards the opposite side of the river. This was very easy; for though the sands were about a quarter of a mile wide, the water was nowhere more than two feet deep. The farther bank was about four or five feet high, and quite perpendicular, being cut away by the water in spring. Tall grass grew along its edge. Putting it aside with his hand, and cautiously looking through it, the hunter can discern the huge shaggy back of the bull slowly swaying to and fro, as, with his clumsy swinging gait, he advances towards the water. The buffalo have regular paths by which they come down to drink. Seeing at a glance along which of these his intended victim is moving, the hunter crouches under the bank within fifteen or twenty yards, it may be, of the point where the path enters the river. Here he sits down quietly on the sand. Listening intently, he hears the heavy monotonous tread of the approaching bull. The moment after, he sees a motion among the long weeds and grass just at the spot where the path is channelled through the bank. An enormous black head is thrust out, the horns just visible amid the mass of tangled mane. Half sliding, half plunging, down comes the buffalo upon the river-bed below. He steps out in full sight upon the sands. Just before him a runnel of water is gliding, and he bends his head to drink. You may hear the water as it gurgles down his capacious throat. He raises his head, and the drops trickle from his wet beard. He stands with an air of stupid abstraction, unconscious of the lurking danger. Noiselessly the hunter cocks his rifle. As he sits upon the sand, his knee is raised, and his elbow rests upon it, that he may level his heavy weapon with a steadier aim. The stock is at his shoulder; his eye ranges along the barrel. Still he is in no haste to fire. The bull, with slow deliberation, begins his march over the sands to the other side. He advances his foreleg, and exposes to view a small spot, denuded of hair, just behind the point of his shoulder; upon this the hunter brings the sight of his rifle to bear; lightly and delicately his finger presses the hair-trigger. The spiteful crack of the rifle responds to his touch, and instantly in the middle of the bare spot appears a small red dot. The buffalo shivers;

death has overtaken him, he cannot tell from whence; still he does not fall, but walks heavily forward, as if nothing had happened. Yet before he has gone far out upon the sand, you see him stop; he totters; his knees bend under him, and his head sinks forward to the ground. Then his whole vast bulk sways to one side; he rolls over on the sand, and dies with a scarcely perceptible struggle.

Waylaying the buffalo in this manner, and shooting them as they come to water, is the easiest method of hunting them. They may also be approached by crawling up ravines, or behind hills, or even over the open prairie. This is often surprisingly easy; but at other times it requires the utmost skill of the most experienced hunter. Henry Chatillon was a man of extraordinary strength and hardihood; but I have seen him return to camp quite exhausted with his efforts, his limbs scratched and wounded, and his buck-skin dress stuck full of the thorns of the prickly-pear, among which he had been crawling. Sometimes he would lie flat upon his face, and drag himself along in this position for many rods together.

On the second day of our stay at this place, Henry went out for an afternoon hunt. Shaw and I remained in camp, until, observing some bulls approaching the water upon the other side of the river, we crossed over to attack them. They were so near, however, that before we could get under cover of the bank our appearance as we walked over the sands alarmed them. Turning round before coming within gun-shot, they began to move off to the right in a direction parallel to the river. I climbed up the bank and ran after them. They were walking swiftly, and before I could come within gun-shot distance they slowly wheeled about and faced me. Before they had turned far enough to see me I had fallen flat on my face. For a moment they stood and stared at the strange object upon the grass; then turning away, again they walked on as before; and I, rising immediately, ran once more in pursuit. Again they wheeled about, and again I fell prostrate. Repeating this three or four times, I came at length within a hundred yards of the fugitives, and as I saw them turning again I sat down and levelled my rifle. The one in the centre was the largest I had ever seen. I shot him behind the shoulder. His two companions ran off. He attempted to follow, but soon came to a stand, and at length lay down as quietly as an ox chewing the cud. Cautiously approaching him, I saw by his dull and jelly-like eye that he was dead.

When I began the chase, the prairie was almost tenantless; but a great multitude of buffalo had suddenly thronged upon it, and looking up I saw within fifty rods a heavy, dark column stretching to the right and left as far as I could see. I walked towards them. My approach did not alarm them in the least. The column itself consisted almost entirely of cows and calves, but a great many old bulls were ranging about the prairie on its flank, and as I drew near they faced towards me with such a grim and ferocious look that I thought it best to proceed no further. Indeed I was already within close rifle-shot of the column, and I sat down on the ground to watch their movements. Sometimes the whole would stand still, their heads all one way; then they would trot forward, as if by a common impulse, their hoofs and horns clattering together as they moved. I soon began to hear at a distance on the left the sharp reports of a rifle, again and again repeated; and not long after, dull and heavy sounds succeeded, which I recognized as the familiar voice of Shaw's double-barrelled gun. When Henry's rifle was at work there was always meat to be brought in. I went back across the river for a horse, and, returning, reached the spot where the hunters were standing. The buffalo were visible on the distant prairie. The living had retreated from the ground, but ten or twelve carcases were scattered in various directions. Henry, knife in hand, was stooping over a dead cow, cutting away the best and fattest of the meat.

When Shaw left me he had walked down for some distance under the riverbank to find another bull. At length he saw the plains covered with the host of buffalo, and soon after heard the crack of Henry's rifle. Ascending the bank, he crawled through the grass, which for a rod or two from the river was very high and rank. He had not crawled far before, to his astonishment, he saw Henry standing erect upon the prairie, almost surrounded by the buffalo. Henry was in his element. Quite unconscious that anyone was looking at him, he stood at the full height of his tall figure, one hand resting upon his side, and the other arm leaning carelessly on the muzzle of his rifle. His eye was ranging over the singular assemblage around him. Now and then he would select such a cow as suited him, level his rifle, and shoot her dead; then quietly reloading, he would resume his former position. The buffalo seemed no more to regard his presence than if he were one of themselves; the bulls were bellowing and butting at each other, or rolling about in the dust. A group of buffalo would gather about the carcase of a dead cow, snuffing at her wounds; and sometimes they would come behind those that had not yet fallen, and endeavour to push them from the spot. Now and then some old bull would face towards Henry with an air of stupid amazement, but none seemed inclined to attack or fly from him.

For some time Shaw lay among the grass, looking in surprise at this extraordinary sight; at length he crawled cautiously forward, and spoke in a low voice to Henry, who told him to rise and come on. Still the buffalo showed no sign of fear; they remained gathered about their dead companions. Henry had already killed as many cows as we wanted for use, and Shaw, kneeling behind one of the carcasses, shot five bulls before the rest thought it necessary to disperse.

The frequent stupidity and infatuation of the buffalo seems the more remarkable from the contrast it offers to their wildness and wariness at other times. Henry knew all their peculiarities; he had studied them as a scholar studies his books, and derived quite as much pleasure from the occupation. The buffalo were a kind of companion to him, and, as he said, he never felt alone when they were about him. He took great pride in his skill in hunting. He was one of the most modest of men; yet in the simplicity and frankness of his character, it was clear that he looked upon his pre-eminence in this respect as a thing too palpable and well established to be disputed. But whatever may have been his estimate of his own skill, it was rather below than above that which others placed upon it. The only time that I ever saw a shade of scorn darken his face was when two volunteer soldiers, who had just killed a buffalo for the first time, undertook to instruct him as to the best method of 'approaching'. Henry always seemed to think that he had a sort of prescriptive right to the buffalo, and to look upon them as something belonging to himself. Nothing excited his indignation so much as any wanton destruction committed among the cows, and in his view shooting a calf was a cardinal sin.

To Cure Sometimes

Katharine Tottenham

Very often we come upon or hear of injured or ailing wild birds. For most people they are understandably a difficult matter to deal with, but this author turned herself into a real 'Bird Doctor' who successfully treated hundreds of winged patients. Lucky is the person who can consult such an expert when faced with an injured-bird problem.

Of the physician's three ancient precepts, *To cure sometimes*, *To relieve often*, *To comfort always*, the amateur bird doctor can usually hope to achieve little more than the first. Even today we know so little about what makes a bird 'tick' that treating it as a patient must be a matter of trial and error, and the onus for weighting the scales one way or another rests in the last resort with the bird itself. If it decides to live, then it will live under the most fantastic conditions.

A classic example of this was shown by a robin that lived and bred for three seasons while carrying a sliver of wood diagonally through its body; by some unknown mischance the point had penetrated the bird's breast and emerged from the middle of its back, having miraculously by-passed the vital organs.

The cage-bird enthusiast has problems enough when illness strikes one of his pets, but cage-birds are at least tame and accustomed to human hands. Nursing wild birds presents the additional problem of fear, which must be conquered if the patient is to be treated at all. But this is not so difficult, because of an inexplicable bond that often springs up between humans and birds: an odd affinity that, obviously, owes nothing to any physical likeness but may be due to the avian capacity for extra-sensory perception (otherwise telepathy), which has recently been put forward as an explanation of many hitherto unexplained mysteries of bird behaviour. I believe this to be true. The amazing aerial evolutions of a flock of dunlin are more easily understood on the basis of control by a so-called mass mind.

Some people have an unconscious horror of birds that is outwardly unnoticeable, but is discernible by the hypersensitive individual bird, giving it a feeling of unease which it expresses in wildness. Other people with the best will in the world lack the imagination and experience that would give them enough confidence to handle the delicate bundles of palpitating feathers. But the average person with a gentle touch will find birds easy to manage after a little practice. Confidence inspires confidence, and slow decisive movements and a calm voice will soothe the wildest breast.

By establishing a small-scale home clinic for wild birds, one can make a very real contribution to local conservancy, and at the same time have unique opportunities for studying various species at close range. Most children are interested in a bird hospital and soon learn how to collect casualties and bring them for treatment without inflicting further damage, and this gives them a new sense of responsibility towards all animals – a lesson that is absent from the curriculum of the average school.

I have kept a record of birds treated over a period of several years, detailing the symptoms, the action taken to cure them, the diet and the final result. This list shows a steady upgrade from a miserable ten per cent to a present ratio of eighty per cent of patients completely recovered and released.

Whatever our views on birds in cages, it must be admitted that without the cage-bird keeper and the manufacturers who supply his demands, the care of wild birds in temporary captivity would be very much more difficult than it actually is. Packaged seeds, insectivorous and rearing-foods are readily obtainable nowadays, and with modern deep-freeze methods it is even possible to feed sea birds from a carton in an emergency.

Gone are the days I squeamishly remember when mashing earthworms, insects and hard-boiled egg and biscuit-meal was a daily task. Now I have a larder of packages that provide for the arrival of almost any species of bird.

Rearing baby birds is a reasonably easy business when a little skill has been acquired. Nursing accident victims is more difficult. In this case one has to deal with broken bones, the possibility of internal injuries, the effects of shock and the bird's own choice between living and dying.

I experienced an odd example of this with two sea-gulls. The first arrived with a broken wing, which after a couple of weeks was mending nicely; then the second one arrived, outwardly un-damaged but clearly very sick. I put them together in a comfortable pen, thinking that the sight of each other would be an encouragement, but I have never been so wrong. Within half a day number two was dead, reasonably enough of internal haemorrhage as autopsy showed, but soon afterwards gull number one was in a coma and died. There was no practical explanation for its death beyond some strange telepathic 'death-wish' infection. So I learned to keep the chronically ill separate from the convalescents.

A high percentage of accidents result in broken legs and wings.

Other than fracture cases, the general run of accident victims are suffering from shock and minor injuries, and they often recover with no active help on our part. What they need is safety from predators, a supply of good food and absolute quiet: in these surroundings they can, metaphorically, lick their wounds and mend themselves.

In all cases the sands of time are running out during the period from the moment disaster strikes to the arrival of the bird for treatment. The peculiar hollow structure of bird bones makes them susceptible to exposure to air in the case of serious fracture and, besides this, the effects of shock are busily at work. This time lag has accounted for a large proportion of my twenty per cent of failures, but it is an uncontrollable feature of the work that has to be accepted.

Another question to be faced squarely is whether a case is hopeless. A too sentimental approach can result in real cruelty, and I make myself kill quite a number of maimed birds, much as I hate doing it. There are three types of casualty: the first has every prospect of complete recovery; the second is badly injured and in obvious distress; and the third has a good chance of recovery but will never be fit to return to the wild.

It is important to make an honest assessment as soon as a bird arrives, destroying it promptly if it falls into the second category, and choosing the common-sense and humane alternative for a bird that can only spend its future in an aviary. Some will flourish and live contentedly under these conditions, but for others such a life is out of the question. Swallows and swifts are an example: they are built for an entirely aerial existence; indeed, swifts even sleep and mate while airborne. Keeping such birds in permanent captivity would be most unkind, and the same applies to ocean birds, like auks and petrels; but a gull will settle down happily to a domesticated life, and so, surprisingly, will some of the waders.

The final decision must be tempered by the facilities one has for keeping a species in suitable surroundings, or the possibility of its being acceptable to a zoo with properly designed enclosures. The maxim should always be, *when in doubt, destroy*.

Various methods of destruction are recommended, but I have found that the only quick and sure means is to give the bird a sharp blow on the base of the skull, which procures an instant and painless death. Anaesthesia in any form is unsuitable for birds, as they resist it and die slowly and unpleasantly.

To return to the birds with a future, the housing question is important. In most places passerines will form the majority of patients, and these will do well in box cages of the type used by canary and budgerigar fanciers. Wire fronts, fitted with doors, can be bought at pet stores or corn merchants and attached to the open side of wooden packing-cases, and these will make good temporary quarters for many of the smaller species; or one can, of course, buy these cages ready-made at a price. A useful size is about two feet long, by one foot wide, by eighteen inches high, as this will be suitable for any sick bird up to the size of a pigeon.

Many people make the mistake of giving a bird patient too much freedom, turning it loose in an attic or shed, where it will do nothing but damage itself in attempts to escape. What it needs is a shaded and restricted compartment which impresses it as a sanctuary and, strange as it may seem, a small box cage makes a frightened and bewildered bird settle down in a very short time. All-wire pet-bird cages are quite unsuitable, as they appear to be prisons from which the bird may escape if it can only batter its way through the bars.

Perches are usually arranged so that they rest on the first cross-bar of the cage front, but for the new arrival all but one should be removed, and this fixed about one inch above the floor. Food and water pots must be inside, and if the cage is fitted with outside feeders, these should be removed and the pop-holes blocked.

If the bird is ill enough to spend its time sitting on the cage floor, it will appreciate a soft bed of rags or meadow hay; but if it is able to perch, the floor can be littered with either sawdust or peat moss for insectivores, and dry sand for seed-eaters. All species, except birds of prey, need grit in order to digest their food, and if this is not provided as a floor covering, it should be available in a separate container.

Curiosity is strongly developed in birds, and their investigations will soon teach them how to use glass and plastic water founts clipped to the bars of the cage. These are excellent appliances and can be obtained at most pet stores. All my perching birds have learned to use them within twenty-four hours, and one blackbird enjoyed watching the air bubbles rising in the tube so much that she drank enormous amounts of water every day.

Cages for larger birds, such as a rook, should be of the same design but of rabbit-hutch proportions. Sea birds can rest for the first few days in a basket or tea chest, bedded with soft hay, and then convalesce out of doors in a wire-netting run. Old, shallow, kitchen sinks are usually to be begged, or bought for a few shillings, from a builder's yard, and these make good ponds for water birds.

The design and construction of aviaries depends largely on the question of finance. It is essential to have some kind of enclosure where the patients can be rehabilitated before release, and provided it is about six feet in height and allows shelter and room for flying-exercise, the other dimensions are a matter for individual choice. In fact, I made a useful small aviary out of odd lengths of timber quartering, a few planks and five yards of half-inch wire netting, at a cost of little more than thirty shillings.

Equipped with two or three cages, an aviary and an open enclosure, the bird hospital is established, but there is still the catering department to consider. I keep two basic foods which suit all adult passerines: the first is a Dutch product called Sluisfood, and this will be eaten by most insectivores; the second is Capern's Finch Mixture, which can be given to sparrows and buntings, as well as finches.

Some live food is necessary for insectivorous birds, and this can be provided in the form of meal-worms or 'gentles'. Meal-worms are clean and not too unpleasant to handle. They are the larvae of a beetle, *Tenebrio molitor*, which is found in flour mills, and an ounce of them, which can be bought at pet stores for about half a crown, will multiply in a cake tin to provide a constant supply. The tin should have a few air holes drilled in the lid, and then be filled with alternate layers of newspaper and broad bran, which is very slightly moistened from time to time.

Meal-worms are rather rich and indigestible and, for this reason, a ration of six a day is plenty for a thrush-sized bird, while a fledgling of the same type should not have more than one.

'Gentles' is a nice trade name for ordinary maggots. These are revolting creatures, although they are cleaned before being sold;

but birds love them and thrive on them, and they have the great advantage of softness, which makes them a suitable food for the smallest nestling.

These foods are a general stand-by. Some rarer bird visitors will thrive on the oddest diet when their natural one is impossible to obtain, and this calls for imagination and ingenuity.

Medical supplies are necessarily limited, and the medicine cupboard can only be a very modest affair, as antiseptics are not used for birds and there are few effective drugs available. However, it should be possible to obtain on veterinary prescription a small quantity of sulphanilamide powder, for use on wounds; and a seventeen-per-cent solution of sulphamezathine, which will often cure internal complaints of virus origin, as it is a specific for coccidiosis in poultry. It is given at the rate of one teaspoonful to a pint of water.

It is useful to collect a number of quill feathers dropped by species of birds of various sizes, as the stems can be cut off and split lengthwise to make very good splints for leg fractures. If a close fit is obtained, this kind of splint will be kept in position without bandaging or plaster, but it may be as well to bind it once round, top and bottom, with Scotch tape. The great advantage of this method is its lightness, which is an important aspect, particularly with small birds.

Unfortunately, wing injuries are the commonest accidents and the least likely to respond to treatment. Dislocation, with local muscular damage, of the shoulder joint is, in my opinion, hopeless. Fractures of the upper and forearm are not promising either, but if treatment is not delayed these breaks *will* mend – with luck.

An injury that is often mistaken for a broken wing is subluxation of the carpal joint. For the sake of simplicity, one can look on this as a dislocated wrist, and it is often described as 'aeroplane wing'. The sufferer is grounded, and the wing tip, which supports the heaviest feathers, is twisted and useless. The treatment in this case is simple and effective: the flight feathers are clipped back as close as possible, without drawing blood, and the patient is kept caged until it moults through a new set of wing feathers. By this time the joint will, usually, have returned to normal, and after convalescence in an aviary the patient can be released.

Another type of casualty which appears serious, but can be cured, is the bird that has lost its tail. Many of them, particularly birds that hop rather than walk, lose all sense of balance, and fall over backwards every time they stand up. Blackbirds seem to be the most frequent victims of this accident, possibly in the course of hair-breadth escapes from cats. Again, the treatment is simple. All that is required is board and lodging for about four weeks, when nature will have supplied a new tail. It is odd that tails are replaced so promptly, while wing feathers can only be grown when a bird moults.

Wounds, with or without haemorrhage, should be bathed in cold water, and if necessary the plumage can be cut away to allow clean healing. The high metabolic rate of birds makes them less susceptible to local infection, and one application of sulphanilamide will be quite enough to clean a wound and promote healing. In fact, minor wounds are best left alone and, certainly, antiseptics should never be applied to a bird's skin.

Haemorrhage must, of course, be dealt with immediately. On

one occasion I was called urgently to a neighbour's pigeon which had severed a vein in its leg. The distracted owners were bathing it in a bowl of warm water, which was rapidly filling with the bird's life-blood. I took it from them and held the leg under the cold-water tap for a few seconds, which allowed a clot to form, and bleeding stopped. We then applied sulphanilamide powder and put the now very weak pigeon in a darkened cage. It was given milk to drink, ordinary corn, and one tablet of a proprietary brand of pigeon tonic every day for ten days, and then it was fit to return to its companions in the loft.

Long-billed birds often damage their beaks, and as a general rule, accidents of this kind are totally crippling and the sufferer should be destroyed. Only the horny tip of a bill is capable of regeneration. This is always growing to make good the wear and tear of use, and sometimes one finds rogue growth in budgerigars and in wild soft-bills, such as starlings and blackbirds. In wild birds, the trouble usually rights itself, but the caged budgerigar needs help in the form of objects to chew – natural branches of hardwood, cuttle-bone and such.

Like the beak, claws of captive birds often grow too long, and as clipping necessitates handling and the careful avoidance of blood vessels, it is much easier to rasp the claws by glueing a strip of coarse sandpaper to the underside of one or two perches, so that a bird gives itself a manicure every time it grips the perch.

Occasionally one finds a patient with symptoms for which there is no certain diagnosis. A few years ago a number of birds were found with a leg paralysed and held at right angles to the body. I had a robin in this condition, and I gave him no treatment beyond the normal one of quiet and good food. He gradually recovered and spent his convalescence in a spare room, where he perched or squatted on a radiator, glorying in the heat and possibly gaining some therapeutic effect from it.

A vitamin deficiency affects young waterfowl with leg paralysis, and this will respond to doses of codliver oil and vitamin B complex, which can be supplied in the form of yeast extract. I have known a young heron to suffer in this way, as well as ducklings and cygnets, and these birds are often destroyed in the mistaken belief that they are beyond aid.

This chapter of accidents must end with the saddest casualty of all: the victim of scientific farming and horticulture.* These poisoned birds are generally in the throes of convulsions when they are found, and there is only one thing to do – kill them instantly.

A correspondent in the United States tells me that yeast extract will sometimes save a bird that has taken a mild dose of insecticide, but so far all my cases have been severe and hopeless.

Few species are safe from these poisons. Finches pick it up from dressed seeds at sowing-time; so do mice and voles, which are then eaten by birds of prey; while insectivorous birds are certain victims in areas sprayed with D.D.T. or other toxic chemicals. Besides birds, other creatures like hedgehogs, shrews, snakes and lizards, and even foxes, badgers and stoats and weasels are potential victims.

As an example, an earthworm which has eaten material containing D.D.T. will accumulate the poison, and when it in turn is eaten by a thrush, the bird will again accumulate this dose and

* Written in 1960.

add to it as other polluted insects are digested. This collected poison gradually invades its whole body until the brain cells are reached. Then death mercifully follows locomotor paralysis and convulsions.

Taking Note

Gilbert White

This eighteenth-century parson spent most of his life in the Hampshire village where he was born. Yet his book, 'The Natural History of Selborne', composed mainly of letters to his friends Thomas Pennant and Daines Barrington, had a profound influence on our enjoyment and perception of nature. Though he had, to us, quaint ideas about bird migration, he was one of the first people to study ecology (or oeconomy, as he called it), the inter-relation of plants and animals. Nothing was too insignificant to arouse his interest and he showed by his copious and detailed letters the immense value and pleasure of keeping Nature Study notes.

Sir,   November 4, 1767

It gave me no small satisfaction to hear that the *falco* (this hawk proved to be the *falco peregrinus*; a variety) turned out an uncommon one. I must confess I should have been better pleased to have heard that I sent you a bird that you had never seen before; but that, I find, would be a difficult task.

I have procured some of the mice mentioned in my former letters, a young one and a female with young, both of which I have preserved in brandy. From the colour, shape, size, and manner of nesting, I make no doubt but that the species is nondescript. They are much smaller, and more slender, than the *mus domesticus medius* of *Ray*; and have more of the squirrel or dormouse colour; their belly is white; a straight line along their sides divides the shades of their back and belly. They never enter into houses; are carried into ricks and barns with the sheaves;

abound in harvest; and build their nests amidst the straws of the corn above the ground, and sometimes in thistles. They breed as many as eight at a litter, in a little round nest composed of the blades of grass or wheat.

One of these nests I procured this autumn, most artificially platted, and composed of the blades of wheat; perfectly round, and about the size of a cricket-ball; with the aperture so ingeniously closed, that there was no discovering to what part it belonged. It was so compact and well filled, that it would roll across the table without being discomposed, though it contained eight little mice that were naked and blind. As this nest was perfectly full, how could the dam* come at her litter respectively so as to administer a teat to each? Perhaps she opens different places for that purpose, adjusting them again when the business is over: but she could not possibly be contained herself in the ball with her young, which moreover would be daily increasing in bulk. This wonderful procreant cradle, an elegant instance of the efforts of instinct, was found in a wheat-field suspended in the head of a thistle.

A gentleman, curious in birds, wrote me word that his servant had shot one last January, in that severe weather, which he believed would puzzle me. I called to see it this summer, not knowing what to expect: but, the moment I took it in hand, I pronounced it the male *garrulus bohemicus* or *German* silk-tail,† from the five peculiar crimson tags or points which it carries at the ends of five of the short remiges. It cannot, I suppose, with any propriety, be called an *English* bird: and yet I see, by *Ray's*

* The harvest-mouse.
† The waxwing.

Philosoph. Letters, that great flocks of them, feeding on haws, appeared in this kingdom in the winter of 1685.

The mention of haws puts me in mind that there is a total failure of that wild fruit, so conducive to the support of many of the winged nation. For the same severe weather, late in the spring, which cut off all the produce of the more tender and curious trees, destroyed also that of the more hardy and common.

Some birds, haunting with the missel-thrushes, and feeding on the berries of the yew-tree, which answered to the description of the *merula torquata,* or *ring-ouzel,* were lately seen in this neighbourhood. I employed some people to procure me a specimen, but without success.

Query – Might not *Canary* birds be naturalized to this climate, provided their eggs were put, in the spring, into the nests of some of their congeners, as goldfinches, greenfinches, etc? Before winter perhaps they might be hardened, and able to shift for themselves.

About ten years ago I used to spend some weeks yearly at *Sunbury,* which is one of those pleasant villages lying on the *Thames,* near *Hampton-court.* In the autumn, I could not help being much amused with those myriads of the swallow kind which assemble in those parts. But what struck me most was, that from the time they began to congregate, forsaking the chimneys and houses, they roosted every night in the osier-beds of the aits of that river. Now this resorting towards that element, at that season of the year, seems to give some countenance to the northern opinion (strange as it is) of their retiring under water. A *Swedish* naturalist is so much persuaded of that fact, that he talks, in his calendar of *Flora,* as familiarly of the swallow's going under water in the beginning of *September*, as he would of his poultry going to roost a little before sunset.

An observing gentleman in *London* writes me word that he saw an house-martin, on the twenty-third of last *October*, flying in and out of its nest in the *Borough*. And I myself, on the twenty-ninth of last *October* (as I was travelling through *Oxford*), saw four or five swallows hovering round and settling on the roof of the county-hospital.

Now is it likely that these poor little birds (which perhaps had not been hatched but a few weeks), should, at that late season of the year, and from so midland a county, attempt a voyage to *Goree* or *Senegal*, almost as far as the *equator*?

I acquiesce entirely in your opinion – that, though most of the swallow kind may migrate, yet that some do stay behind and hide with us during winter.

As to the short-winged soft-billed birds, which come trooping in such numbers in the spring, I am at a loss even what to suspect about them. I watched them narrowly this year, and saw them abound till about *Michaelmas*, when they appeared no longer. Subsist they cannot openly among us, and yet elude the eyes of the inquisitive: and, as to their hiding, no man pretends to have found any of them in a torpid state in the winter. But with regard to their migration, what difficulties attend that supposition! That such feeble bad fliers (who the summer long never flit but from hedge to hedge) should be able to traverse vast seas and continents in order to enjoy milder seasons amidst the regions of *Africa!*

> With all due deference and regard,
> Your most obliged and most humble servant.